SKIING SIMPLIFIED

SKIING SIMPLIFIED

By Doug Pfeiffer
and the Editors of *Skiing* Magazine

Illustrated by Anthony Ravielli

GROSSET & DUNLAP
A FILMWAYS COMPANY
Publishers · New York

ACKNOWLEDGEMENTS

It wouldn't have been possible to produce portions of this book without the help of many capable people—instructors, photographers, writers, and editors. Among those deserving special thanks are the following: John Jerome and Dr. Hans Kraus for the chapter on conditioning, and for the exercise drawings; Sven Coomer, Virginia Sturgess, and Ed Crist for photographic assistance; Emery "Woody" Woodall for advice on skis and boots, and Gordon Lipe on bindings; John Henry Auran, Al Greenberg, and Robert Scharff for editorial work; and of course, Tony Ravielli, the illustrator.

Dust jacket photo of three skiers enjoying the wide open slopes and powder at Sun Valley, Idaho, was taken by George Schwartz.

Frontispiece photo of Verbier, Switzerland, and equipment photos were taken by Virginia Sturgess.

Introduction

Skiing—the young answer to the old cry for excitement. The thrills of fast driving and speedboat racing with few of the dangers. At nowhere near the cost. Some of the freedom of flying—without the noise. Everyone can have fun out there in the cold and blustery. Everyone, that is, who takes lessons—at least for a couple of days—to overcome the gawkiness we all once had to overcome.

Why the fun? It has something to do with the personal aspect of the sport, I guess. The challenge is You Against The Elements. It's classic. Eternal. Not you against another person. You have only yourself—your skills—to depend upon. Beat the hill, and you swell with pride. Fail, and you are not about to be put down until you go down all the way, standing up. It's a great, personal, never-ending challenge, mixed in with all kinds of healthful, heady sensations. Skiing's grip has held me fast for the last 35 years, and in case you find its hold on you to be weakening—or if you'd like to experience its powerful grasp—I've put this book together from the best of my Instruction Corner articles which have been appearing in SKIING for the last six years. My intent is: Information for the newcomer, rejuvenation for the old-timer.

Skiing Simplified is a good, descriptive title for this book—I hope. But, don't expect it to be a purely "how to ski" affair, or a "how to ski like me" book. Don't expect it to be conventional, or to say this is the way—the only final form way—to come down a mountain. If it's anything that can be put into a slogan it's a how-to-understand book. A book that tries to get at the soul—the nitty gritty—of technique. I just happen to be one of those types who never seem to lick a muscle skill without first understanding clearly just what it is that I have to do. Years of teaching have led me to believe that a lot of you are the same type.

I'm also the kind of person who is inclined to believe that the orthodoxy of teaching skiing may have been wrong all these years. Basically, what people have been taught—force fed, really—has been a series of maneuvers. The traditional goals have been the snowplow, the snowplow turn, the stem turn, the stem christie, and finally, if you hung around long enough, wedelning or some other form of parallel skiing. The error is that these maneuvers are thought of as tools —something concrete, as if each were given its own shape and that all a learner had to do was pick up the right one and hammer or saw away. Read christie, or wedeln or whatever for those last two verbs.

But it's not so. A christie is composed of a series of skills—techniques, really.

And it's these skills or techniques which you should learn. It's no mere coincidence that until now none of the world's champion racers has come up through the ranks of the ski school, where the constant emphasis on maneuvers over-trains—molds you, really—into a statue-like copy of national style. Who ever heard of putting a marble statue through a ski race?

Rigidity is the last thing you want. Snow changes constantly. Terrain changes constantly. You cannot force a body position onto snow or terrain. You must adapt—let your body move into whatever constantly changing positions it must. You must learn to f-e-e-l your way. You—your movements—must become a function of the snow, the shape of the hill, your equipment.

The total picture of skiing, as I see it—and ski it—is this:

FIRST—You need equipment which is right for you.

SECOND—You need a few basic maneuvers—the usual "walkie-talkie" stuff which every beginner should learn in ski school.

THIRD—You need balance. Lots of it. Everybody has some. Everybody can get more, because there are skills—many of them—which can be learned to improve balance.

FOURTH—You need to develop edge control skills—plenty of them. The development of them is what your instructor (or you teach-yourselfers) should stress in every maneuver or exercise you try. Edge control is a final goal. The stem turn or the stem christie are not.

FIFTH—You need to understand the big picture about that fabulous turned-on, turning world of the parallel christies. The technique mystique is not that unfathomable.

SIXTH—You need to know some of the major skills of the christies—like un-weighting, and powering your skis into the turn.

SEVENTH—Then, put the skills together—in your own way—and develop a nice, relaxed manner of letting your body movements adapt to the snow-clad mountains.

EIGHTH—Then, if you want, fill in the gaps in your knowledge, the weaknesses of your skills—and polish yourself into a shining example of stylish efficiency.

This book has been put together with this scheme in mind. The overall philosophy is simple, the details, more involved. Please, don't try to read this volume as you would a novel. When you go through it, don't let yourself become snowed by the details. There are many. I've done my best to present an overview at the outset of each chapter, then the details, in a whole-part-whole system—a sort of inspection, analysis, then synthesis. Take the chapters in easy bites—a bite from here, a bite from there. Before long you'll be able to put together your own way of understanding. Do so, and I could guarantee that with practice, you'll become a good, if not a superior skier.

The information compiled in this book is due in part to the help of those great racers, very capable, certified ski instructors, equipment engineers, manufacturers, and authors of ski books whose brains I've picked these past 25 years. Thanks to Tony Ravielli, whose talented fingers have etched my likeness onto so many of the pages in this book. And thanks to the editors of SKIING Magazine who have so often blue-pencilled my typewritten words into coherent thoughts.

Doug Pfeiffer
Sept., 1970

Contents

1

EQUIPMENT
Your Tools For Fun

Do It With the Right Gear

Skiers haven't always carved up the slopes with such self-assured speed and finesse, amid such moguls—and crowds—as they do now. We do things today which just five years ago were virtually impossible. Almost phenomenal developments in equipment have made the difference; skis of lightweight fiberglass and epoxy; high-backed boots, and also even the more conventional ones that have superb lateral support; lightweight poles; bindings that bind firmly, yet can release during a nasty, ear-bending tumble.

Skiing techniques of today have developed only as fast as advances in boot and ski design have permitted. And that has been fast. So fast, in fact, that a big problem facing any skier is how to choose equipment properly suited to individual needs. At first, you will have to rely on someone's advice. As time goes on, however, best learn to be your own expert counselor. This chapter, dealing with each piece of equipment separately, will start you on your way.

BOOTS

Only a very strong, athletic person would be able to ski the graceful and precise modern styles without the modern ski boot to support and stabilize the ankle and foot during rapid consecutive turns on hard packed and usually bumpy slopes.

Boots are the skier's vital links to his skis. The boots must prevent the foot from sliding, twisting, or lifting; simultaneously, they must stiffen and strengthen the ankle laterally while permitting the ankle to be flexed forward freely and comfortably. The boots must absorb all the strains of the pull against the bindings, which, with the increasing popularity of step-in and turntable types, have become more and more inflexible, forcing the boots themselves to take all the strain. They must keep the skier's feet warm and dry in all sorts of weather. And, in spite of this abuse, they must last several seasons while performing all these miracles.

Buying a new pair of ski boots is often a nearly mystical experience, with the future of your feet in the hands of the salesman serving you. It is to be hoped you will consult a real expert and be told that "the best pair is the one which fits you best," and with this advice obtain a pair of boots which will give comfort and improve your skiing. Unfortunately, defining good fit is not easy. Here, we'll make an attempt to analyze some of the more important aspects of boot design

1

that contribute to that end. As you set out to find that best pair, bear in mind the complex function ascribed to a ski boot in the beginning of this chapter. Only a skilled skier with experience in fitting will be able to do a competent job of helping you. Each pair of feet represents an individual problem. Feet are as different as faces, and each skier represents a different complex of needs, skills, and desires.

How the boot should fit. First of all, the length, width, and shape of your foot will have to be accommodated. You should shop in a store that carries a full selection of widths, and where, if necessary, you can select from more than one manufacturer's last.

You should be aware that the foot is held from the ball of the foot back through the instep and into the heel cup, which is designed to hold the heel down. Throughout this whole area, the boot should be consistently snug without your having to tighten the fastenings excessively. The toes should have ample room for warmth. If the length is correct, short-toed skiers will have some extra length. Otherwise, the toes will be pinched in the narrow front, and the shaft of the foot won't fit correctly. Conversely, skiers with longer toes should be careful to choose a boot with a sufficiently long cap for toe room—not just a longer boot—or the important fit from ball to heel will be lost. In addition to the area around the foot itself, the ankle area must also fasten snugly.

Small areas of pressure on bunions, protruding bones, or wider parts of the foot will be dealt with in a competent shop by localized stretching of the boot, not by selling you a boot too big or too wide simply to give comfort in that one tender area or wide spot. If you try to compensate in this manner, the boots will soon fail to hold your foot securely, and movement will produce greater irritation, bigger swellings, and bone spurs. Those skiers with truly different feet should consider custom-made boots, or the latest in boots foamed to your feet, available in most better ski shops.

In this connection, it should be pointed out that wrinkled ski pants and heavy seams located over the bones of the feet are among the major sources of irritation and soreness usually blamed on the boots. It is useless to spend hours selecting ski boots, only to wear them over pants which don't fit properly. Sometimes, shortening the strap under the instep will correct the situation by pulling the pants seams down away from the pressure areas. In other cases, retailoring is necessary. Boots should always be fitted with pants on. Without ski pants, it is impossible to judge correctly the fit in the heel and ankle or the proper boot length—unless the skier always wears knickers or the new over-the-boot pants.

When trying on boots, you ought to use the new cushion-foot sock. Somewhat lighter than the traditional rag sock, and almost as warm, it lacks any cable or ribbed pattern to irritate the feet. An additional silk or very light woolen sock can be added to conserve additional warmth; but avoid socks that are too thick or have too many layers, for, inside a properly snug boot, they will cut off circulation and allow the foot to roll.

As you succeed in finding a pair of boots with the correct length, width, and shape for your feet, the question of good fit should be considered in a new light. No matter how well the boots seem to conform to your feet, this is not enough. To ski, you must bend the ankles. It is

Figure 1-1. *First in the plastic revolution was Lange.*

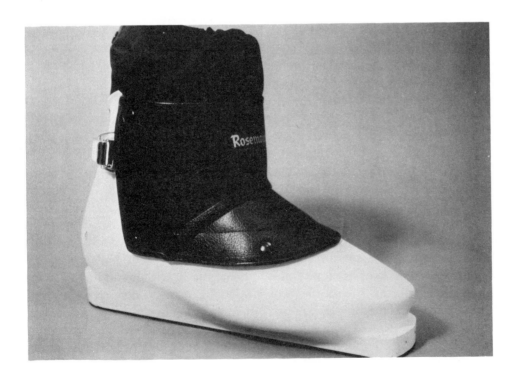

Figure 1-2. *Rosemount's hard shell—an engineered boot.*

not always easy to find a pair of boots which flex easily enough and yet give this needed support, but until you find the pair that can do this best for you, you have not found a good fit. One of the saddest sights in skiing is the skier, perhaps but not always a beginner, wearing a fine pair of ski boots perfectly fitted to his feet, unable to bend his ankles and having no luck at all trying to ski. The boots often are quite expensive, but weren't fitted to him. With ski boots, "fit" must also mean "function."

Stand up in those new boots, and flex your knees and ankles. It may take some pressure, but you should be able to achieve a full forward ankle bend without severe discomfort. If you can flex your ankles, the boots will get easier with each successive bending. If you cannot, don't be misled by the myth that the boots "will break in." Boots not flexed don't break in or wear out. *You* do! (This is not to say leather boots don't soften or stretch with use. They do, but not necessarily to give you greater comfort. As boots break down, they fail to hold the foot securely. Many professional skiers, who break their boots down rapidly by skiing daily, forestall this tendency by using two pairs of boots in rotation.)

As you flex your ankles, note whether the boots wrinkle or bow out and lose close contact in the instep and heel region. Boots that do, soon soften and require constant tightening to keep the foot down. Your heel should remain anchored when the boot is flexed and you are standing normally with the boot heel caught under something to keep it down. If you pull straight up, you will probably be able to lift your heel, but a pull in this direction would result in a hard forward fall while skiing. Pointing

the toe will also lift the heel, but you are already sitting in the snow when you achieve this kind of bend on skis. If the heel stays down when you flex your ankle, and the boot retains contact all over the foot, you will not have problems with lifting your heel.

A tendency for the boot to cut somewhat along the top edge of the tongue or upper can be relieved while the boot is very new by loosening or not using the top lace or fastening on the boot. Distinguish, however, between a local tendency to cut, which is relieved by this method, and a general failure of the boot to flex and follow the angle of your shin as it does so. In this whole process, new boots must be given some time to shape to your feet. They have been packed in a box for months and have lost shape. A minimum of half an hour on your feet in a warm room and several refastenings are needed to judge how well they can conform to your feet.

Now that you have gotten this far into choosing a ski boot, you have surely become aware of the wide variety available in ski boot designs. Some choices will perhaps be ruled out by cost, but within the price which you must pay for a pair of durable boots today, there is bewildering variety.

There has been a noticeable trend toward selective reinforcement of the ankle region using plastic inserts and bonded-in fabric layers which cannot stretch. The plastic counters in the heel region of most boots have strengthened them greatly without adding to stiffness. The aim of the bootmaker is to build a boot that when new has an acceptable level of stiffness for the average skier and maintains this stiffness for a reasonable length of time.

Basically, the durability of the boot

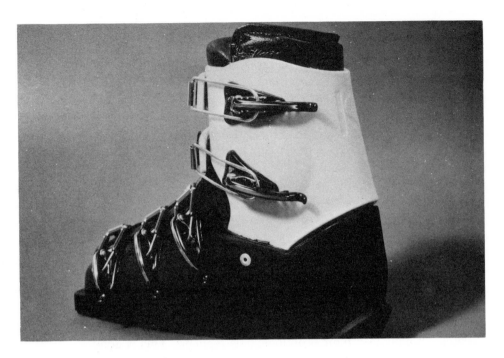

Figure 1-3. *And now, Peter Kennedy and foamed fit.*

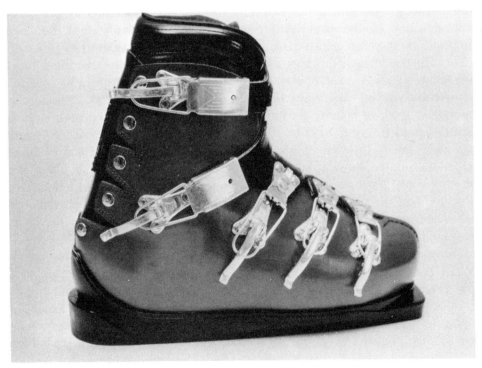

Figure 1-4. *Speedy buckling, synonymous with Henke.*

depends on the quality of the materials used. Leather quality is extremely hard to judge and has nothing to do with stiffness or thickness. The laminating of various plastics to the leather hasn't made the task of judging quality any easier. Cheap boots, no matter how good they look or feel, are seldom a bargain. Buy the brands—and from shops—that have proved they can deliver quality.

What to look for in buckles. The biggest selling point of buckle boots has not been so much the speed with which they can be fastened, as their claim to better comfort, fit and support. Some people who say their feet have always given them trouble in a laced double boot swear by the buckled varieties. Some skiers even say the buckle has completely changed their outlook. Skiing, they've learned, does not necessarily mean aching feet.

In general, the overall performance of a buckle boot is related more to the boot than to the buckle. If the leather or plastic shell of the boot's exterior is inferior, the tension exerted by any buckle will soon stretch the boot to the point where it gives no support. Then too, a weak rivet can render any buckle inoperative. And, of course, if the last is not designed for your foot, or if you have been given the wrong size, no buckle, no matter how efficient, can make the boot fit you.

Buckle boots, excluding certain hardshell plastic ones, come in four-, five-, and six-buckle models. A word of caution is in order here. An individual's foot size does not remain constant. One can't predetermine the buckle stops and assume the boots will always fit properly at the adjustment. The body's fluid balance changes even during the course of a single day. A certain skill is needed. As a matter of fact, most people do not know how to put on a buckle boot. The procedure is quite different from donning a lace boot, and if this difference is not properly understood, no buckle boot can do its job.

With the lace boots, skiers learned, by and large, that it was important to get the heel all the way back into the boot. A smart kick on the floor with the back of the boot before lacing the inner boot was the usual method. This would not be sufficient with a buckle boot. It is necessary to put the foot straight down into the heel area and tap it back, but not all the way back. The proper procedure is then to buckle up each buckle starting at the front, using the loosest setting possible until the fourth buckle is reached. This is generally attached to a notched strap which should be set so that the loosest buckle notch will provide moderate tension. Close this to achieve moderate tension, then half stand, flex the ankle against the strap so that the heel is forced back, and then reset to achieve tension again; flex forward once more to make sure the heel has been forced all the way back, and again reset for a tight adjustment. Particularly with a new boot, this repeated adjustment and flexing is neccessary to guarantee that the heel is back where it belongs. Then, and only then, should the instep buckles be readjusted to tighter settings. The top buckle should then be loosely fastened, at least until the boots are broken in.

Note that tightening the buckles in any manner will not force the heel back into position. On the contrary, it will prevent the heel from sliding into place. With the heel forward, tightening the buckles will cause pain. Eventually, if the skier doesn't break down, the boot will. Note also that the fourth buckle (the third on four-buckle models) is the only one that must be tight. If that is properly adjusted, the heel will stay snug during a forward flex even if all the other buckles are open. Because all buckles operate on a leverage principle, the great danger is that boots will be closed too tightly. If the boots are put on correctly in the first place, the mistake can be avoided. Since we have made so much of the importance of the fourth buckle in proper buckle adjustment, we might just as well mention here that this does not apply to boots with only four buckles. Such boots must of necessity compromise proper fit. The third buckle and the top buckle have to do some of the job normally done by the crucial fourth buckle. Some ingenious diagonal strap arrangements, however, come pretty close to providing adequate support for the intermediate skier using such a boot.

If the danger of overtightening is great because of the tremendous leverage available with all buckles, it is greater with those buckles that don't permit fine selection. With some buckles, the only adjustment possible is from one notch of the buckle arm to another. Others have loops that can be screwed longer or shorter or plastic flippers that permit in-between fit selection. Still others work on a track with half-step adjustments provided via a hinge at the base of the bail. Most of these in-between adjustments are for the instep area. Almost all models provide additional adjustment in the ankle area via straps to which the buckle bail is attached.

Very much related to speed of adjustment and flexibility of adjustment is the ease of adjustment in buckles.

Many a pair of frostbitten toes can be attributed to the fact that a skier, knowing his boots were laced too tightly, just didn't want to be bothered with the task of unlacing and relacing his boots—particularly on the top of some windy mountain. With buckle boots, he can actually loosen them while riding the chair lift and then, in a matter of seconds, tighten them back to the proper tension. And he can do this without taking off his gloves—provided, that is, that the parts of the buckle are easily grasped. Not all are as well designed in this respect as some of the leading models. It is a relatively important consideration.

The final advantage of the buckle— and one that has won the loyalty of racers in particular—is the increased amount of support to the foot that the buckle makes available. As we have seen, all buckle boots permit more pressure than is needed. Over-tightening is more apt to result than with lace boots. But with care, this tremendous leverage can be put to good advantage.

Some models pull the boot past the desired tension, then slacken up as the buckle locks into position. This is much the sort of action that an experienced skier uses when lacing. A different model locks at the point of maximum tension for each setting. This has the advantage of not stretching the boot material more than necessary but the disadvantage that there is less tolerance for improper adjustment. If the buckle is too loose, it will open. This encourages overtightening which in turn can lead to stretching the leather.

No matter which principle of tightening is used, the buckle permits spot tension. This is particularly important for the racer. Instead of a solid column of laced leather, as he got in an old-fashioned boot, the buckle models permit him to select the areas where he wants more tension—the ankle, for instance. Here the diagonal effect of the buckle approximates the tension racers have always sought with long thongs. Down through the instep, too, he can pick which buckles to tighten, which to loosen. Such selective tension is not possible with laces, but all buckles provide this feature.

Naturally, the materials of the buckles are important. Loops, for example, should be of tempered steel wire. Riveting must be carefully done or the tension of the buckle will lift the plates and pull the rivets right out of the boot. Even the best design can lose its effectiveness if workmanship or material is shoddy.

Because of the already established popularity of buckles, however, it can be expected that inferior fasteners will continue to come on the market. Fortunately, we can also expect that additional improvements will be made on the many fine models presently available. If in doubt, the wise skier will seek the advice of a reputable ski retailer. With a little care, he will find he has invested in a new world of foot comfort, effective support, and convenience.

Ski boot materials. Leather for years was the traditional material employed in ski bootmaking. In such construction, the durability of the boot depends on the quality of the leather used. Leather quality is extremely hard to judge and has little to do with stiffness or thickness. Except in the cases of obvious attempts to deceive, our panel of boot experts at *Skiing* had to admit they could not tell either, unless they could

cut up the boot for testing and knew the source and quality of the rawhide and the tanning process used. Adequate quality leather is both scarce and expensive. These were two of the basic causes for the plastic revolution in ski footwear.

Today, plastic is the most popular material for boots. But, wending one's way through the maze of plastic designs is no easy task. Among the plastic-leather laminates, for example, there are as many variations in quality as there were among the old leather boots. Not only are there the variables of leather quality, workmanship, fit, reinforcing, buckle design, and everything else that has always distinguished better boots from the volume-priced models; there are also the variables of the plastic materials used, the way plastic is worked, and the way it is integrated into the boot design.

Another classification might be called the non-rigid plastic outers. Again, this is but a handy grouping rather than a guide to quality. The materials vary from laminated plastics to molded polyurethane, molded PVC (polyvinyl chloride), and other products concocted in test tubes. Inners vary from leather to Corfam, to removable boots.

Finally, there are the hard shell boots—unyielding fiberglass shells. One boot in the experimental stage is even made of a metal shell. Common to all these plastic classifications, though, are greater durability, more lateral rigidity, better control. And the trends spotted recently remain confirmed: locked hinging, ski-width soles, raised heels, increased use of color.

It is to be hoped that this discussion has made plain that none of the many boots on the market or the many design variations available is best simply because of name, or price, or novelty, or because they were used by Hans Hinkelgruber while winning the most recent Olympics. Seek out the best shape for your feet, and seek out the most stiffness you can flex comfortably; this will add control to your skiing. Buy the best quality you can afford, for using is abusing boots. Explore all the new advances in design and materials. They can add real convenience, durability, warmth, and comfort; but whatever their features, beware of boots ill-suited to your needs. It may take time to find a fit that will function for you, but if you do, that pair of fine ski boots will add more pleasure to your skiing than anything you can buy.

As we go to press, a revolution in boot fitting is taking place. Polyurethane or silicone foams are being poured or injected into the hard outer shell of a ski boot—with your foot in it—and in five to fifteen minutes the foam sets up to conform perfectly to your foot. The process is extremely promising, but it is as yet too soon to provide you with adequate guidance because the techniques of fitting and the materials being used are changing every week. Keep in touch with your specialty ski shop for the latest word.

SKIS

To get the most satisfaction, every skier should be equipped with the skis that suit his needs as closely as possible. To help get yourself on the right skis, first learn which are available in your area, their prices, and the purposes for which the various brands and models were designed.

To learn about skis:

1. Ask other skiers about their reaction to their skis.

2. Seek out and read each company's catalogs and sales brochures.

3. Read the advertisements of the various companies.

4. Ski on as many different models as you can. Borrow or rent them (see page 30).

Though the following can't pretend to be anything more than an introductory course on the design and construction of skis, it will help you develop a good broad basic understanding of the subject—enough to permit you to select intelligently a pair that is right for you.

A good place to start is nomenclature. Here is a glossary of the most common features of a ski:

Camber. The arch built into each ski, designed to distribute the skier's weight evenly along the bottom of the ski. Each ski should have from one-half to three-fourths of an inch of camber. In other words, holding a pair of skis bottom to bottom, the distance at the farthest point of separation should be between one and one and one-half inches, slightly more for long, soft skis.

Cut. This refers to the side-cut or side camber of a ski. Note that a good recreational ski for Alpine skiing is widest at the shoulder, narrower at the waist, and wider again at the hip.

Edges. Alpine skis come equipped with steel edges along the bottom. These are a vital, functional part of the equipment, completely necessary for enabling the ski to hold or bite into the snow. Top edges of aluminum or plastic are often supplied to protect the tops from nicks and subsequent water penetration.

Flex. This refers to the flexibility of the ski. Some skis are easy to bend, others hard, and some in between. Some manufacturers produce a product with quite similar flex between each separate pair. Others do not. When they do not, you must determine what the approximate flex is.

Flex Pattern. For most purposes, skis should bend in an even, smooth curve when held at the shovel and heel and depressed over the center of the running surface.

Footplate. That section of the ski upon which the binding is mounted, sometimes referred to as the binding area of the ski.

Forebody. This refers to that part of the ski from the waist (narrowest point) up to the shoulder (widest point).

Groove. The groove runs down the bottom of a ski. It is there primarily to help the ski run straight and to make it move faster.

Length or Size. This is variable. Each model of a good ski usually comes in several sizes, measured either in centimeters, with two-to-three to five-or-more inches of increment between each size. Different manufacturers measure skis in different ways. Most measurements refer to the chord length—a straight line from tip to tail. Some use projected length—a straight line from tail to a point directly below and perpendicular to the tip. Others use sole length—following the curved surface from tip to tail. Depending on which measurement is used, the marked size on one pair could vary by five centimeters from the marked size on another pair of the same actual size.

Torque or Torsion. This refers to a ski's ability to twist along its long axis. In general, a ski with great resistance to torque will bite the snow more than one without this feature. However, if the high torque ski is also stiff in flex, it will be neither as comfortable nor as easy to ski as one that is softer in flex.

Today's skiers are vitally concerned about whether a ski is made of fiberglass and epoxy, metal, or wood. Each of these materials has merits and drawbacks; exactly which material is best is not easy to say with complete objectivity.

Wood, traditionally, has made excellent skis. It is relatively easy to work with and relatively inexpensive. But it is not durable enough to withstand the heavy abuses that today's recreational skier gives it. Modern plastic coatings and laminating processes have made it more durable, but add appreciatively to the cost. For that reason, most of the cheaper skis are made completely of wood.

Actually, no skis are made completely of metal (though a few models are almost completely so). Most metal skis are a sandwich construction wherein wood, used mainly to fill up space, separates a top and bottom skin of metal. The metal provides the bending strength for the ski and the durability. A plastic sole, usually of some type of polyethylene, provides a good sliding surface, and a plastic top provides unlimited design variation for sales appeal and product identity. Metal skis, in general, have great strength and ski excellently. Most are easily repairable and provide years of service.

Almost all successful so-called epoxy skis, epoxy-glass skis, or fiberglass skis are constructed of layers of laminated wood sandwiched between layers of various qualities of epoxy resins and glass fibers. Many of these skis perform beautifully. A few makes have been around for several years. However, some questions still remain about this type of ski's durability, repairability, and long-term camber retention. In spite of this, some top lines are so appreciated for their skiing qualities that skiers would insist on using them even if they lasted only a season. You'll get a good idea of the durability of fiber-reinforced plastic skis (experts refer to these as FRP's) by checking out the manufacturers' guarantees.

What about steel edges? The best, called L-edges because of their shape, present the least amount of metal to the snow. This is an advantage in terms of getting more speed out of your skis, since exposed metal is slow on snow. Some edges are one continuous strip bonded to the ski without rivets or screws. If designed scientifically, this type of edge serves as a functional unit of the ski, adding to its strength, flexibility, and torque resistance.

Other types of L-edges are also used. These are usually made in segments so as not to increase the stiffness of the ski. They are screwed on, with the screws hidden under the plastic sole or else covered with a separate strip of plastic base material. All L-edges are sometimes referred to as hidden edges, inasmuch as about 60 percent of the steel is hidden from exposure.

Almost all edges of the better quality skis not having hidden edges do somehow interlock and overlap so as to present no open gaps when the skis are heavily flexed. Only the cheapest skis have edges which do not interlock or overlap.

All Alpine skis should have steel edges which overhang from the sides one-sixteenth to one thirty-second of an inch. This is so the edge can be filed and kept sharp more easily. Otherwise, when the edge is flush to the ski's side-

Figure 1-5. *Metal skis were pioneered by Head.*

wall, filing is difficult. Overhanging edges are called offset edges.

For ideal performance, the steel edges must be set flush and square with the running surface of the ski. Any deviation from this rule—even as little as 2 degrees—is bound to produce skis which behave in peculiar, unpredictable fashion. In general, the more costly a ski, the higher the grade of steel used for the edges. In the cheapest of skis, the metal is sometimes so soft it cannot even be filed to any semblance of sharpness.

A variety of different types of skis is currently available. Even though

11

many of them are for special uses, you ought to know of their existence. Among the skis used for Alpine purposes (the type of skiing done by almost all recreational skiers) count the Standard, the Combination, and the Slalom, Giant Slalom, and Downhill models. The first two are the most commonly used by the recreational skier. The Slalom model, used for that type of race, is narrower and has more waisting than the Standard. The Giant Slalom is sometimes cut very similarly to the Combination model. It is not quite as suited for quick, continuous turning as is the Slalom model, but it does hold its direction better for traversing and schussing and permits more comfort at faster speeds. The Downhill model is generally wider and with less waisting than other models. It is used in lengths ten to fifteen centimeters longer than usual and has a soft forebody to permit it to snake easily over large bumps and to absorb relatively easily the shocks of high speed skiing.

Two other types of Alpine skis are in use today. They are the Deep Powder models, very soft in flex and used almost exclusively by persons who love to wallow up to their hips in the stuff, and the short-short models. These very short skis, anywhere from two to five feet in length, with proper supervision are a valuable teaching tool and a very pleasant diversion for any recreational skier. Some ski areas offer special instruction for their use. Emotions still run high regarding short-short skis. Many converts swear by their use. Many die-hards still insist on passing them off by saying "You can't really ski with those." The fact is, they are in use increasingly and slowly being accepted as a valuable and pleasant adjunct to the sport.

Among the special-use skis are those for the Nordic aspect of the sport— cross-country racing, ski touring, and jumping. Skis for the first discipline are extremely narrow, very light, and inclined to be fragile. Touring skis are somewhat heavier, sturdier, and often equipped with steel edges. They are also wider, but not as wide as even the slalom skis of an Alpine skier. Jumping skis are the heaviest of the lot, used in lengths up to eight and a half feet, at least four inches wide at their narrowest point. They are designed to provide a jumper with maximum stability and speed while in the air. They are not designed for anything else. Having three or four grooves in the bottom, they are very difficult to turn.

The purchase of a pair of skis is an exciting event. To find which ski is best suited for you, ask yourself these questions: How well do you ski? What are your physical attributes? How much can you spend for skis?

Answer honestly. The difference between an intermediate doing stem turns on packed surfaces and an expert wedeling down any slope has a big bearing on which length ski is needed. So does a difference of fifteen to twenty pounds in weight. Heavier persons need somewhat stiffer or longer or more cambered skis than light-weights. Differences in a person's strength, physical condition, and athletic aggressiveness also make significant differences in skis required. A stronger person can handle a stiffer or longer ski than a weaker person, just as can a more experienced, athletic skier.

If you don't know how much you want to spend for skis, but you do know how much you want to spend overall on ski equipment (skis, boots, bindings, poles), then consider that for skis alone, about

40 percent should be set aside.

In selecting a ski, the first consideration is length. How long should the skis be? As previously stated most skis are measured in terms of centimeters. A 200 centimeter ski is about 6 feet 6 inches long. The word "about" is important: Manufacturers measure their skis differently; thus, one firm's 200 centimeter ski may be slightly shorter than another firm's 195, or slightly longer than yet another's 205. For that reason, we refer to the manufacturer's label of a ski's length as its size. Size, then is an approximation of a ski's length. You should know that about two and one-half centimeters equal one inch. Then five centimeters—the usual increment between sizes of a manufacturer's skis—is a matter of two inches. That difference is not critical when it comes to the exact size of ski for you, unless you are an elite class racer. Or unless you are considering a ski which is already close to the limits of tolerance for your height, weight, and skiing ability.

And that brings us tight up against the nitty gritty of picking skis. What are those limits? What is the normal size ski for you? In general, a ski which reaches to the top of the wrist of your upstretched arm is considered long. And a ski which reaches only an inch or two above the elbow of your upstretched arm is thought of as short—disregarding for the moment the specialized three-, four-, and five-foot short skis. A normal length ski, therefore, is one which reaches to someplace between elbow and wrist of the upstretched arm.

Pick a long ski: if you are heavy for your height; if you habitually ski fast; if you are still growing rapidly.

Pick a shorter ski: if you ski slowly, controlling your speed by turning fre-

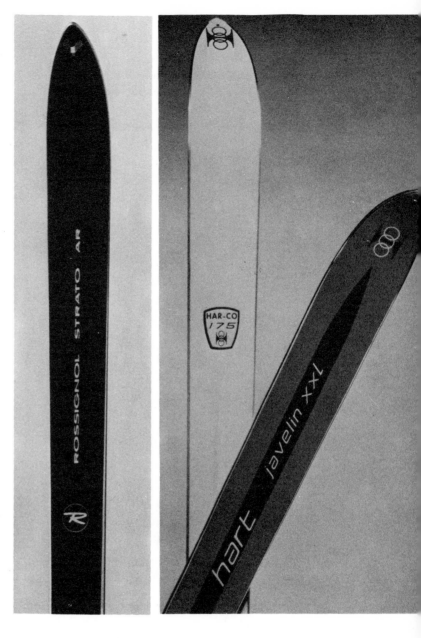

Figure 1-6. *A leading glass ski is Rossignol's Strato (left). Hart (right) offers a combination of metal and fiberglass.*

quently; if you are lightweight; if you have doubts about your athletic prowess. If you seldom ski faster than fifteen to twenty miles per hour, you may be pleased with a ski even as short as your height.

13

Pick a very short ski (anything less than your height) only if you've rented several pairs, in various lengths, and have determined the optimum length for yourself.

Simple enough to here, right? Well, if you don't want to be confused by further facts, better not read on. The foregoing information will get you by as long as you are choosing from among the best lines. Part of what you pay for among the best is something called "quality controls for product consistency." The most conscientious manufacturers strive to make every pair of skis of a certain size and model with an absolute minimum of difference between them. One of the frequently encountered variables is the matter of bending flex—that characteristic of a ski which we refer to as soft, hard, or medium flex. Time was when many skis bore a mark corresponding to their flex. A heavier skier could then select skis on the stiff side of the range; a light skier, the softer flex ski, yet both pairs of skis would have been sized the same. Nowadays, you have to feel the flex by hand which, to say the least, is a very unreliable method at best, filled with arty mystique (and devoid of scientific accuracy). If you want to be sure the flex of the skis which you are about to purchase is reasonably suited to you, try this: Place the skis bottom to bottom. Mark where the soles of the relaxed skis touch at front and back. Then put supports, such as books, under each end of the skis, so they're suspended horizontally at least five inches from the floor, with the marks you've made on the skis hitting the inside edges of the supports. Now stand on the skis, dividing your weight equally between them, placing your feet exactly

where they'd be if the bindings were mounted on the skis. Have a friend see how much the skis bend under your weight. If the skis depress less than an inch below the top of the supports, the skis are too stiff for you.

If, when you stand on the skis, they flex more than three inches below the supports, the skis are considered soft-flexing. These are fine for soft-snow skiing, but will not provide precise control for you on the hardpack.

Two other factors complicate the art of picking a pair of skis. One is the matter of your strength, the other concerns the way you ski. Some skiers christie by pushing around the heels of their skis and frequently shifting weight from ski to ski. This way of skiing is typified by the Austrian and American techniques. Others ski with their weight more or less evenly distributed on each ski at all times, initiating their christies by swivelling both ends of each ski around its middle, directly underfoot. Their way is typified by the French technique and the hot dog techniques of all nationalities. Heel pushers and stronger legged skiers get along best with skis that are on the stiff side. Foot swivellers and the not-so-strong-legged skiers do better on softer flexing skis. Versatile skiers, however, use either flex, adapting their technique to the demands of the skis.

When picking a pair of skis for a youngster, apply the same principles described above. However, because of the relative lack of strength of those under ten or twelve, the size of the skis is best limited to head-height or a few inches shorter. Of course, children quickly grow into longer length skis, but to assure their quick learning as beginners, their skis should not exceed

14

their height by more than four inches.

There you have them—the many subtleties to consider when picking the right pair of skis for yourself. It should now be obvious why you need to know your own mind, strength, way of skiing, and pocketbook, if you are to find the ideal marriage between you and your skis. Chances are, you'll not hit the mark exactly right. But this is no cause for despair. The human mechanism is very adaptable, and with practice, you can learn to like almost any pair of skis, and with more practice, ski better than you ever did before. The information provided here should narrow down your selection to no more than a near miss, and provided the bottom of the skis are properly maintained, you'll soon ski yourself into the ideal pair of skis.

BINDINGS

Most skiers don't *select* a pair of bindings; they accept the recommendations of the salesman. Or of their friends. Unfortunately, this doesn't guarantee that the skier will end up with the binding he should have. Neither does continuing with the brand he has been using for the last five years just because he likes them. "They always release when I want them to" sounds like a pretty good testimonial. The trouble is, every skier with a broken leg would probably have said the same thing—before his accident. After all, only a damned fool would continue to ski with bindings he thought wouldn't work.

If recommendations or even your own experiences are not to be trusted, how can you tell if a binding is any good? Frankly, it's no easy matter. Some performance characteristics can be seen on casual inspection; others require intricate testing. Fortunately, most of the best selling brands are fairly reliable—providing they're properly installed and adjusted.

The Cables. Bindings break down into two main categories: cable and cableless. The former consists of a cable which passes around the heel of the boot, down and along the sides of the ski through cable guides, then up to the front, ahead of the toe unit, where some type of stretching and clamping device is located. With proper mounting, adjustment and maintenance, cable release bindings do operate reliably. But always replace kinked or out of shape cables immediately. Be sure to set the adjustment so that your heel can lift off the ski about one-half inch, then be released. Periodically check the setting and smooth operation of each component.

Incidentally, with one exception, do not consider any type of cable assembly which does not provide a mechanism that pops up, partially freeing the cable and allowing the heel of the boot to lift up in the event of a hard forward fall. A few of these still exist, often as hand-me-downs from friends, which provide no forward releasing factor whatsoever. Since most injurious falls involve some forward and vertical thrust on the heel, this type of cable assembly should be labeled "suicide" and thrown out.

The one exception mentioned above is a cable binding which appeared recently, with the releasing mechanism located in the springs directly at the heel. This device—the Marker Snaplok—is not subjected to the friction problems of the usual type of cable binding, since the cable snaps apart right at the heel. It has met with wide acceptance, and when mounted and adjusted properly, offers good control and releasability.

15

Cable bindings, because of the built-in problems of friction, are fast losing their sales appeal, even though their cost is considerably less than for most cableless types. However, experienced skiers who frequently go ski mountaineering or touring prefer the easy release of heel tension by simply having an extra forward set of cable guides, which lets the heel rise up from the ski for walking on skis.

Cableless Bindings. These bindings are of two types: step-ins and latch-ins. The former require no bending over to insert the boot; the latter do. Both types have gained rapidly in popularity in the last two years, and numerous different models have appeared—too many, actually, to attempt to evaluate them even by category. They all provide some degree of safety. At the end of this chapter some firm guidelines are presented to help you pick the best.

The first step in selecting a binding is to know its intended use: whether for Alpine skiing, touring, or both; whether for a child, a lightweight adult, or a heavy adult; whether for a recreational skier or a racer. Unless the binding is to be used for cross-country touring, dismiss the idea of a cable binding from your mind. With the exception of cables which release at the heel, these designs should be considered outmoded for downhill skiing.

As for the special needs of a child, lightweight adult, etc., they can be met by those bindings which provide for a wide range of adjustment. Tightening or loosening a tension screw can make the same binding safe for both child and racer. Other bindings are more limited and may have special springs for lighterweight people, or, at the other end of the scale, for racers. The only sure way to know is to check them out with an instrument like the Lipe Release Check.

If you can't obtain a release at the setting recommended for your weight and ability, go to a different spring or to a different binding.

Assuming you have made a valid selection in terms of use, the next question is performance—how the unit works. Briefly, here is a checklist of the qualities to look for:

1. *Compatibility of toe and heel.* It is best to buy toe and heel units matched by the manufacturer. In some cases, different brands of toes and heels can be mixed to advantage, but unless you know what you're doing (don't assume the salesman waiting on you is any more knowledgeable than you are in these matters), mixing is a risky practice. With many combinations, the results can be disastrous.

2. *Anti-shock characteristics.* This is the ability of the binding to move off center under a momentary load, and then return to center when that load is removed. *Skiing's* binding consultant Gordon Lipe considers movement of three-eighths of an inch from center without release to be the minimum for lateral flexibility and one-fourth of an inch upward the minimum for vertical flex at the heel. The lateral movement should be equal to both left and right, with return to center.

3. *Low inherent friction*—to prevent jamming of the pivots when high loads are applied (as when the boot is squeezed into place).

4. *Toe units relatively insensitive to changes in forward pressure exerted by the heel units.* If sensitive, such toe units should be combined only with heel units with easily controlled forward pressure.

5. *Consistent releases* (left, right, and vertically).

6. *Consistent contact.* Whatever

Figure 1-7. *One of the oldest — and best — of the step-ins is the American-made Cubco.*

arrangement is used to make contact between the boot and the binding, it should be of such nature that this contact is not changed appreciably by use and wear.

7. *Units that are easy to adjust,* and adjustments that are self-locking.

8. *Ease of entry and exit.* Getting in and out should not change the release pressures.

9. *A good runaway device* — one which does not interfere with the release function.

10. *Low maintenance.* The maintenance required should be easy to perform.

11. *Operation immune to freezing.*

12. *Compatibility with the boots you own.*

In addition to the above characteristics, the following, not strictly related to performance, would be added bonuses: visible adjustment settings, handsome appearance, light weight, function easy to understand, mounting easy to do, clear instructions provided by the manufacturer.

How do you go about checking all these points? Some are obvious, of course. You can look at the binding and know if it is handsome, or if the adjustment settings are visible. You can read the instructions and know if they are clear, easy to understand, and whether the binding is easy to mount and adjust.

Other points are more subtle and may require a more practiced eye. For example, you don't have to ski with the bindings for a couple of years to find out if they are easy to maintain or relatively immune to freezing. Units with simple design and rugged construction —

17

pivots completely open or completely sealed — are the ones that will cause the least maintenance problems and which will not allow ice to be compressed during the release action. (Silicone spray applied to any binding, by the way, will reduce maintenance and icing problems.) All this is visible on inspection.

More careful examination is required to determine some of the other performance features. Most shops have bindings displayed on what are known as demonstration boards. If the complete binding is mounted on the board, you can use it to assess performance, though frequently such bindings are mounted with special demonstration springs and therefore cannot be used to determine the range of adjustment. But, with the aid of a tester such as the Lipe Release Check, which most shops have, you can discover a good deal about the performance characteristics.

Shock absorption, for example, is measurable. With the boot in the binding, apply lateral pressure at the toe. If the binding releases before the boot toe moves a minimum of one-fourth of an inch off center, it has insufficient shock absorption. This should be checked in both directions, and in each case, the boot toe should return to center when pressure is removed. The Lipe Release Check plunger is a good device for applying this pressure.

At the heel, apply upward pressure, and if the binding releases before the boot travels three-sixteenths of an inch vertically, again you know it has insufficient shock absorption. And again, if there is sufficient vertical travel, the binding should return to normal position when the pressure is removed.

Determining whether the binding has a low friction design is not quite as easy. Probably the best you can do is to look for smooth action as you release the boot from the binding. At no point during the release should you feel any restraining action which might prevent full release.

To determine if the toe unit is relatively insensitive to changes in forward pressure from the heel, take the lateral release pressure reading with a series of different forward pressure settings. If the lateral release pressure changes, the toe unit is affected by forward pressure changes. When this is the case, hairtrigger adjustment is required to get the proper settings at both heel and toe. On the other hand, even if the lateral release pressure doesn't change, the forward pressure could affect the toe in other ways. For example, too much could reduce the amount of shock absorption or even negate the shock absorption by preventing the toe unit from returning to center. And in the case of a toe unit that requires forward pressure for proper engagement of the boot, too little could allow the notched boot to slip away from the teeth of the toe unit.

Such problems can be resolved if you have a heel unit that provides separate means of adjusting hold-down tension and forward pressure. A heel unit that utilizes the same spring for down and forward pressure is not a drawback, however, if the relationship between hold-down and forward pressure is well-balanced and the effect on the toe unit is minimal. But it is largely because of the possible ill effect forward pressure can have on the functioning of the toe unit that mixing the toe unit of one manufacturer with the heel unit of another is such a dangerous practice.

18

Figure 1-8. *Marker's Simplex toe requires notches in the boot to drive the unit.*

Figure 1-10. *A shock-absorbing toe requiring no notches is the Look Nevada II.*

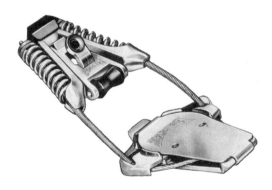

Figure 1-9. *The Marker Rotamat is a lightweight latch-in unit used by many racers.*

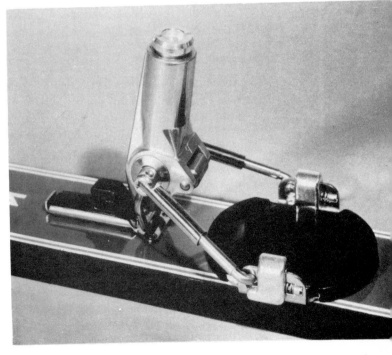

Figure 1-11. *The Look Grand Prix heel unit is an enclosed cam-operated step-in.*

To test for consistent releases, note the Release Check number required to open the binding at a given setting, then repeat the release action several times. You should get the same reading every time. Be sure to check for consistent left and consistent right releases.

You should also check to see that your boots are compatible with the unit you are considering. In a cup-type of toe unit, a boot that is too narrow could penetrate too far into the cup for proper leverage. An asymmetrical boot toe could cause unequal release to the left and right. A sole that is too thick or too thin might not fit the range of the toe-hold-down lug (always allowing for a one-sixteenth of an inch clearance), or the hold-down lug at the heel.

Bear in mind, too, that the boot is an essential part of the binding. It is your responsibility to keep in good condition the part of the boot that contacts the binding. Worn out notches on old boots should be refurbished by installing sole protectors. If you buy new boots to fit bindings that require notches, it is wise to install the sole protectors at the outset. Some of the newer bindings do not require notching, but proper function of all release bindings (except the boot plate types) is dependent on proper shape and condition of the sole area contacting the toe unit. Properly fitting sole protectors will provide more safety and longer boot life. Remember also that boot curl drastically affects toe release pressures. The more the curl, the more the friction between the ball of the foot and the ski. Either purchase a binding that won't require toe height adjustment (boot plate types), or units which can be adjusted to compensate for the curl. Rigid soles, of course, like those on almost all of the modern plastic boots, largely eliminate this problem as does proper storage of boots in a boot press. In any event, remember that care of the boot is the biggest factor in maintaining consistent contact between boot and binding.

Visual inspection will tell you if the unit is easy to adjust. But even a practiced eye can be fooled about self-locking characteristics of adjustments; extended use is the best test of this factor.

Similarly, whether getting in and out of the bindings changes its setting is something you can't determine without extensive use or testing. However, in most cases, whether the binding is easy to get into and out of should be apparent. Bindings with teeth that require boot notches are harder to line up than the cut-type. Bindings that are not rigid on the ski are bound to be difficult to put on, particularly on a steep slope. Less apparent to casual inspection are the difficulties connected with putting on bindings which are highly sensitive to snow under the boot. This can be a particularly sticky problem in deep snow. Any step-in binding, for that matter, is apt to be difficult to put on in soft snow. When it comes to deciding which binding is for you, consider your own tolerance for such difficulties: Would you rather have to bend over to latch on a unit (relatively easy to put on in deep snow) or would you rather be able to merely stamp down on a step-in (relatively harder to put on in deep snow)?

Checking out a good runaway device is fairly simple. This could be a ski stop —a spring loaded lever that prevents the ski from sliding on its own—or an Arlberg or various other kinds of straps that hold the ski to the leg after the binding releases. The only caution is that it should be attached in such a manner that no hardware rubs on the boot to interfere with lateral release, or that in forward release, the strap doesn't prevent the boot from rising off the ski. You can check this visually.

Finally, there is the range of adjustment. All you can do is ask the shop to make sure to give you the proper spring for your weight. You can check this out only when the bindings are mounted on the skis. Of course, everything should be checked at this point to make sure the bindings have been properly mounted and adjusted for your weight and ability.

One final note. The biggest contributor to binding malfunction in an otherwise properly functioning unit is the friction between the boot and ski. Some devices to reduce this problem are now on the market. The various friction pads provided by most manufacturers are also some help, as is the use of silicone spray. A binding that functions smoothly, produces low friction, and that gets the highest degree of retention at the lowest settings is the goal. If you can't get satisfactory results with one brand, try another.

Remember that the biggest mistake made when buying, especially by a beginner or intermediate skier, is to try and save money by choosing an inferior binding with the idea that your skiing technique does not require the best. Actually, the poorer a skier's ability the better the binding he needs. When it comes to releasable ski bindings there is only one standard a skier should consider—buy the best regardless of cost.

POLES

For the beginner selecting his first ski outfit, poles are frequently an after-thought. In going through his early ski maneuvers, he may have been told by his instructor to hold the poles parallel to the slope. That doesn't look as though they're very necessary. But he has probably learned that they are an aid when he is climbing, indispensable when he has fallen and is struggling to get back up. Still he probably doesn't plan to do much climbing, hopes he won't continue to do too much falling. As a result, he buys the cheapest poles he can find, though as likely as not, these will soon be bent out of shape and he'll be replacing them with something better.

How do you tell a good pole? It is impossible for the layman to distinguish between a shaft of high-tensile strength, aircraft aluminum alloy, and one of lesser grades. Price differentials can be assumed to reflect quality differences not discernible to the untrained eye. There are some objective ways to choose a pole that's right for you.

Length. Regardless of quality, proper length is essential. Ski poles that reach to your armpit are long. Those that reach to your waistline are short. Long poles provide extra leverage for stunts and gelandesprungs. Short poles can be moved quickly, which makes them useful to mogul-tamers who go from one turn to another in a hurry. Normal length poles, when they are gripped and placed correctly, should allow your forearm to remain nearly parallel to the ground. An inch or two longer or shorter than normal makes little difference to most skiers. If in doubt about what length you prefer, buy your poles long and have them shortened an inch or two at a time—until you find what's comfortable for you.

Weight. A fifty-four inch pole weighs anywhere from about ten ounces to over a pound. Steel poles are usually heavier than aluminum poles. But overall weight is less important than balance or swingweight. The weight out at the tip is what contributes most to fatigue. Therefore, rather than weigh a pole, swing it to get the feel of its balance. If more of the weight is up near the handle, the pole will be easier to manipulate than if the weight is concentrated out near the basket.

Taper. One of the ways pole designers accomplish good balance is by swaging the shaft of the pole into a gradual taper. If the taper begins near the handle or at least thirty inches from the point and extends the full length of the shaft, it is said to have a long taper. If it begins nearer the basket, it is said to have a shorter taper. If the shaft is of even diameter right down to the basket, there is no taper. And if the shaft tapers upwards from the middle to the handle as well as from the middle toward the basket, this is called a double taper.

Swaging is a process of hammering a tube down to a smaller circumference. This results in lengthening the pole and in a thicker layer of metal which, in turn, means added strength and a lighter end. The longer the taper, the lighter and thicker the end. Assuming equal grades of metal, the choice between a properly swaged short taper, long taper, or double taper is primarily a matter of esthetics.

Handle. Various grades of plastic, rubber, or leather are used in pole handles, the better materials being more resistant to cold, moisture, and wear. Most top quality poles use vinyl. The shaping of the handle can be important. For example, if the handle is notched for finger grips, it could prove awkward to a skier wearing mittens. If the notch-

ing or molding results in holding the pole with the end protruding an inch or so beyond the top of the clenched hand, this could be dangerous in a fall. Some pole handles are tilted or so shaped to make it easier to plant the poles far enough ahead while skiing. Others are shaped or clearly marked to differentiate the right pole from the left. Most of these considerations come down to a matter of personal preference.

Strap. Pole straps are straight or shaped (to fit more comfortably around the wrist), adjustable (with a buckle) or non-adjustable. Some are also releasable so that at a given pull, rather than jerk your arm off, the strap will release from the pole. Even the so-called non-adjustable straps, however, should be adjustable. When leather gets wet, it stretches. Over the course of a season, the stretching could amount to a couple of inches. A strap that is too long gives no support to the hand in gripping the pole. One that is too short, doesn't permit a proper grasp of the pole and it restricts hand movement. Most better poles have a screw or pin going through the top of the handle, through both ends of the strap, into a plug of wood inserted in the top of the pole shaft. To shorten a strap fastened in this manner is simply a matter of removing the screw and strap, cutting off the necessary amount from one end, making a new hole in it, and re-inserting both ends and the screw. Incidentally, if you want to be fastidious about it, when shortening a strap in this manner, put the ends back so that the lower strap curves off slightly to the right on one, to the left on the other. The thumb should rest on the lower strap (for minimum fatigue). If you get two poles that are not a pair, it is relatively simple, when there is a screw at

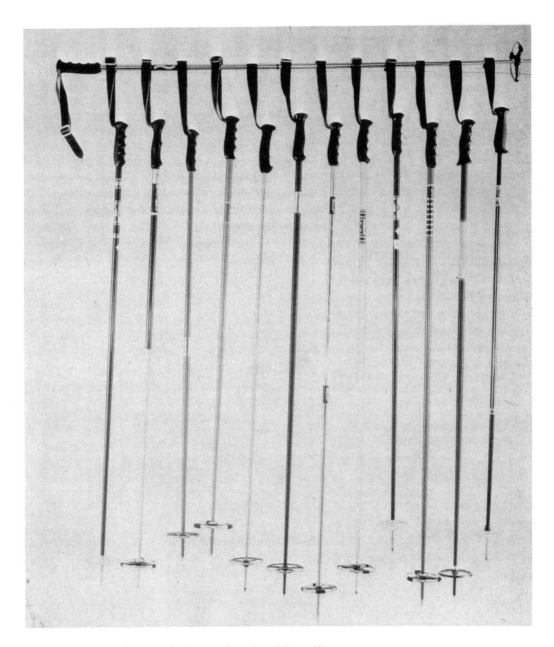

Figure 1-12. *Poles are lightweight, durable, efficient.*

the top, to make a pair by reversing the straps on one.

Basket. The basket consists of a ring, usually of metal, and spokes—of leather, rubber, or plastic. The plastic must be joined to a drive-fit ferrule in the center of the ring. It is attached to the shaft by friction in order to keep weight to a minimum; that is to say, rather than cotter pin, nuts and bolts or the like, most pole manufacturers use rubber grommets or other friction devices, which are not always foolproof. Baskets do slip off, usually in very cold weather, when rubber loses its elasticity. Top quality, new baskets are very inexpensive. A simple way to put the basket back on is to place the basket

23

over a bathtub drain, wet the tip of the shaft with detergent, and press the shaft into the basket.

Most baskets are about four and a half inches in diameter. The distance from the tip of the pole to the place where the basket sits on the shaft should be about three inches. The spokes should be flexible—which is why the distance from the tip to the basket must be in excess of the radius of the basket, else the ring would slip over the tip. There are baskets with three spokes, four spokes, five spokes, and some with almost solid centers. Some manufacturers provide poles with special deep powder attachments— wider baskets, essentially. There is disagreement over whether such attachments are an advantage.

Point. For skiing where the surface is frequently packed or icy, it is essential that the tip of the pole be sharp enough to penetrate. Swaging a steel pole right down to a point works fine. With aluminum shafts, an integral point is not hard enough if a good deal of ice is encountered. In many aluminum poles, therefore, a separate hard steel point is inserted. Epoxy glues—or swage-fit or drive-fit—make this bond about as permanent as an integral point, so that whether a point is integral or inserted is no indication of how good it will be. Dulled points can be re-sharpened. For cross-country skiing, poles have a special point curved on one side to eliminate sticking as the pole is pulled out.

SKI CLOTHING

The first function of ski clothing is to keep you warm—if you can also be beautiful and fashionable at the same time, that's all to the good. The theory of keeping warm calls for keeping body heat in, not keeping cold air out. This is most effectively accomplished via layers of clothing which trap the heat from your body between them. At the same time that you're piling all those layers on, you must be sure they fit loosely enough to allow proper circulation. A too-tight pair of stretch pants, no matter how expensive the fabric, won't keep you as warm as a less expensive, but properly fitted pair.

For a skier, the layers usually consist of: underwear (shirt and long johns), turtleneck shirt, stretch pants, sweater, parka, or lift coat or windbreaker. On the extremities go socks, gloves, and hats or headbands.

You are well-advised to shop for all of those items in a specialty ski shop or department, for several reasons. The specialists will have a larger selection not only in styles and colors, but in price ranges; employees in a ski shop are usually skiers themselves and can give you good advice on the clothing you will need and how it should fit you.

PARKAS. A parka is the item of ski apparel which offers you most protection against the cold and wet. It should be warm, water resistant, and wind resistant. It should be lightweight and flexible.

Parkas are usually made of three heat-trapping layers of material: a nylon outer shell, an insulating middle layer or fill, and a lining. Still the most popular fabric for the shell is nylon, which can come disguised as taffeta, silk, oxford cloth, or even velvet. Other fabrics include poplin, wood, and "Astro-cloth." Whatever the fabric, it should be treated to resist water and wind. Some nylons can be coated to make them completely waterproof. Like vinyl, these are usually too warm, because air cannot penetrate and perspiration cannot evaporate.

The fill provides the most efficient layer for trapping warm air from your body. It can be made of down—the warmest and most expensive; or of resilient synthetic fibers; or of acetate wastes. The latter are least expensive but tend to pack together and lose their insulating qualities. The fill is frequently fastened to the outer shell by quilting. The lining is usually of nylon.

Increasingly popular are streamlined jackets made of stretch fabric to match pants. They will not keep you as warm as a filled parka, but some people are willing to sacrifice warmth for chic. Manufacturers are experimenting with lightweight inner linings which add to warmth without destroying the sleek look.

Fur parkas come into a category by themselves. Real fur parkas, whether rabbit or mink, need no middle layer. They also tend to be naturally water resistant. Synthetic fur or pile fabrics are not as warm as the real thing and may not even be as warm for skiing as the traditional triple-layered parka.

Recently, the tapered-leg stretch pant has yielded ground to all sorts of trouser-legged pants, often as not made of non-stretchable, ciré nylon fabrics. These over-the-boot pants have several ingenious cuffs designed to keep snow out of your boots. Their prime advantage—a better mating of boot to foot.

What to look for in fit. Parkas range from waist length to mid-thigh length—one long enough to cover your fanny when you are sitting on a chairlift is preferable. The long, mid-thigh lift coats, should have side zippers at the bottom to enable you to maneuver freely when necessary. Some parkas have a detachable or foldup panel to give you extra coverage as you want it.

Parkas should be cut fully enough to fit comfortably over a ski sweater when necessary; wrists should be snug without being constricting; so should necklines. Swing your arms back and forth to be sure there is no pull across the back or chest. Look for zipper closings—buttons or snaps will not keep cold air out; look for enough pockets and for a device for attaching lift tickets—all are details which indicate a well-made parka.

Pants. Most skiers today wear stretch pants, not only because they are flattering to both men and women, but because they are warm and comfortable. Stretch fabrics are available in assorted qualities with characteristics depending on the original fibers and how those fibers are woven together. Most stretch fabrics combine a stretchable nylon fiber with wool or with a synthetic such as rayon or an acrylic. Competing hard with the stretch nylon fiber is a synthetic elastic fiber called spandex—its generic name. Spandex can also be combined with wool or another synthetic, and it has up to eight times the stretchability of nylon. Pants made with spandex are fitted as standard stretch pants are. What you do get from spandex is long wear, great flexibility, and almost 100 percent "recovery"—return of the stretched-out fiber to its original shape.

Many of today's stretch pants are machine-washable; others should be dry cleaned. If you've picked up mud or dirt on your pants by falling or getting shoved in a cafeteria line, let the pants dry and then brush them carefully with a good clothes brush. In most cases, the soil will be removed. In fact, it's a good idea to brush them after each wearing anyway.

A good pair of stretch pants will last several years—longer if you don't ski frequently. If you do ski only a few weekends a year, a moderately priced pair of stretch pants will suffice. For the sake of variety, women in particular often prefer to buy two pairs of moderately priced ski pants rather than one pair of expensive ones.

What to look for in fit. The biggest problem in buying ski pants is finding the proper fit. Pants deviate in their proportions from manufacturer to manufacturer to such an extent that one manufacturer's size 34 Regular may fit you perfectly and another's 34 Regular may leave you gasping for breath. Here, an experienced salesperson can save you time—he will already know which brands run small, which run large and which run true to size.

The fit you should look for is taut, not tight. Pants should be smooth but not strained across the seat and abdomen and should not cut under the fanny. The line from hip to ankle should be straight and tapered. The waistband should ride on the hips, slightly below the natural waist. If it's higher than that, the pants may be too long; if it pulls too hard on your hips, they are probably too short.

UNDERWEAR. One set of long underwear is a must. The two-piece sets, top and tights, are most popular. Tops may be made of multi-layered thermal cotton, soft imported wood, cotton-lined wool, or a combination of natural and synthetic fibers. Tights can be made of pure silk (some people swear by silk, others say it offers no warmth at all); double- or triple-layered thermal fabric; a wool and nylon combination; cotton, or plain stretch nylon. Some have feet, some do not. There is a difference in construction between a dancer's tights and a skier's tights—the former may not be warm enough.

SOCKS. Skiers do suffer from cold feet. One of the reasons is poor circulation, another is that feet locked into ski boots have very little opportunity to move and flex and keep going what circulation there is. Most skiers wear two pairs of socks, a lightweight inner pair and a heavyweight outer pair. If underwear tights are the kind with built-in feet some skiers add only a single pair of heavy socks.

Socks should be carefully fitted. If they are too large, there will be bulky lumps to rub against the foot; if they are too small, they will restrict circulation. You should be able to move your toes freely inside the sock.

The inner pair of socks can be made of lightweight cotton, silk, or a synthetic. The outer pair can be Ragg wool (frequently called the Norwegian sock), a multi-layered thermal sock, or the new so-called cushioned sock. Experiment with the various combinations to find which suits you best—the cost is small when the reward is warm feet. But, a caveat to beginners; one of the signs of a beginner skier is socks worn outside the pants. The top of a sock sticking out between boot and pant not only breaks the trim line of the pants but serves as a wick to absorb moisture from the snow. It might be wise to have a pair of heavy socks available to wear when you're trying on pants in the store to insure a proper fit at the ankle.

SWEATERS AND TURTLENECKS. Sweaters and turtleneck shirts are probably the most practical of all ski purchases because they can be fitted into your nonskiing life as well. They're good for skating, sailing, informal parties—some women even team the turtlenecks with suits or jumpers for office or town wear.

Ski sweaters can be of the hand-knit wool, elaborately patterned, imported-from-Europe variety to a simple synthetic yarn machine-knit, made-in-U.S.A. Some skiers buy sweaters by weight, operating on the theory that the heavier it is, the warmer it is. That's not necessarily true—many synthetic-yarn sweaters are lightweight, but as warm and at least as long-wearing as wool.

Which style is a matter of individual taste. Cardigans are popular with men and can be worn over a coordinated pullover for skiing or with a shirt for after-ski. Turtleneck pullovers look smart under a collarless or mandarin-collared stretch jacket. V-necks are useful for after-skiing and general sportswear.

A word about sweater fit: A pullover should fall about mid-hip. The bottom of the sweater should be firm but not tight around the hips; the shoulder seams should fall at or slightly below the shoulder; cuffs should be snug at the wrist. There should be enough room to maneuver arms and shoulders with no strain or pull across the back.

Today, turtlenecks are available in patterns and an increasing variety of solid colors. They're made of fabrics ranging from all cotton through nylons and polyesters to pure merino wools and silks. Cotton reinforced with nylon or a polyester is probably the best buy in the medium-price range. But, since a turtleneck is the layer of clothing which begins to trap body heat most effectively, at the neck and wrists in particular, it should be snug enough to keep warm air from escaping. In fact, some warm-blooded skiers dispense with an underwear top altogether and begin their layers of clothing with an absorbent cotton turtleneck.

HEADGEAR. U.S. Army cold weather studies indicate that more heat is lost through the head than through any other part of the body. Wear a hat when you're skiing—a hat, not a headband, unless it's a warm, sunny day. Hats that convert from caps to hoods are good insurance for uncertain weather. Knit hats are practical, usually inexpensive, and come in a multitude of styles and colors.

Fur hats are warm, luxurious, and can double for street wear. Avoid wearing them in very wet weather, however, as wet fur will flatten and mat.

GLOVES OR MITTENS. Mittens are warmer than gloves, but skiers seem to prefer gloves for their flexibility. Leather gloves with Curon- or foam-type interlining and a silk lining seem to be most popular. For extra warmth, wear an additional silk or wool liner. If you're going to be using a rope tow a great deal, look for a heavy-duty glove with special protection against the rope.

GOGGLES OR GLASSES. The two pairs of lenses which usually come with a skier's goggles or glasses are not to color-coordinate with your new sweaters. The dark lenses are for protection against the glare of snow under a bright sun; the yellow lenses are to lend depth and dimension to terrain under the flat light caused by an overcast. Goggles also offer protection against wind and flying snow.

TRIP GEAR

Are you ready to go skiing when the time comes? Do you pack in a hectic

27

rush-hour way, hoping the right things will land in your suitcase? There's an easier way to do it, and to help you make sure that you've remembered all the equipment and clothing necessary for a ski trip, *Skiing's* editors have compiled a checklist of what to take with you. First, before the season starts, check off the items you already have, and buy what you'll need. Second, keep this list handy, and use it for guidance each time you pack for a skiing trip.

If you drive to the slopes, you've free rein over what to take. But if you're flying, check baggage regulations before packing—not all airlines have a special rate for skis, which will consume fifteen to twenty-five pounds of your weight allowance. Pack accordingly.

Essentials

☐ Skis
☐ Poles
☐ Boots and Boot Tree
☐ Wax
☐ Parka
☐ Sweater
☐ Turtleneck Shirt
☐ Hat/Headband
☐ Goggles/Glasses with yellow and green lenses
☐ Lip and Sun Cream
☐ Ski Lock
☐ Ski Ties or Carrier
☐ Stretch Pants
☐ Thermal Underwear
☐ Socks—Heavy, Light
☐ Mittens/Gloves
☐ After-Ski Boots
☐ Binding Tool, Silicone Spray
☐ Tissues, Band-Aids, Aspirin, Sewing Kit

Options

☐ Additional Sweaters
☐ Lightweight Parka
☐ Warm-up Suit, Pants
☐ Fanny Pack, Belt Pouch
☐ Camera, Film
☐ Foam Padding for Boots
☐ Nylon Windshirt
☐ Skier's Release Check
☐ Extra Stretch Pants
☐ After-Ski Sweater or T-Neck
☐ Knickers, Knee Socks
☐ Face Mask
☐ Additional Underwear, Socks, T-Necks, Glove Liners
☐ Edge File
☐ Repair Kit

Ski Vacation

☐ Pajamas, Robe, Slippers
☐ Extra Apparel
☐ Pant Suit, Cullottes, Long Skirt for Girls
☐ Flannel Slacks, Blazer or Sport Jacket
☐ T-Necks for Men
☐ Dress Shoes
☐ Dress-up After-Ski Boots
☐ Jacket, Coat, Cape
☐ Gloves
☐ Handbag or Ski Pouch
☐ Tie or Ascot

SKI CARE

Your ski equipment is a good-sized investment, thus it's wise to take good care of it. Here are a few tips that you should keep in mind:

Boots. Plastic boots require little care, except for cleaning them after use. This should be done as directed by the boot-maker. Leather boots, on the other hand, must be kept on a boot press or strong shoe trees when not in use. Never attempt to dry them too rapidly, such as in front of a fire. During the season, ordinary paste shoe polish keeps boots looking well and in good condition.

To prepare leather boots for the coming winter, clean thoroughly with mild soap and water solution, if needed. To leather soles, apply commercial sole sealer (available at specialty ski shops) to soles only. Apply several coats of good quality boot polish, as needed. Have all stitching repaired as needed.

SKIS. It is particularly important to protect the steel edges of skis during storage. A coat of paste wax is an easy way to do this, and it is better than oil which deteriorates and softens polyethylene. Any ski that has been carried back and forth to ski areas on the top of a car, over salted highways, will develop rusty spots on the steel edges in a short time if not cleaned. Skis should be wiped with a clean damp cloth after a trip by car if the highways in your area are salted. The bindings suffer also, and any small opening in the ski may let in salt water to corrode and delaminate the skis. Poles should also be cleaned when exposed to such conditions.

For top performance, your skis must also be waxed. Yes, they may be fast enough for you now. Possibly they are, much of the time. But unless you have skied on waxed skis over a period of time, you will fail to realize how much more easily a waxed ski turns and how much more easily you can get those skis to slip and bite and control speed when necessary. The regular use of wax markedly postpones the wearing away of the polyethylene base. A pair of skis can go all season without serious wear if they are waxed every skiing day — unless you try to ski on rocks. Some things even

the best of waxes can't handle.

Hot wax is recommended, especially for skiing on abrasive snow. Paste wax from a tube as a daily skiing treatment will improve the running characteristics and protect the base somewhat. Paste waxes are certainly convenient enough to apply, and easy to reapply to a damp ski in the middle of the day.

If you are concerned about the appearance of your skis, the new plastic-cleaning liquid preparations available in most hardware stores will do wonders for them. Follow up the cleaning with a coat of a good grade of liquid car wax, and the surface scratches will be less obvious even in a black phenolic surface.

All skis, but wooden ones in particular, require some care when stored. They should be always wiped dry and should never be stored near heat. In summer, each wood ski should be fixed against a flat wall by clamps placed near the shovel and tail of the ski; insert blocks of wood about one inch thick between the center of the skis and the wall. This method of storage will help preserve the camber. Metal and FRP skis don't require this summer care; but like wood, should be kept in fairly cool, dry conditions.

When preparing your skis for a new season's use, remove any accumulated rust with fine steel wool. Repair defects in the plastic soles. Tighten all screws holding the steel edges, tip and heel protectors. Coat sides and top of skis with thin layer of floor wax or paraffin. This will help prevent absorption of moisture and will keep snow from sticking excessively to the tops of the skis.

BINDINGS. The moveable parts of your ski bindings should be lightly oiled during the season with a thin gun oil which won't turn stiff or gummy. If the mechanism appears to be clogged with sludge, dis-assemble, wipe clean, and re-oil (or grease). Wipe all exposed metal binding parts with a lightly oiled rag to prevent rusting. Set adjustment mechanism to proper release load in accordance with your build and skiing technique.

POLES. Replace badly worn baskets. Have straps shortened to fit snugly over your gloved hand.

RENTAL EQUIPMENT

As we have implied several times already, it takes time and experience to select the best ski equipment for you. Since there is a wide range of gear available, a good way to experiment, before making the initial investment, is to rent boots, skis and poles. The bindings are always fixed to the skis.

Most ski shops in major ski areas have a rental department stocked with a wide array of skis and boots. Try out the different types of skis—metal and fiberglass—on a rental basis to help determine your preference. Do the same for boots, trying the various types. But, remember that a rental service is only as good as the organization which runs it. It takes time for the operator to help you select the correct length of skis, to adjust the pressure points on the release bindings, and to obtain proper fit of boots. When a horde of skiers all seeking rentals descends upon a harried shop operator there is a good chance that the service will be slow and mistakes made in choosing proper equipment. To prevent this, it's wise to place your order beforehand. In this way, he can put the equipment you desire aside. In most cases, deposits in advance are required for this service.

2

LESSONS, LANGUAGE, LIFTS, AND LAWS

Talk It Like a Pro

LESSONS

At most ski areas, a typical ski school offers both group or private lessons. Nowadays, many schools also offer lessons in what has become known as GLM (for graduated length method), in which you start out on three-foot skis the first day, then move up to four-footers, and finally normal-length skis.

Group lessons, which may vary in size from four to one dozen students, last about two hours and at most areas are given twice daily — at 10 a.m. and 2 p.m. The cost of group lessons is rather inexpensive and thanks to various package instruction plans can be downright cheap when you consider what you get.

After one two-hour group by a competent instructor on the proper terrain, most new-comers to skiing are able to make simple changes of direction, to stop, to fall safely, possibly even to ride some form of slow up-hill mechanical transportation, and to enjoy themselves thoroughly. Progress from then on depends upon how efficient the instructor is, how capable the student is, snow conditions, and how many consecutive days are spent skiing. Assuming that "learning to ski" means to make stem christies on the average prepared slopes, then as little as four all-day les-

sons may do the trick, with eight to ten being the more common number, provided the days are consecutive. More time will be required if lessons are taken on weekends only.

Moderately more expensive private lessons offer several advantages for special problems; for instance, if you are self-conscious about performing in front of a group, or if you are especially timid about taking up skiing or going faster, then private lessons may be worth more to you than their actual cost. Also, if your skiing requires aid on one or two persistent pesky points about which nothing can be done in a group class because of lack of time, a private lesson can open new worlds of pleasure.

Many ski instructors are members of the Professional Ski Instructors of America (PSIA), and teach what has come to be called the "American Ski Technique." This method of ski instruction evolved over a period of some twenty-five years and derives its base from the Austrian theorists of the 1950's. By enrolling in a school that employs the American Technique, you can be assured of receiving *almost* uniform instruction no matter where you go in the United States. But, the more you know about your skiing ability the easier it is for ski school directors to quickly and accurately place you in the ski school class which will best meet your needs. In the schools that teach the American Technique, six levels of skiing ability are identified. The following information will help you to evaluate yourself with reasonable accuracy.

BEGINNERS *Class A.* First-time Beginners. For those who have never been on skis before, or who have not skied for many years. Maneuvers taught: walking, climbing, falling, getting up, straight running, kick turn, and possibly the snowplow. You probably will not have to take this class more than once.

Class B. Second-time Beginners. For those who are familiar with all of the maneuvers of Class A. Maneuvers taught: snowplow, traversing, use of easy uphill conveyances, polishing of Class A maneuvers, and usually the snowplow turn. You may have to take this class at least twice to learn the maneuvers satisfactorily.

INTERMEDIATES *Class C.* Beginning Intermediates. For those who are familiar with most of the foregoing maneuvers. Required ability: to snowplow with good control over your speed. Maneuvers taught: snowplow turns (if not taught in Class B), stem turns, side-slipping, and many exercises designed to improve confidence, balance, and coordination. You may have to repeat this class at least three times before progressing to the next.

Class D. Advanced Intermediates. Required: at least a rudimentary ability to sideslip and to make stem turns on slopes pitched at about 15 degrees. Maneuvers taught: stem christies and many exercises designed to improve ability to traverse in good form at medium to fast speeds, to sideslip and make uphill

christies. Also, many exercises to prepare you for parallel christies. You may have to repeat this class at least four times and possibly many more.

ADVANCED *Class E.* Parallel Christie Class. Required: a good ability to sideslip at various speeds, and sufficient confidence to ski on 20-degree slopes at medium-fast speeds. Maneuvers taught: parallel christies with numerous exercises designed to help eliminate the stem. You may have to repeat this class at least five times.

Class F. Wedeln Class. Required: ability to make parallel christies on slopes generally considered "intermediate" or better—15 to 20 degrees. Material taught: close-linked parallel christies and polishing of all maneuvers learned so far. This class should be repeated as often as necessary.

NOTE: Minor variations in the classifying of ski school students occurs because each school director must arrange the sequence of maneuvers into a pattern which best suits the need of the terrain and snow conditions available at his area. Consequently, not all maneuvers mentioned above will be taught in exactly the same class. Larger ski schools may offer classes on racing, deep snow techniques, stunts, etc.

THE LANGUAGE OF SKIING

Skiers, especially ski instructors, have their own special language—about technique . . . about equipment . . . about competition. To swing with them, know what they're talking about . . . on the slopes . . . at the bar . . . and in the magazines. As they say, dig the action in this section. You're practically guaranteed to become a better listener, a better talker, and maybe even a better skier. No doubt about it—understand some of this technical language and you will learn much faster. Become as familiar with the technical definitions here as you are with your favorite phone number, and who knows? You may even become an instructor.

ANGULATION. The bending away from the slope (or the turn) by the upper body which compensates for the movement of the knees toward the slope (or turn). Angulation helps to change edges, control edges, and shift body weight from ski to ski.

ANTICIPATION. The twisting and moving of the upper body in the direction of the next turn *before* the turn begins.

BACKWARD LEAN. Body position placing the center of gravity of the skier behind the balls of the feet.

BANKING. The leaning of the entire body toward the imaginary center of a parallel christie causing the skis to change from riding on their uphill edges, to being placed flat on the slope, to being inclined on their inside edges (of the turn).

CHANGE OF LEAD. On a traverse the upper ski always leads. Therefore, as a christie progresses the inside ski of the turn must advance, either automatically or deliberately, to change the lead.

CHECK. Any maneuver used to slow down the movement of the skis.

COUNTER-MOTION. Motion around the vertical axis of the body opposite the direction of the turn.

COUNTER-ROTATION. The movement of the upper body in a direction opposite, or counter to, that in which the lower body turns. The opposite of rotation.

EDGE CONTROL. The control of the angle of the running surface of the skis to the slope.

EDGING. A means of controlling the sideward slippage of the skis by setting the skis at an angle (by angulating) to the snow so that they "bite" the surface.

FALL LINE. An imaginary line from wherever you stand indicating the most direct and steepest way down. When schussing you ski in the fall line. To increase speed, turn into the fall line. To decrease speed, turn off the fall line.

FORWARD LEAN. For most skiing conditions, in order to maintain balance, the waist, knees, and ankles must bend forward so that more of the body's weight presses on the ball of each foot than on the heel.

LEVERAGE. Accentuated, temporary forward or backward lean.

HEEL THRUST. A muscular force or pressure applied to the heels so that the tails of the skis are displaced sideways. Same as *heel push.*

ROTARY HEEL THRUST. The result of counter rotation from a high body position by down-unweighting.

HOP. A means of up-unweighting. The general meaning of the word describes the action quite adequately.

NATURAL POSITIONS. The body should not be placed into positions which are not necessitated by the dynamics of skiing.

POLE PLANT. The quick placement in the snow of the inside ski pole on a turn to serve as a sort of pivot for the turn.

PROJECTION CIRCULAIRE. Term used in the French system. A complex of movements used to initiate a christie, consisting of up-unweighting, increase of forward lean, banking, and rotation. The same as *anticipation.*

RISING MOTION. Relatively slow

rising, resulting in change of body position—it is not used for the purpose of unweighting—it in fact increases the weighting of the ski.

SINKING MOTION. A slow down-motion used as a preparation for an up or rising motion.

BLOCK, BLOCKING. A contraction of any or all of the rotary muscles of the body which transmit the turning power generated in one portion of the body to another part. For example, if the shoulders are used to supply the turning force, then the muscles which would allow the hips and legs to swivel around at the ankles must be blocked at the right time so that the torque generated by the shoulders is passed on to the feet . . . and skis.

FOLLOW THROUGH. A phrase somewhat obsolete in current skiing nomenclature, though the movements are still to be observed in the actions of good skiers. In golf, the energy from the wind-up and swing not dissipated at impact with the ball must be absorbed by a follow-through. So, too, when a skier swings his arm or ski pole in the direction of an intended turn, the energy not dissipated once the turn gets under way must be absorbed by a curving, forward motion of the outside arm and pole.

FOOT SWIVEL. A form of turning power where the strength of the lower legs is used to swing both ends of the skis, so that they swivel or pivot around directly underfoot. Often used to initiate parallel christies. Same as *foot pivot.*

KNEE CRANK. The knees, either singly or together, can exert a strong turning force when they are pushed in toward the center of an intended turn.

SWING. An arm or pole can be swung around in the direction of the turn and can provide a considerable amount of turning power. Hence, the phrases, pole swing or arm swing.

STEERING. Snowplow and stem turns are often spoken of as steered turns because the strength of the legs and feet are used to steer the skis around.

TIP THRUST. By using the heels or the tail ends of the skis as pivots, the tips can be thrust or pulled to either side to induce a quick change of direction. Same as *tip pull.*

TURNING POWER. Any of the forces used to initiate or continue a turning movement of the skis.

WINDUP. Akin to counter-rotation, except that a windup is used only before a turn is initiated and not to initiate it. Windup is a preparatory movement— somewhat like in tennis or golf—of a ski pole, or arm, or shoulder, or hip, or all of these, to permit a swing of great power and amplitude.

ROTATION. A twisting of the upper body in the same direction as the intended turn. The movement is often led by the outside arm and shoulder, but sometimes by the hips which rotate in the desired direction of travel.

RUADE (say, roo-AHD). A French word for horse kick. A means of unweighting the tails done by simultaneously retracting the legs and lowering the upper body. Often, though erroneously, called by many a *"hop."*

SKI POSITION. Relative position of one ski to the other; closed, opened, stemmed or advanced.

SETTING THE EDGES. A quick movement of the knees toward the slope (an increase in angulation) and a quick upwards movement of the body causing the edges to grip very positively. Used to end a parallel christie, and often used to check speed or prepare for another christie, as in short swing turns.

TOTAL MOTION. All movements in skiing should be smooth and rhythmic, constantly conforming to the dynamics of skiing. In no case, should the body merely be *put* into a position and held in that position.

TWISTING ANGULATION. A combination of counter rotation and angulation performed simultaneously. The result is familiarly referred to as the "comma" position.

TURNING. The act of changing direction on skis.

UNWEIGHTING. Any of several movements which can be used to momentarily lighten pressure of the skis on the snow.

UP-UNWEIGHTING. If the body is suddenly raised from a low position, the pressure of the skis on the snow will be virtually non-existant during the brief time that the body reaches its maximum height.

DOWN-UNWEIGHTING. The skis are virtually weightless during the time that the body is lowered quickly from a relatively upright position. In actual practice, a combination in one degree or another of UP- and DOWN-unweighting is generally used. A ruade or hop is also an effective means of unweighting.

WEIGHT SHIFT. A rapid transfer of weight onto one ski or the other, aided by changes of angulation from side to side. Same as *weight transfer.*

MANEUVERS OF SKIING

When instructors speak of a skiing maneuver they have in mind a precise one. Here are definitions of the more commonly used and confused ones.

CHRISTIE. A contraction of the word Christiania; any turn in which the skis are in a parallel position as the turn is completed.

STEM CHRISTIE. The turn is approached with one ski pushed out at an angle to the other. As soon as the turn is begun, the skis are brought parallel as early as possible and the turn is completed with a curving sideslip.

PARALLEL CHRISTIE. No stemming is involved in this turn, not even a slight amount. The skis are kept parallel to each other throughout the turn. This does not mean that they must be close to each other at all times.

UPHILL CHRISTIE. A turn "into" the hill with skis parallel. The completion phase of all "christie" turns.

GARLAND. An exercise in which the skis are alternately slipped downhill and traversed across the hill. Variations are stem garlands, sideslip garlands, etc.

GELANDESPRUNG. A German term meaning terrain jump; an aerial maneuver to clear obstacles by springing into the air, using both poles for support.

HERRINGBONE. A basic method of climbing on skis, performed by placing each ski up the hill in alternate steps, maintaining a V-position with its point to the rear. The poles are used for support.

MAMBO. A technique of skiing in which the upper body twists in the direction of the turn well before the skis do. Utilizing a hip-wiggling, rhythmic motion, once the skis start to turn, the upper body twists in the opposite direction to them.

KICK TURN. A means of reversing direction on skis when in a stationary position, by first kicking one ski around, then bringing the other one after it.

STRAIGHT RUNNING. This is the same as *schussing,* where the skier moves straight down the slope. The skis ride flat on their soles.

TRAVERSING. The skier moves across the slope with skis on their uphill edges, so that the direction of motion is exactly the same as that in which the skis point. No sideslipping should be present.

STEP TURN. A method of gradually changing direction while walking on skis.

SNOWPLOW. The skier moves down the fall line with his skis placed in a "V" position, the tails apart and the points held close together. The body is kept centered over both skis so that weight is equally distributed on each foot and the inside edges of the skis grip the snow equally.

SNOWPLOW TURN. A turn done at slow speeds, in which the skis never lose their snowplow position. These turns are usually linked together.

STEM TURN. From a traverse with skis parallel, one ski is opened out into a half-snowplow (stem), the other ski then stems as the turn progresses into the fall line. Once the lower ski points in the direction of the new traverse, the upper ski is brought parallel to it. Another definition: A snowplow turn is used to link a traverse in one direction with a traverse lower down the hill in the other direction.

SIDE STEP. A simple method of climbing a slope; similar to walking up a flight of stairs sideways.

SIDESLIPPING. The skier moves at an angle to the direction in which his skis point. Numerous variations exist such as: *Lateral* or *vertical*—the skier slips sideways down the fall line with skis kept across the slope continuously.

Diagonal, or on the bias—the skier moves obliquely across the slope by going slightly forward and sideways simultaneously.

Curving—The tails of the skis are permitted to slip more than the fronts so that a turn into the hill is effected.

WEDELN. A series of closely linked parallel christies performed in quick succession without any appreciable braking action.

SHORT SWING. Similar to wedeln, but braking action by setting the edges is noticeable and varies from a slight to a great amount.

STEMMING. A separation of the tails of the skis, so that the skis are in a "V" position with the apex at the tip. A snowplow is sometimes called a double stem. Virtually all ski schools teach an *uphill stem*.

TERMS COMMONLY CONFUSED

In the special language of ski instruction the words left and right are seldom used. Instead words which indicate your relation to the hill or the turn are used, as follows:

When traversing, all parts of the body or ski equipment on the side closest to the slope are referred to as *uphill* parts. Examples: uphill edge, uphill ski, uphill arm and shoulder, uphill pole, etc. All parts on the side farthest from the slope are referred to as downhill parts. Examples: downhill arm, downhill ski, downhill edges, downhill pole, etc.

When turning, all parts of the body on the side closest to the center of the turn are referred to as *inside* parts. Examples: inside arm, inside pole, etc. All parts of the body on the side farthest from the center of the turn are referred to as *outside* ski, outside pole, outside arm, outside hip, etc. Be careful not to confuse the words *inside* and *outside* when they are used in relationship to the body positions alone. For example, when snowplowing the *inside* edges of the skis must be used. The *outside* edges of the skis are kept off the snow.

Some further examples. When a skier makes a turn toward the fall line from a traverse, his uphill ski becomes the outside ski until he has turned just past the fall line, at which time the ski could be referred to as the downhill ski. In the same situation, his original downhill ski becomes the inside ski, and then the uphill ski as the turn progresses off the fall line.

PHASES OF TURNING

Instructors speak of four basic types of turns: static, steered, skidded, and jumped. *Static turns* are kick turns, and step turns which do not require speed or direction of motion to perform. *Steered turns,* like snowplow and stem turns, require a definite muscular effort to direct and guide the skis throughout the turn. *Skidded turns*—the stem christies and parallel christies—may be started by a steering action, but once initiated they are made to continue on a skidding (or side-slipping) curve by relying on the proper use of the shape of the ski. *Jump turns* are those initiated by jumping the skis off the snow and turning them in the air.

Almost every turn can be broken down into the following four phases. Learn the phases and you'll be better able to analyze skiing mistakes.

PREPARATION PHASE—*"Get Set"*—The period of time during which the movements are made to prepare for the turn, though no actual change of direction takes place as a result, except as noted below in the completion phase.

INITIATION PHASE—*"Go!"*—During this period of time the skis are actually displaced toward the new direction. This phase is the most difficult and is where most errors begin to develop which cause falls in the next two phases.

CONTROLLING PHASE—*"Keep Going"*—During this period of time the length and sharpness of the turn is controlled. It is sometimes referred to as the fall line phase.

COMPLETION PHASE—*"Stop"*—The period of time during which the turn in one direction is brought to a definite conclusion. When turns are being linked together, this phase blends in with the preparation phase.

SPEEDS OF SKIING

How fast is pretty fast? Pretty slow? Really moving out? The following brief explanations will give you an idea. But don't get it into your head to break the world's speed record. It now stands at 108.6 mph.

SLOW SPEED. Not more than five or six miles per hour. The speed of the beginner and lower intermediate. The speed at which snowplow turns and stem turns are effective.

MEDIUM SPEED. Approximately six to fifteen miles per hour. The speed at which stem christies are comfortable for the intermediate skier.

FAST SPEED. Comfortable speeds for parallel christies, from about sixteen to twenty-five miles per hour. The range of speeds most generally used by the advanced skier.

HIGH SPEED. The speed comfortable only to the expert, ranging from about twenty-five to forty-five miles per hour. Close linked turns become increasingly difficult to do at these speeds.

RACING SPEED. The speed of the downhill racer. Speeds seldom attained off the race course or by skiers not in training for racing.

THE COMPETITION LANGUAGE

In this book, we do not go into techniques of racing competition. To get the full picture of skiing, however, it's important to have some knowledge of this phase of the sport. But to understand what racing is all about, to be able to communicate with a competitor, you must understand the basic frame of reference for competition. First off, a competitor is either an *amateur* or a *professional.* The pro uses his name or his likeness for advertising purposes or competes for cash prizes or prizes having a significant cash value. An amateur, supposedly, competes only for sportsmanship and glory. The few pros around today are former great amateurs. Unfortunately for them, few pro races are held. Skiing for money prizes just hasn't come completely above board yet.

In the USA today about 15,000 persons—the majority of them under eighteen years old—hold amateur competitor cards issued by one of the eight regional associations affiliated with the United States Ski Association. The USSA in turn is affiliated with the Federation International de Ski. The FIS is the world governing body for skiing competition.

A card-holding competitor generally takes part in one of two disciplines—the Nordic events or the Alpine events. The former consist of cross-country races of various lengths, plus jumping. The Alpine events are the downhill, the slalom, and the giant slalom. Some collegians may bear the coveted title of *Skimeister,* which means that at some important meet they came out with the highest overall standing in four or five events. (Sometimes the giant slalom is not included.)

Jumpers win events through a combination of points given for distance and for style. In a special event, called *Ski Flying,* only distances count. A new world record in this event was established in 1969 by Jiri Raska, who flew 541 feet after leaving the take-off.

Cross-country runners race against the clock on prepared courses having approximately one-third of the terrain flat, one-third uphill, one-third downhill. They cover distances as much as fifty kilometers (31.4 miles) in about three hours.

The Nordic discipline is closest to the hearts of the Scandinavians and the peoples of eastern Europe. For western Europeans and North Americans, the Alpine events are the most popular.

Alpine competitors race against the clock, leaving the starting gate at sixty-second intervals. They win their events sometimes by the merest shadow of a second—by a few hundredths. They do this despite the fact that they race over courses which at best provide quite dissimilar snow conditions. In an effort to establish some semblance of course similarity, a complex system of points has been devised by the FIS. The winner of a race gets 0.00 FIS points. Each successive finisher receives points commensurate with the time elapsed between himself and the winner. For any given event, the fifteen competitors having the lowest points are classified—or seeded—into a group called a "seeding." The first seeding will be the first group to leave the starting gate. The second seeding then contains competitors whose FIS-point totals rank them in sixteenth to thirtieth place. And so on, for the third and subsequent seedings. To determine starting order, the fifteen names in each seeding are drawn by lot.

A modern downhill usually requires two to three minutes to complete. It should avail itself of natural, but not dangerous, changes in terrain, requiring only long sweeping turns. Ideally, only a few (ten to fifteen) control panels (gates) set no closer than thirty-three feet to each other, should be required to mark the way down the two- to three-mile course. Some of the most famous downhill races in Europe are: Arlberg, Kandahar, Hahnenkamm, and Piste Verte. In the USA some of the more famous downhills are held in Aspen, Sun Valley, Stowe, Vail, and Jackson Hole.

The downhill race is a test of endurance, daring and a certain skill with brute strength and speed. The slalom, on the other hand, tests agility, quickness of response, and skill in turning quickly in one direction then another. On a slalom course racers seldom exceed twenty miles per hour. They race between gates—consisting of two flagged poles—and combinations of gates. The poles of each gate cannot be set closer than ten feet to each other or one and a half feet between each set of gates. A modern slalom course is set with gates and combinations so that the winning skier must make a turn about every second. A top race through sixty to seventy gates will require about a minute to complete.

Giant slalom is something of a compromise between slalom and downhill, being run at speeds faster than the former, slower than the latter. In the GS, as this event is often referred to, poles for each gate must not be set closer than sixteen feet to each other. No combinations of gates may be used.

Hence not as many turns are encountered and speeds are commensurately greater. A world championship calibre GS course should cover about one mile, having a vertical drop of 1,500 feet, through fifty gates, and should require about one hundred seconds for the winning time.

TOWS AND LIFTS

In the early stages of learning to ski, walking and climbing on skis is one of the most useful parts of your training. It strengthens those muscles which are absolutely necessary to controlling your skis, it increases stamina, and it gives you practice in edging as well as a better feel of the skis. But, as you progress through Class B, the advanced beginners' class, you'll want to take full advantages of tows and lifts. And the advantages of tows and lifts are quite obvious: They save the time and effort of climbing, and give you a chance to rest before the next downhill run.

There are three major categories of tows and lifts. The first type permits the skier to stand on his skis on the snow and pulls him up the hill. Rope tows, T-bars, J-bars and Pomalifts are included in this category. When riding the second type the skier keeps his skis on while the conveyance lifts him off the ground and carries him uphill. Chairlifts of various designs belong in this category. The final type is the one in which the skier rides to the top of the slopes without his skis on. Gondola lifts and cable cars are the two examples of this group.

TOWS THAT PULL UPHILL

The Rope Tow. This Canadian invention first appeared in 1934. Until 1955 or thereabouts it was the most widely used form of uphill transportation for skiers, but is now quickly disappearing from the skiing scene. This type consists of an endless rope, going around two pulleys, one at the top of the slope and one at the bottom. The rope is driven by a motor.

Before riding a rope tow, you should have had at least an hour's walking and climbing with skis on. To ride one, carry both poles in your outside hand. Then side-step into the tow line, placing both skis in tracks a few inches apart. With the hand which is closest to the rope, squeeze the rope gradually and slide with it as you tighten your grip. For support, once you are moving at the same speed as the rope, place your outside hand behind your back and grasp the rope from underneath. As you gradually squeeze, lean back slightly to avoid being pulled forward onto your face. Be sure to keep the knees flexed to absorb the bumps and ruts. To get off, let go of the rope and use your momentum to ski away. You may have to use the step turn to get away from the rope. In any case, move as quickly as possible from the tow and the skiers coming up behind you.

The T-Bar. A motor-driven cable runs high up, on pulleys mounted on towers, and from the cable hang metal bars in the shape of an upside down T. The T-bar lift is best ridden with another skier.

To ride a T-bar lift, step into track, skis parallel and pointing uphill. Hold the poles in the outside hand, away from the bar. Then, while watching the bar over your inside shoulder, grasp it with the inside hand, pulling it down gently and letting it catch against the back of your thighs. Place your outside hand against the bar, close to your thighs.

While riding, lean against the bar, but don't sit on it. Keep your knees flexed to absorb minor terrain changes. At the get off place, at the top of the hill, stand full on your skis and push away from the bar. Keep going until you're well out of the way of successive up-coming skiers.

The J-Bar. Actually the J-bar lift is a single T-bar. That is, the metal bar, instead of being an upside down T, is in a shape of J and it carries only a single skier. The Pomalift is similar to the J-bar type, except that it has a metal disc or platter, which is placed between the legs. The actual riding technique of the J-bar and the Pomalift is the same as for the T-bar.

TOWS THAT LIFT TO THE TOP

Like the T-bar, the chairlift operates from a high cable running on towers. Chairs are suspended from it, and in these the skier sits while he rides to the top. While there are some single-chair lifts still in use in America, most of them employed today carry two skiers at a time. A few have wide bench chairs which carry three, and even four, persons.

To ride a chairlift which has double supports (having an upright post at each end of the bench), step quickly into position indicated by markers or by the attendant. Holding the poles in the inside hand, watch for the oncoming chair over your outside shoulder. As the chair approaches, grasp the post with your outside hand to slow it down, and sit gently.

When riding a center-supported type of chair, step quickly into the indicated position in the same manner as for the double supported chair. Hold your ski poles in your outside hand and watch for the chair over the inside shoulder. As the chair approaches, grasp the post with your inside hand, sit down gently, but fast, so the chair does not catch you behind the knees. In either type of chair-lift, keep your ski tips pointing up throughout the entire ride to prevent their catching in the snow.

When you reach the top, stand up on both skis. If there is a ramp directly ahead to lead you out of the way of the moving chair, ski down it in your normal running position and make a snowplow turn to stop. If the unloading spot is just a level area, stand up on your skis and push away from the chair, a little to the side if you can manage it, and get out of the way of the next skier coming up.

CARS THAT GO TO THE TOP

Cable cars and gondolas provide luxury travel to the top and carry from two to one hundred and twenty skiers. When traveling in such vehicles, the skis come off and you stand, or sit, protected from the elements. Since most of these devices load and unload in a stationary position, little problem is encountered getting in or out.

LAWS OF THE SLOPES

Frankly, what follows has nothing to do with law. More appropriately, the title could have been "Safety Rules," or "Sportsmanship and Safety." But the "l" alliterates nicely with the other words of the chapter heading. As taught by most ski schools, the topic is divided into three general parts:

1. Conduct (traffic rules on the slope).
2. Courtesy (toward other skiers).
3. Safety (tips for safer skiing).

Let's look at the rules of these three categories more closely:

SKIING CONDUCT—*Rules of the slope for skier traffic.*

1. Ski in control. Be able to stop when necessary and avoid other skiers. Don't be a schuss boomer.

2. Leave the ski lift unloading platform quickly to make room for skiers behind you.

3. Check skier traffic before starting. Look uphill for oncoming skiers before descending.

4. When overtaking another skier, avoid the skier below or beyond you. He may not see you.

5. Let the skier know on which side you are passing. State audibly "on your right" or "passing left," etc.

6. As a moving skier, you must avoid stationary skiers and pass at a safe distance.

7. Stop at the side of trails or at visible locations which will not impede or block the normal passage of other skiers.

8. As a skier entering a main slope from a side or intersecting trail, you must yield to skiers already on the slope.

9. When approaching another skier on an opposite traverse to yours, pass to the right to avoid collision.

10. After arriving at the bottom of the slope, do not stand in the flat runout at the end of the trail. You may be in the way of other skiers moving very fast.

SKI COURTESY—*The golden rules of skiing.*

1. Carry your skis so they point high over your shoulder to avoid hitting others.

2. Wait your turn in the lift line; line cutting is reserved for ski school classes and working ski patrolmen.

3. Do not walk on ski slopes without skis. The hole left by a boot may cause a skier to fall. If you must walk, do so at the edge of the slope.

4. Follow posted instructions at the ski area. Ask the lift operator, ski patrol or ski instructor if you don't understand.

5. Fill your sitzmarks (the dent in the snow caused by your fall). Tramp the snow with your skis to smooth the area. A hole must not be left to cause a fall for another skier.

6. Wear ski retaining devices to avoid losing your skis should they inadvertently come off (two-point fixation, safety straps, or a type of ski stop). Shout a warning to those below when a ski is loose. A runaway ski is dangerous and can cause serious injury.

7. Give way to the beginner. His control may not be as good as yours.

8. Don't swing or bounce while on chairlifts. Don't "snap" Pomalift platters, T-bars or ropes. This may cause other skiers to fall off or derailment of the rope or cable.

9. Cooperate with the Ski Patrol. They will assist you and give you information about the ski area.

10. Remember that courtesy to your fellow skiers makes your skiing more enjoyable.

SKI SAFETY—*How you and your friends can enjoy safe skiing.*

1. Be physically fit. Get a good night's sleep.

2. Eat a good breakfast. Stop for lunch. When skiing, as when driving, don't drink alcoholic beverages.

3. Drive safely to and from the ski area.

4. Dress for the weather; wear non-breakable sunglasses or goggles; use anti-sunburn lotions even on cloudy days; check for frostbite on cold days.

5. Use proper equipment; check it often.

6. Use properly adjusted release bindings with a ski retaining device.

7. Follow posted instructions at ski lifts and on slopes.

8. Learn the meaning of the uniform trail signs: green-square—easiest; yellow-triangle—more difficult; blue-circular—most difficult. Consult a ski area map for slope difficulty.

9. Be aware of danger spots. Look for the red-diamond-shaped sign. It means *Extra Caution.*

10. Obey trail closure signs. A fluorescent orange octagonal sign means *Avalanche Closure.*

11. Ski within your ability. Improve by taking lessons from a certified ski instructor.

12. Loose clothing and long hair are hazards on rope tows and ski lifts.

13. When riding any lift, carry ski poles by the shafts with the points back. Don't have straps around your wrists, except on rope tows. Take straps off wrists when skiing in trees or bushes. The jerk caused when the ski pole basket becomes caught may dislocate a shoulder.

14. Keep ski tips up when riding chair lifts.

15. Avoid deep powder snow until you've learned how to ski in it.

16. When ski touring away from the ski area, check out and check back in with the Ski Patrol or other responsible individuals. It may be worth your life.

17. Ski with companions when skiing remote runs or areas. Four or more

is recommended. If an accident occurs, one stays with the victim, two go for help.

18. When an accident occurs, cross a pair of skis upright in the snow *above* the victim. Be sure to report the *exact* location of the accident to the Ski Patrol or lift operator. At least one person should stay with the injured person until the Ski Patrol arrives.

19. Stop skiing when you are tired or when visibility is poor. Allow sufficient time to complete your last run before the Ski Patrol "sweeps" the slopes.

20. Ski defensively; be aware of other skiers; be ready at all times to react to the unpredictable movements of others.

3

THE PRELIMINARIES

Learn These Your First Day

Skiing is no magic art. Everyone who really wants to can learn. But, don't expect too much at the outset. As a beginner, you should not start off on steep slopes. Your domain is the beginner's (practice) slope. If you practice systematically, going from the easier to the more difficult maneuvers, you'll be surprised at how fast you'll progress — especially if you take lessons. And you *should* take lessons, especially for your first few sojourns.

Before putting on your skis, be sure they have been left outside for *at least* ten minutes so that they will cool off to the temperature and won't ice up on the bottom. Also, keep the soles of your skis out of direct sun. If a ski is warm, or becomes warm, and is then placed on cold snow, snow will melt to water, then quickly freeze once the ski has cooled off, causing ice to form. A thin layer of wax will prevent the ice from adhering.

On a level spot, place your skis flat on the snow and parallel to each other. Then set your poles firmly in the snow on either side of the skis. Stand between the skis and insert the toe of the left boot into the toepiece of the left ski. (Mark your skis L and R just in front of the binding, not so much for the sake of the skis as for the proper mating

of boot and binding.) Now complete the closing of the binding. Put on the right ski, following the same procedure.

Correct holding of the poles comes next. As shown in Figure 3-1, the hand, thumb included, should pass up from underneath, through the loop of the strap. Then fingers and thumb should clasp the grip as shown. The strap should pass low over the back and provide firm support to the heel of the hand. The strap must be shortened if more than a half-inch of pole protrudes above the gloved hand. The fingers must not have to squeeze hard to make the pole swing as a unit with the hand.

And now you're ready for your first adventures on skis.

WALKING ON SKIS

You learn to walk on skis for obvious reasons, but also to develop a sense of rhythm and a feeling for the skis as they glide over the snow. To start walking, first stand squarely on your skis, unsupported by your poles. The feet and legs should be comfortably apart and the skis should be flat on the snow. At first take small steps, learning to slide the skis along rather than to lift them. As you develop rhythm, allow your arms to swing naturally, with ski

44

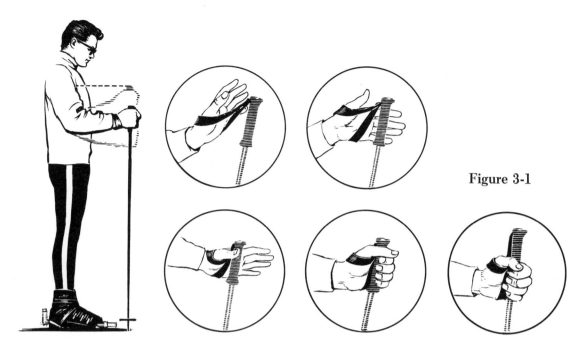

Figure 3-1

poles dragging. When that feels natural, then concentrate on coordinating each step with a pole plant.

It's important to keep in mind that the two main differences between the ski-walking step and walking without skis are these: On skis, you don't lift your foot, but slide it forward; and on skis you help your walk with the ski poles. That is, in ski-walking, you keep both skis on the snow and slide first one forward and then the other, without lifting. As you slide forward, emphasize your weight on the leading ski, and move the poles as you move your arms when walking—left foot forward, right pole forward; right foot forward, left pole forward. As each ski pole is brought forward, its point should not be placed in the snow further ahead than the toe of the leading foot. The ski pole should be brought forward so that it always slants backward as shown in Figure 3-2. That way, the instant the pole is placed in the snow just ahead of the leading foot, it's in a position to have your arm pull against it immediately. This strong pull, plus the push of

the shoulders once they have glided past the backward-slanting pole, will insure you a smooth glide after each step. Repetition of these steps, with increased pushing power, will increase speed. Remember that a good glide will give you more distance per step than increasing the length of the step.

When walking on the flat, as just stated, ski poles should be used to push you along and not as constant props to keep you from falling. If you need constant support it is likely your ankles roll first, causing you to list and lurch to one side or the other, as in the Figure 3-3.

Why? It could be because your boots are too wide for your feet or not buckled securely enough (often true of children's boots). Or maybe the leather has softened so much that lateral support has gone. Or, the problem could be you, perhaps not having enough control or strength over your ankles. To ski well and learn fast, it pays to get in shape at least a little *before* you take up the sport. After all, each foot and ankle has to control more than ten pounds of

45

Figure 3-2

WRONG

RIGHT

A. Ravielli

WRONG

Figure 3-3

RIGHT

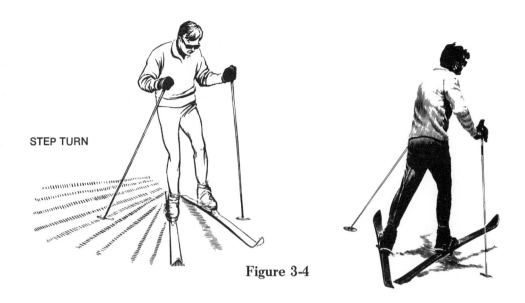

STEP TURN

Figure 3-4

equipment. Another cause: you could be trying, before being ready, to walk with your feet and skis too close together, making you walk as if top-heavy.

To walk correctly, first remedy the boot situation. An inexpensive partial help is to use an Arlberg Strap to wrap around your boot for extra support. In addition, spend an hour or two of leisurely walking on skis for each of your first few ski jaunts. While doing so, concentrate on the following: 1) Watch where *you* are going (not the skis); 2) keep the legs and feet comfortably apart; 3) keep the skis flat on the snow; 4) take small gliding steps. Do these things and you'll rapidly increase your level of physical fitness as well as your ability to walk on skis and to master the slopes. After all, if you can't control your edges on the flat, how could you possibly do so on the hill side?

STEPPING AROUND
AND TURNING

Soon after you put on your skis, you'll need a way to change direction. The two most common ways of doing this on the level is by the step-around turn and the kick turn.

STEP-AROUND TURN

Until you are at ease in maneuvering those long pedal extensions and have developed a feel for the nuances of sliding on skis, rely on this as the method to come about. The best approach to the step turn is to think of it as marking off the segments of a pie you're about to slice up. To do it, raise the tip of one ski off the snow and move the raised ski tip away from the other ski, keeping its tail in the snow. Set the tip down and shift your weight to the ski you've just moved. Then raise the tip of the other ski, and move it toward the first ski. Set the ski down and shift your weight onto it. Repeat this several times and you'll be right back where you started. At first, practice on level ground where there is no danger of your skis slipping away from you.

A variation of the step-around turn is to move the tails of your skis and pivot around the ski tips. You can avoid crossing the tips of the skis by following this simple rule: imagine the tips to be tacked in place at the shovels as shown in Figure 3-5. Then all you do is pick up the heel of the ski and move it and

47

Figure 3-5 .

Figure 3-6.

yourself over as if trying to mark off a pie-shaped section on the snow. Remember that the wider apart you spread the tips of the skis, the further apart must you also spread your legs. Stepping around is usually easiest when you take fairly small sideward steps.

An additional word of advice: Learn to do maneuvers such as this without having to stare at your skis. You'll develop your senses of motion, timing, and balance much faster if you don't constantly look at your skis. An occasional glance at what you are doing is all that should be necessary.

You can use the step-around turn on gentle slopes or at the bottom of a slope. If you're facing uphill, open the tips. Open the tails if facing downhill. By edging your skis inward and using your poles for support, you'll be able to turn without slipping.

If you have to step around on a steep slope, you will have to brace against the poles to prevent your skis from running away. Be sure to plant both poles below and far enough ahead of the tips when starting to step around so that you have the best possible support as your skis are stepped into and beyond the fall line (as shown in Figure 3-6). Then, as you step, pivoting around the poles and the ski tips, you will end up in the correct position without any difficulty. Note how the hands, placed as they are over the end of the pole which rests firmly against the heel of the palm, allow you to keep your arms directly in line with the ski poles. This position supplies you with maximum support with a minimum of energy and strength needed.

KICK TURN

The kick turn is a more awkward though quicker method of turning

Figure 3-7. *The kick turn.*

around from a stationary position. It can be done on the flat or on a slope and you can start it with either ski. Initially, choose a flat spot where you will slide neither forwards nor backwards.

If you are beginning with the left ski, place your right pole to the front and your left pole to the rear, close to your skis. Now swing your left ski forward and upward, lifting the tip until the ski is straight up and down, with the tail resting on the snow. Remember this: don't just try to pick up the ski, kick it up. To do this, first swing the foot and ski straight backward, then swing it forward easily, then swing it back again, more vigorously this time, and finally, *kick* the foot forward and up. If need be, practice this swinging action several times with each foot, so that you can keep the ski moving directly forward and backward without any awkward side movement. Keep the tail of the left ski on the snow and swing the tip outward and down, parallel to the right ski, but pointing in the opposite direction. Now, shift your weight to the left ski, lift the right ski around, and place it parallel to the left, bringing the pole around at the same time. You'll find the task easier if you keep the boots close together as you turn the ski to its right place beside the ski which is already pointed in its new direction. Practice kick turns with each ski, until you can do them in either direction.

Here's a way to prevent a fall which results from tripping over your own ski poles while kick turning. The method works especially well on a side hill. First, make sure the skis are directly across the fall line, on their edges, so they will slip neither forward nor backward. Then, while maintaining the position of the skis, twist your upper body toward the valley. Then place the tips of your ski poles in the snow on the uphill side of your uphill ski. Practice will teach you to place them where you will get the firmest support. Then kick around the first ski, but hold your ski poles in place. Then start to bring around the second ski. keeping it close to the snow and close to your standing foot. Once the second ski has been brought partially around, then (and not before) bring around the corresponding ski pole. With practice you will be able to do this as one rhythmic movement. The same twisting of the upper body for locating the position of the poles may be used on the flat, except that you may twist in either direction since you have no uphill or downhill side.

If you sometimes fall backwards into the slope, when doing a kick turn on a hillside, your problem may be simply that you do not correctly position your poles. To avoid future falls, learn to place your poles as in Figure 3-7D, with both of them planted in the snow on your up-hill side. The phantom drawing shows how to obtain a tripod support effect by placing the poles further up-hill than normally, then placing your fists against the buttocks. This position lets the hips lean back toward the hill while the upper body leans down-slope slightly, resulting in a very stable platform from which to start your kick turn. Hold this position until the first ski is completely around in its new direction. Make sure it is securely placed, then start to bring around the other ski, relinquishing your tripod position and bringing around the ski pole right after the ski.

While on the subject of kick turns, familiarize yourself with the handy kick-back. There are a number of

Figure 3-8.

Figure 3-9. *The toes-down kick turn.*

reasons for getting into the position illustrated—Figure 3-8. You can inspect the bottom of your ski to see if it needs waxing. Or if ice needs to be removed from the sole. Or if a screw has come loose from the edges. Have a friend apply the wax. Or remove the ice with the spine of a hard pocket comb, the shaft of a ski pole, or even a thumb nail. If a screw is loose, hie yourself to the ski shop for a quick repair job.

To get into this position, first find a flat spot, or else place the ski which you intend to stand on in a firm, no-slide position. Then swing your leg sideways, kicking back from the knee, while allowing the tip of the ski to skim the snow. The pole on the kicking side

will have to be pulled out of the way to let the ski tip pass. Then re-plant the pole to maintain balance. Once you've inspected the running surface of the ski and had the maintenance performed, lift up your foot to pull the tip free from the snow, and swing the ski back into place. Follow the same procedure with the other ski if it also needs inspection.

The Toes-Down Kick Turn. This kick turn is *not* for the beginner, but rather for the intermediate and advanced skier. It is a fine way to turn when you've been dead-ended on a steep slope and here's how it's done:

1. Stamp out a secure platform for your upper ski.

2. Twist your upper body toward

51

Figure 3-10. *The sidestep.*

the valley, placing your ski poles as shown. (Figure 3-9.)

3. Lean into the hill slightly, bracing youself against the poles. Make sure your upper ski will slip neither forward, backward, nor downhill.

4. Now, kick around the lower ski, placing it parallel to the one you are still standing on. Push yourself away from the hill slightly so as to shift your weight to the turned ski.

5. Bring around the upper ski pointing the toes downward as you do so. This frees the tail of the ski from the hill and allows the ski to swing around freely. Keep the boots close together as you swing the ski around.

6. Once that ski is more than halfway around, bring along the corresponding ski pole, and begin to stand upright once again.

CLIMBING

In the good old days, before the advent of lifts, slopes had to be climbed before they were skied. But even with today's wide use of ski lifts, everyone, sooner or later, is going to have to do some climbing. In addition, climbing is one of the best ways, especially for the beginner, to warm up the skiing muscles and condition the body to the demands of the sport.

There are two basic ways to climb: the sidestep and the herringbone. Let's examine both.

SIDESTEP

The initial downfall of many a beginning skier comes with the learning of the sidestep, or stairway step. As a matter of fact, the sidestep is the modern Alpine skier's major climbing maneuver. He needs it to get up steep lift ramps. Beyond that, it's the first stage in learning edge control, which is the real key to skiing. The sidestep appears to be two simple motions, but actually there are three. First: lift the upper ski. Second, move it smartly to the side as though about to cut a real step into the snow with your uphill edge. Be sure to cut that step at right angles to the fall line. If you find yourself slipping when you put weight on that ski, then you have not edged it enough. Make a small spray of snow fly every time you take a step. Finally, bring the lower ski up alongside.

In other words, as you stand with your skis across the fall line (horizontal to the hill), your weight should be on the downhill ski and the downhill pole planted below it. Now pick the uphill ski off the snow and step it up the slope about 12 to 18 inches. Move the uphill pole up at the same time. Don't just place the ski down flat on its bottom surface. Make a small spume of snow fly uphill as you slam the ski into its own step. As the ski is set, shift your weight to the uphill ski. Then, lift the lower ski and pole and bring them alongside, thus completing the step. Repeat over and over again as you climb the hill. If you find that you are slipping down the slope, edge your skis more.

"Edging" means setting the skis on their uphill corners so that the steel edges on the bottoms of the skis will bite into the snow and give you a grip on the hill. This is most easily done by pushing your knees sideways toward the slope. Don't try to edge too much by rolling your ankles into the hill. Ski boots are purposely constructed to minimize lateral movement of the ankles for better support when the skis are edged. Actually, good edge control begins with boots which provide firm lateral support to the ankles. Test your boots by standing on a hard floor, like this: Maintain your entire weight on one foot with the boot tilted over on the edge of its sole, as illustrated in Figure 3-11. If the sole of the boot rolls back almost flat to the floor, and the uppers remain canted to the side, then the boot fails to give you enough support. Buy a new pair. A few degrees of play between the boot upper and the sole is not harmful, and in fact, tends to make the problem of edge control less critical, though control becomes less precise.

Good edge control is improved by having good edges on your skis (Figure 3-12). They must be perfectly flush with the sole of your ski. Their sides must be perfectly square to their running surface. Preferably, the edges should project about one-sixteenth of an inch beyond the sidewall of the ski, providing an extra margin of bite for hard surfaces.

In side-stepping, don't be over-ambitious. It's a tiring maneuver at best, and by taking large steps you make it more tiring still. You will preserve energy by taking smaller steps at a greater frequency, and making sure the lower ski remains edged as you move

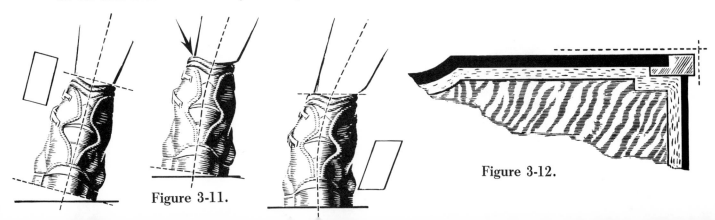

Figure 3-11.

Figure 3-12.

Figure 3-13.
The herringbone.

WRONG

Figure 3-14.
Proper use of poles.

RIGHT

the upper. Also consider the sidestep as a safety measure: You can step down (as well as up) out of a spot you may feel incapable of handling.

A popular variation of the sidestep is the so-called diagonal sidestep, or half stairway step. This maneuver combines walking and sidestepping. That is, you start to side step, but lift the ski forward as well as up the hill. The uphill ski is then edged well into the snow. With the weight on the uphill ski the downhill ski is picked up and brought forward and parallel. The poles move as in walking—right leg, left pole, left leg, right pole. At the end of a traverse, you do a kick turn or herringbone step-around and continue up the slope. Thus, you climb up the fall line in a zigzag fashion, first in one direction, then in the other until the top of the hill is reached. The diagonal sidestep is less tiring than ordinary sidestep and works well on wide slopes.

HERRINGBONE

While more tiring than sidestepping, the herringbone is an easier, quicker, and more direct way to climb gentle to moderately steep hills. It's also a good preliminary exercise for learning to skate and for developing a feel for the edges.

To start the herringbone, face straight up the hill and spread the tips of your skis out so that they form a wide V. Exert pressure inwards with the knees to roll the skis onto their inside edges. Step off in the direction in which the ski you're moving is pointed. Take a good brisk step—almost a lunge—making sure that the ski is placed down at an angle to the intended direction of travel and far enough ahead for its tail to be clear of the stationary ski. Then take the next step. With each step, make a deliberate effort to make the edges bite so that you don't slip backwards as you push off for the next step. Also be certain that the tails of the skis clear each other as you lift them alternately up the slope creating the herringbone pattern for which this maneuver was named.

By learning to step off into the direction toward which you point a ski, and by taking a wide step, you'll avoid the unpleasant crossing of the tails of the skis. Practice will help you to judge how far the tips should .be separated as required by the steepness of the slope which you climb. As a rule, the steeper the hill, the wider the V must be, and the more edge bite you will need. Practice will also tell you how much this bite should be. (Figure 3-13.)

When herringboning up a hill, the ski poles should be used just as they are when walking on skis (3-14). When an arm is brought forward, the pole should be kept slanting backward so that its point will jab the snow about even with the boot of the leading foot. To help you get the right pole action, bend forward from the waist. This will also put your upper body in position to give a powerful push on the pole as you move past it. When you lift your leg, the natural tendency of the ski is to hang down, with the shovel (the widest part) remaining on the snow. Then, when you swing the leg forward to take a herringbone step, the shovel drags, causing the tail of the ski to cross over and rest on the other ski once the step is completed. When you try to pick up this other ski to swing it forward, of course you can't. You are standing on it. Save yourself the awkwardness and raise that shovel by pull-

Figure 3-15. *Herringbone exercise.*

ing up on your toes. Although your steps should be vigorous when herringboning, don't slam your skis into the hill, or you will risk inadvertent release of your bindings.

•The herringbone is a rather ungainly maneuver. It calls for the use of usually un-used muscles. Here's a simple exercise that you can do at home to help develop and tune up the necessary muscles. Walk around the room with low-heeled shoes on, keeping your knees fairly close together, your feet pointed outward and well apart. Walk with a very definite transfer of weight onto the inside edge of each shoe, with each step taken. Do so for at least thirty seconds daily. This exercise will definitely help the new skier become used to the impact created—and help develop the strength needed—when steel-edged skis are forced into hard packed snow. Ski poles may be used with the exercise to help develop the hand and foot coordination required for herringboning up a slope. (Figure 3-15.)

FALLING AND GETTING UP

Everyone falls sooner or later, so here are a few things to keep in mind about falling:

1. Relax and don't fight the fall once you feel sure there is no chance of recovery.

2. Press your knees and feet together and try to land on your seat or hip. If a fall is unavoidable, fall backward and to one side. If you fall forward try to roll up into a ball.

3. Let go of your poles and keep the skis from crossing, or digging into the snow.

4. Keep your eyes open—you'll have a better chance to react.

5. After you've taken a spill, catch your breath and immediately get up and out of the way of other skiers coming down.

Anybody can auger in. It happens to the best of us, so don't feel badly just because you took a tumble. Learn to get up from a fall without wasting precious energy—of which a beginner never has enough. Even before getting up, get yourself untangled and arrange yourself on the slope in such a way that your skis are below you and cannot slide either forward or backward once you begin to start standing on them again. Then pull the skis toward you, bending your ankles. The idea is to get your hips ahead of your heels, then to push yourself directly above your skis, then simply to straighten the legs. On steeper hills, you may be able to get into a position above your skis by pushing against the snow with your hand. However, on flatter slopes and in deep or soft snow this may not give you all the leverage and support that you need. In that case, use your poles as shown. Take special care to assume the proper body position: knees pressed forward so that the ankles are bent; a pronounced bend at the waist. Now, pull

Figure 3-16. *A difficult way to get up.*

Figure 3-17. *An easy way to get up.*

A

Figure 3-18.

B

C

D

E

with the higher hand, push with the lower. Keep your hips forward, so your center of gravity stays ahead of the heels. "Walk" your lower hand up the pole as you push your body away from the slope. Then, once you are in a position like that achieved when you reach down to pick up something from the floor, merely stand up.

The Sit Turn. Use the sit turn to save energy, save time, and save face. For example: After a fall, once you've properly positioned your skis for getting up, you realize you'll want to be facing in the opposite direction. Then save time and energy by turning around while you are still sitting down.

Another use for the sit turn is when you've become bottlenecked on a slope and you're too tired or too unsure of yourself to use a kickturn. Just sit down on the snow for a few moments rest. Be sure you will not slide once your skis have been hoisted as shown in the Figure 3-18. Then save face by using the sit turn. But several important points must be observed to perform an easy sit turn:

1. Always raise the downhill ski first (Figure 3-18B.)

2. Rest the heel of that ski on the snow so the ski points up in the air (Figure 3-18C.)

3. Then, and only then, bring the other ski up toward it. (If you bring the first ski clear over onto the snow, it will trap the uphill ski.)

4. Now allow both skis to fold over into the new desired position (Figures 3-18D and E.)

HOW TO STOP

Skiers stop by turning. And let's face it, modern Alpine skiing is essentially a matter of turning. But turning requires practice. You have to develop the basic skills. So, until you know how to turn, it's easy to get into trouble. Fortunately, there are ways to keep out of trouble even as you learn these skills.

1. Before you know how to turn, limit your skiing to short easy slopes with no obstacles and which have a natural flat run-out.

2. Sitting down in the snow is a rudimentary way to stop, but it is an important decision to make before you gain more speed than you can handle.

3. If the slope is steep enough to give you too much speed, then ski across it, choosing whatever angle allows you to move more slowly.

4. A first simple turn to use for slowing down is to take several small skating steps toward the hill. (By stepping toward the bottom of the hill, you will speed up.) If you step turn enough, you will soon run out of momentum and stop.

5. When going straight down you can slow up and stop by keeping the tips of your skis together and pushing the heels of your skis apart. (You're then using a snowplow.) The resulting V-position of the skis exerts enough friction on the snow to stop you.

6. On slopes pitched more than 10 degrees, you can dissipate speed by allowing yourself to skid sideways. This is called sideslipping.

4

THE USUAL MANEUVERS

Learn These Your First Week, or Sooner

STRAIGHT RUNNING

Nothing seems simpler than skiing straight down a hill. Yet straight running, or schussing, is so fundamental to good skiing, its importance cannot be overstressed. As a matter of fact, all other maneuvers, from traversing to wedeln, are departures from the straight line of descent.

Your first attempts to schuss on very gentle slopes with a safe runout should be done with the feet and legs kept comfortably apart. While learning, the steadiest position is to have each foot directly under its hip. (Figure 4-1.) Only as you gain proficiency, should you try bringing the feet closer together. For the sake of good balance, as you improve, you must resist the temptation to "walk the tightrope" by locking one knee behind the other, one foot slightly advanced, with its heel snuggled into the slight hollow created by the instep of the other boot. This position puts you on such a narrow base that you use the arms for balance much as a highwire artist does to keep from falling.

While learning to schuss, the best rule-of-thumb is this: Stand on your skis so that you feel solidly supported on the ball of each foot. Don't worry about keeping the feet together until

you have developed good balance and confidence. The weight of the body should be distributed over the whole sole of the foot, not just on the toes or heels.

The arms should hang somewhat naturally with a break at the elbows and the elbows held loosely away from the body. The hands, with the knuckles facing forward and downward, hold the poles so that the poles point to the rear, their baskets only occasionally dragging on the snow.

There is a certain stance for skiing

Figure 4-1. *Stance for first schussing.*

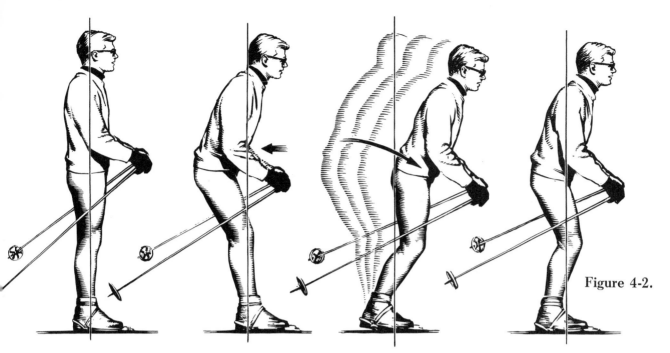

Figure 4-2.

which assures you good balance. It is not quite identical for everybody, but the sensations and general overall positions are. They involve feeling your weight rest more or less on the balls of both feet most of the time, and the feeling of being as steady as a rock at all times. To do this, to have this basic balanced stance (Figure 4-2), follow these directions:

1. From a normal, upright posture, with weight equally distributed on each foot, and with forearms raised slightly . . .

2. . . . push your hips backward while bending forward from the waist and backward from the ankles. Your weight now rests on your heels.

3. While maintaining a slight though relatively constant bend at the waist, move your hips ahead of your heels. Rock back and forth several times to feel the transfer of weight pressing alternately on the toes, then on the heels. Find the position where your weight rests on the ball of each foot and stop the rocking action. You now have. . . .

4. . . . the correct basic stance for balance. This is your own, individual place on which to stand on your skis. Mind you, it is not a position. It is an active, alert posture, one which allows you to move backward and forward at will, compensating for many of the forces which tend to pitch you to your face, or set you back on your hindquarters.

And don't—for good balance's sake—ski with your feet and legs glued together, unless you've got the natural sense of balance and the edge control of a super expert.

You can improve your balance by exercise. Participation in any sport helps. Keeping in shape helps. And the knowledge that you can recover after being knocked askew also helps. To build up this kind of confidence and quick reflexes, stand on one leg, bending forward slightly from the waist, and then move the free leg about in any direction. Allow the upper body and arms to move as necessary, in any compensating direction—but try to avoid moving the arms above or behind the shoulders, since such movements while skiing will tend to throw you back and to the inside. Balance on one leg for at least twenty seconds, up to a minute

Figure 4-3. *Balance exercise.*

if possible. Repeat, standing on the other leg. Repeat daily.

FORWARD LEAN

The phrase, leaning forward, means many things. It means, primarily, keeping your weight on the front of each foot, on its ball. It means having the weight of your shoulders ahead of the hips. How much ahead is a matter of feeling. You should feel balanced at all times. You should never feel as if you are about to fall over backward. That's why instructors say, you should try to get ahead of yourself, feeling that the skis are coming along behind you. You should always lead them ever so subtly. But, to learn to lean forward, "bend-zee-knees" is hardly an appropriate direction to keep in mind. To do that would be to "sit," and that movement puts your weight on your heels and nine times out of ten, unless you are wearing the very latest type of competition boots, a fall will result. A more cor-

62

rect concept is this: Push the knees forward. This movement will produce a forward bend at the ankles, which is most desirable and which makes it easier for you to keep the hips where they should be most of the time—ahead of the heels. If you must think with an accent, then think: Forvard mit zee knees.

•To lean forward, you must be able to bend at the ankles. The more easily you can bend the leg forward from that joint, the more easily you will be able to lean properly. And the more easily you will be able to absorb the ceaseless shocks of skiing. A good forward ankle bend requires a sufficiently long Achilles tendon. Months of disuse of the ankle, or of wearing high-heeled shoes, shortens that tendon. To lengthen it, and to strengthen the calves and thighs at the same time, do this: Place an inch-thick book under your toes. Bend forward slightly from the waist. Maintain this slight bend throughout the exercise. Keeping your heels on the floor, lower your body position by pushing the knees forward, forcing the ankles to bend. Do this to the count of *1-2-3-4, 2-2-3-4,*

Figure 4-4.
Forward lean exercise.

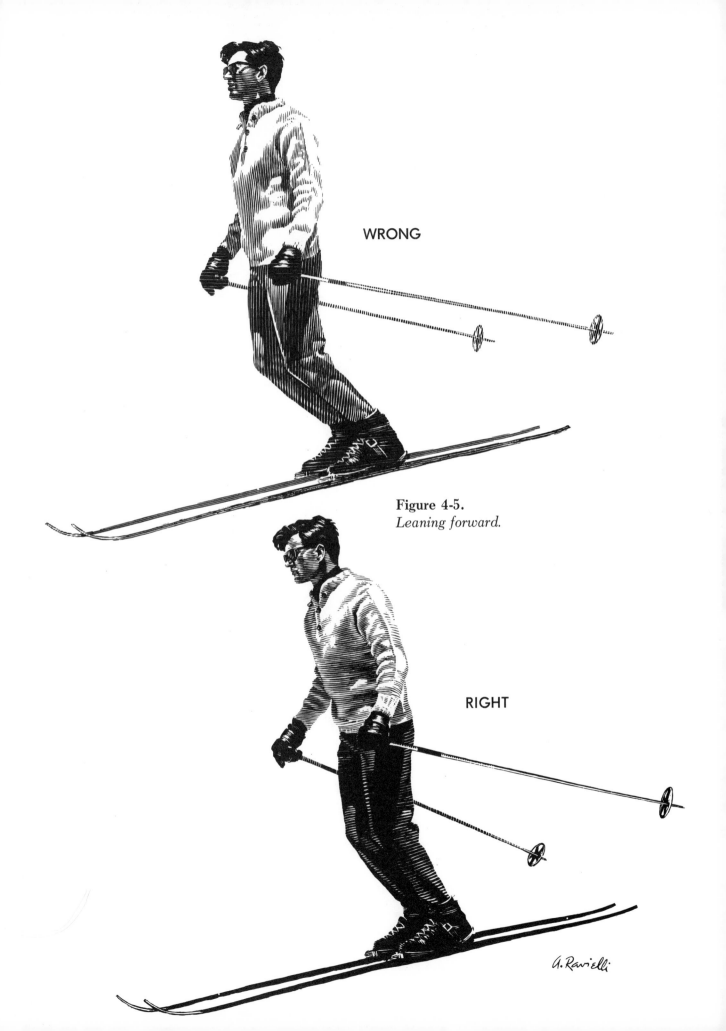

WRONG

Figure 4-5.
Leaning forward.

RIGHT

A. Ravielli

Figure 4-6. *Schussing exercise.*

3-2-3-4, etc., for at least twenty times. Repeat daily. Gradually increase the thickness of the book until you can flex the ankle deeply, heel on the floor, even while using a large metropolitan telephone book as a prop for the toes.

Once you have trained your muscles to hold your basic balanced stance, you must begin to develop the active, alert portion of standing on your skis correctly. For this, most important is the hinging, or flexing action of the knees and ankles. These joints must become as responsive to the demands of varying terrain as the most efficient, smoothly operating piece of shock-absorbing equipment ever devised. And this takes practice—practice of the sort illustrated (Figure 4-6). Schussing practice involves going straight down the fall line of, first, gentle slopes, then gradually increasing your confidence and ability to schuss a slope of at least twenty degrees. The important thing, however, is not just the schussing, but the using of your "accordion" hinges to first flex up and down smoothly and continuously as you descend, then increasing the amplitude of the flexions as illustrated here. To become an expert skier you must deliberately practice using the ankles, knees, and waist to soak up the shocks of skiing. Look for features of the slopes where you can practice. After choosing a bumpy path, traverse it at moderate speeds whenever you get a chance. Practice, as an old maxim has it, makes perfect.

STRAIGHT SNOWPLOW

Before you can safely attempt to ski down a slope of any considerable length, you must learn to stop yourself or to check your speed at will. The easiest—though certainly not the best—

way of accomplishing this is to learn the straight snowplow. This maneuver is used for braking or controlling speed when moving straight down the fall line. The heels of both skis must be pushed apart equally and slightly tilted over on the inside edges, both edged and weighted equally. Instructors say of this position that both skis are equally "stemmed." This allows you to stand directly over the center of the two skis, held there, in effect, by the equal resistance provided by both skis.

Use a gentle, smooth, packed slope to practice snowplowing, and keep your weight resting slightly more on the ball of each foot than on the heel. Keep your hips directly over the heels by slightly pressing knees and ankles toward each other so as to cause the inside edges of the skis to grip the snow more, preventing them from spreading uncomfortably apart and forcing you to sit on your heels excessively. To control your speed effectively, the tips of the skis must stay close together. Learn to turn the front of your feet toward each other—pigeon-toe fashion—at the same time that you press outward on your heels. The inward turning of the feet must be maintained all the time while snowplowing. But remember that this maneuver should be performed with the whole leg, not just from the knees down. If you are unable to spread all of both legs, you may be trying to snowplow on a slope which is beyond the level of confidence for you to handle. Try a gentler slope with a safe, flat run-out. If this does not help, your skis may be too long for the strength of your thighs. Get shorter skis.

There are occasions in skiing when it is safe to sit back—i.e., to carry more weight on your heels than on the balls

Figure 4-7. *The snowplow.*

of the feet—as when you slow down by snowplowing. That's because, as your feet and skis slow down, your upper body will tend to pitch forward. Hence, by sitting back somewhat as you "apply the brakes" (by edging or widening your plow), your upper body can resist the forward thrust. You also get a bonus: the extra weight on the tails of the skis helps slow you down faster. But be cautioned: Sit back too much and you'll stop, bottom down.

If for any reason you can't do an even tracking, smooth snowplow straight down the fall line, then you'll certainly not be able to perform good, accurate snowplow turns. And quite probably, not good christies either. However, your problem may lie with the skis, not with you alone. Generally, skis stiff enough to provide good bite at medium to fast speeds are too stiff for easy snowplowing at slow speeds. Skis too stiff for your weight are difficult to hold in the plow position since you may not get an even contact of the edges with the snow. What you lack in weight you have to make up for in strength. If your skis have a marked tendency to cross at the tips, the bottoms of the skis may have become concave, causing the front edges to grip excessively. A knowledgeable instructor can spot these problems very easily when you demonstrate your ability (or lack of it) to do a straight snowplow. The cure, of course, is repairs or another pair of skis.

A weak ankle is another possible failing of yours which he can spot. If you have trouble displacing both heels an equal distance from the fall line, chances are that the ski which gets displaced the least each time is controlled by an ankle which is weak. If your body,

for example, insists on tilting to the right while you persist in going to the left, either your right ankle collapses inwards too much, or your left ankle bends outward too much. To verify this, examine your ski tracks and note if your right ski leaves a straight line, indicating an edged ski, while the one on the left plows over the snow. Figure 4-9 shows this, but remember that the skier's right ski is the one on the left in the drawing.

Some people have this same problem except that the movements are reversed. That is, the body tilts left and the skier moves right. He moves to his right because the left ski is edged more than the other. If you find that your ankles are weak, a corrective exercise should be done. Here's one that can be done at home: Stand on the floor with feet and legs apart, toes turned in, in the usual snowplow stance. The soles of the shoes should rest flat on the floor at the start, at the count of ONE. On TWO, force knees and ankles toward

Figure 4-8.
Sitting back during the snowplow.

Figure 4-9.

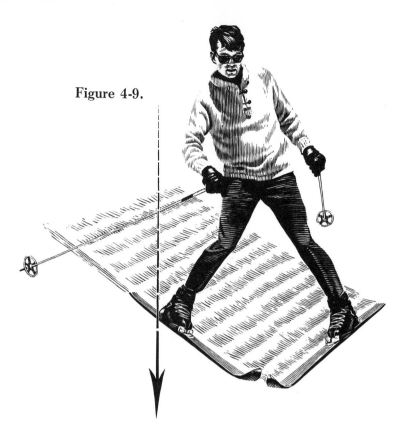

Figure 4-10. *Exercise for snowplow.*

the starting position. On FOUR, repeat TWO, which is the increase of edging by forcing knees and ankles toward each other. Keep the feet turned toward each other throughout. Count 1-2-3-4, 2-2-3-4, etc. Repeat at least twenty times daily. Skis and ski boots may be worn.

SNOWPLOW TURN

Many beginning skiers' first great sense of achievement comes with the learning of the snowplow turn. For many others, it comes with the first christie (or skid) into the hill. Once you have learned to come straight down a gentle hill in a snowplow, you are almost ready to link a series of snowplow turns together.

Before trying the snowplow turn, it's a good idea to improve edge control. Here's how. Choose a gentle, smooth-packed slope that would be ideal for snowplowing (about 8-10 degrees). Start down the fall line in a well-controlled snowplow position. Now, move your right knee and ankle inwards, caus-

ing the right ski to edge markedly, while simultaneously bending outward the left ankle to release the edge of the left ski. You will now move toward the direction in which the edged ski points. The change of direction will be more pronounced if you weight the edged ski (Figure 4-11).

Allow yourself to slide in this sideways fashion for a ski length or so, then reverse the position of your edges. That is, move the left knee and ankle inwards to edge that ski, while bending the right ankle outward. Weight the edged ski. You should now move in the direction in which the newly edged ski points.

A word of caution. No turning or twisting of the body or feet is used in this exercise. Your tracks should not indicate any turning action of the skis whatsoever. Invariably, every skier finds that one ankle provides better control than the other when first attempting this exercise. And just as invariably, the weaker ankle is the same one which happens to be on the outside of the

68

skier's weakest turn. Concentrate a few minutes each day on bending or rolling it outward. Do this while you are skiing, do it while you sit at your desk, and do it by attempting to walk on the sides of your feet, preferably on a carpeted floor. The very slight and subtle sideways bending of the ankles used in skiing is difficult for some people to master, and this is why they never manage to make good christies, or for that matter, good linked snowplow turns.

Once you have a degree of edge control and have mastered the straight snowplow, let's see how to make a snowplow turn. Imagine yourself snowplowing down the fall line. You want to turn to your right? Then push both knees forward and twist them (and your feet) to the right, toward the imaginary center of the turn. Since your body remains centered over both skis, as you turn off the fall line, it will be leaning progressively more away from the slope, and a gradual transfer of weight to the outside (lower) ski takes place. Now, turn to the left, still keeping the body centered over both skis, push both knees forward and twist them (and your feet) to the left, toward the imaginary center of your left turn.

For the moment, disregard the fact that this explanation may not be in vogue with the current explanations of how to turn with a snowplow. There are at least a half dozen variations. Yet they all embody the same two principles—weight transfer (or weight shift) and a rotary force. The way I've explained turns you in the most natural of body positions—if you can imagine standing pigeon-toed, legs spread wide, to be in any way natural—and it allows you to concentrate on the action of the edges and the skis.

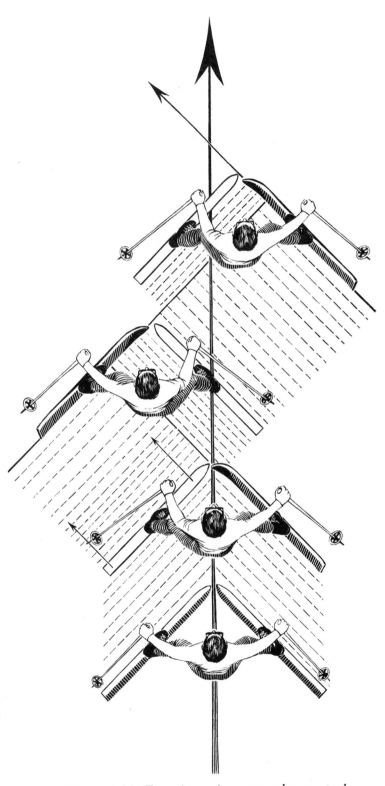

Figure 4-11. *Exercise to improve edge control.*

69

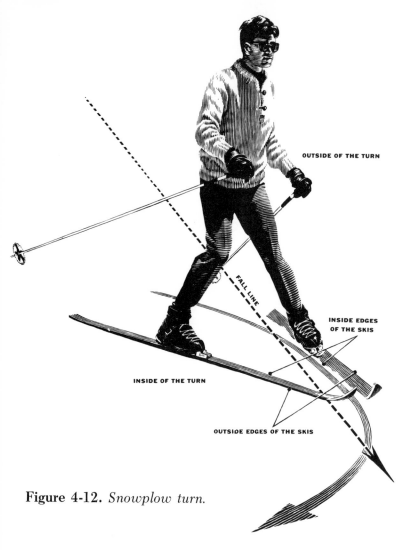

OUTSIDE OF THE TURN

FALL LINE

INSIDE EDGES
OF THE SKIS

INSIDE OF THE TURN

OUTSIDE EDGES OF THE SKIS

Figure 4-12. *Snowplow turn.*

The object in a snowplow turn is to make the outside ski carve around and the inside ski glide or skid around. (To understand what follows, read slowly and associate the words with the maneuver, otherwise they become nonsensical.) To do this, make just the front inside edge of the *outside* ski bite so that you can push its heel around. And you simultaneously ease up on the amount of bite on the front inside edge of the *inside* ski so that its tip can be pushed and skidded over the snow.

The twist of the knees and feet helps do that for you. When you push the outside knee forward and toward the center of your turn, you are, in effect, applying more bite to the front inside edge of that ski and at the same time pushing around

its heel. When you push the inside knee forward and twist it toward the imaginary center of the turn you are helping to release its front inside edge as you push the tip in the desired direction.

Trouble invariably occurs for most skiers in imprecise carving of the outside ski and the hanging up or dragging of the inside ski. The former problem can occur even in a parallel christie; the latter, in all of the plow and stem maneuvers, including the stem christie. These mistakes show up, almost in slow motion, when you attempt snowplow turns, and you or your instructor can see them immediately, analyze them, and start work on corrective exercises.

As was previously stated, there are numerous variations to the snowplow. Currently, the American Technique emphasizes weight shift as a primary turning force. In the start of Figure 4-13, note that my body is kept comfortably centered between skis, that my weight rests relatively flat-footed along the entire sole of the foot, and that there is a slight bend forward at the waist to maintain balance. Now, follow me down the hill: I begin to turn by pushing both knees forward and in toward the center of the intended turn to the left. If the slope isn't too steep, the skis will turn to my left. As I begin to turn off the fall line, my weight gradually transfers automatically to my right ski (the one on the outside of the turn). I can increase the turning rate by leaning over that outside ski, which adds more weight to it, and by increasing the bite of its inside edge.

To turn to the right, I push both knees forward and in toward the imaginary center of a turn to the right. This gradually brings me into the fall line again and right off it if I keep up the twisting action. As before, I can speed up the rate of the turn by leaning out over my out-

Figure 4-13.

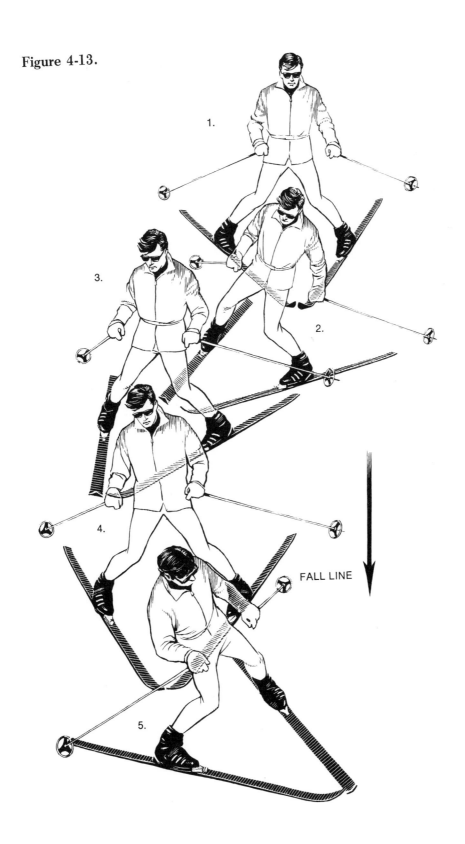

1.

3.

2.

4.

FALL LINE

5.

71

side ski—once that ski has begun to point toward the new direction—while simultaneously pushing my outside knee more forward and toward the inside of the turn.

Many learning skiers have trouble with the snowplow turns. This is not surprising, since the basic position for snowplowing is unnatural and uncomfortable. Remember that once the outside ski of the turn (my left ski in Figure 4-12) has crossed the fall line, that ski should receive more weight than the other one. Make sure it does by concentrating on pushing your outside knee forward and in toward the center of the turn, while forcing or dropping the outside shoulder downward and outward. These movements make that outside ski edge properly and force it to carve its way around the turn.

If you have trouble in trying to complete a snowplow turn, learn to apply more pressure to the inside of the foot which controls the inside edge of the offending lower ski. This is done by pressing the knee and ankle forward and toward the inside of the turn. The lower, or outside, ski of a snowplow turn will only carve its way off the fall line if it's edged enough to support more than half of your weight.

Practice making snowplow turns both to the right and to the left until you can make them smoothly in both directions. Then try linking together right and left turns as you ski down the slope, making controlled turns all the way. Start with a turn to either the right or left, as you did previously. But now, don't turn off the fall line so far that you stop. Instead, don't complete each turn, keeping the skis heading slightly downhill at all times. Remember that it's important to maintain the proper snowplow position when linking turns. Try to develop a sense of rhythm as you turn and turn again.

The snowplow turn as a distinctive turn dates back to 1896 when Mathias Zdarsky, an Austrian eccentric, developed the first formal system of ski instruction. Ever since, controversy has raged over the maneuver.

Experts on instruction agree that every skier must learn to snowplow at some stage of his development, if for no other reason than to have a means of slowing down without changing direction. But agreement is far from complete regarding the snowplow turn. The anti-snowplow turners argue that snowplow habits are bad habits that have to be unlearned if the skier is to climb up the learning ladder. So why teach it in the first place? The pro-snowplowers argue that the turn's value lies in its ability to inspire confidence in the neophyte skier and to enable him to come down a gentle slope under control sooner than by any other means. However, even they admit that excessive snowplowing does develop bad habits, and they usually try to get the beginner out of this phase as fast as possible.

Considering its drawbacks, what has made it possible for the snowplow to survive? For one thing, it is convenient (perhaps too convenient) to teach. The reason the snowplow turn lives a charmed life is that it can be readily adapted for teaching, in crude form, the more advanced movements of any technique that happens to come along.
•*The Turned-around Plow.* This seemingly awkward maneuver may look like a who-needs-it one to you. But learning to snowplow while sliding backwards, as shown in Figure 4-14, will give you a better understanding and feeling for

72

your skis, the positioning of your bindings, and the bite of your edges. It helps build confidence. It is also a practical help when the rope tow or T-bar stops unexpectedly as it pulls you up a steep slope.

Practice first on a gentle slope. In a backward plow, the heels, instead of the tips, are together and as in the conventional version, it is the inside edges that bite and provide the braking. To slide, release the inside edges slightly by rolling out the knees and ankles. To brake, re-edge. If the tails of your skis do not have enough turn-up, you may not be able to slide backwards, but otherwise, the turned-around plow should prove to be a welcome addition to your repertoire of skiing maneuvers.

Figure 4-14. *The turned-around plow.*

IMPROVING BALANCE

A good command of balance on skis implies a certain amount of maneuverability not unlike that which you enjoy without skis on. Many times an obstacle can be avoided by the simple act of stepping out of its way, or stepping one foot over it. Practice is necessary to do this, at all speeds.

•The two exercises illustrated (Figure 4-15), with movements somewhat exaggerated to put the point across, will do wonders for your "loss-of-balance" problems by providing you with a new-found sense of confidence, maneuverability, and ability to recover from what formerly were "upsetting" situations. The first exercise: Schuss a slope which you can handle, then alternately lift one ski off the snow, keeping its sole parallel to the hill, replace it, then lift the other one. The second exercise, a more difficult one when speed begins to exceed ten miles per hour, consists of stepping

sideways one way and then the other while you are traveling down the fall line. Invent your own variations, making small skating steps if you wish. But whatever you do, do it as you put into practice the active, alert, basic balance stance described on page 61.

•Even when you do begin to master the basic stance for balance, occasions will arise when you must do something extra to recover your poise. Prepare for this by deliberately practicing the exercises shown (Figure 4-16). First, alternately lift one ski then the other, and keep the shovel of the lifted ski in contact with the snow. Note that the upper body begins to lean sideways toward the same side as the lifted ski. Just at the moment when you are about to lose your balance, the pole on the side corresponding to the lifted ski is jammed momentarily into the snow—to restore your equilibrium. Another exer-

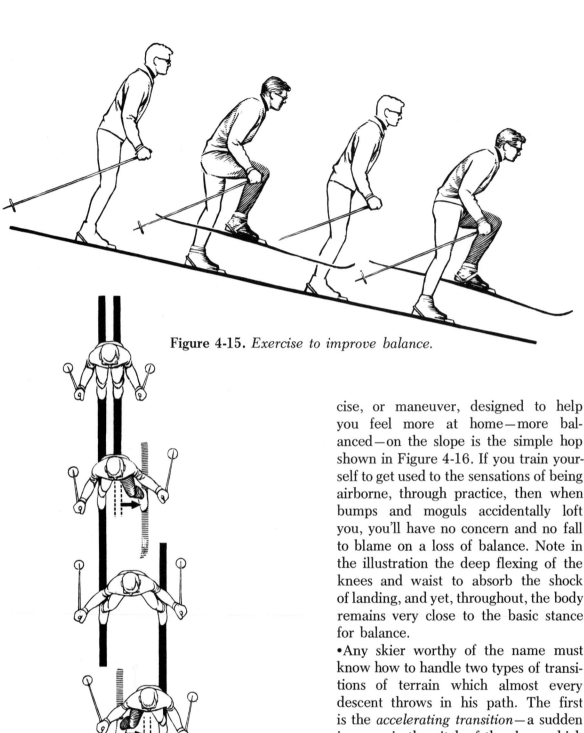

Figure 4-15. *Exercise to improve balance.*

cise, or maneuver, designed to help you feel more at home—more balanced—on the slope is the simple hop shown in Figure 4-16. If you train yourself to get used to the sensations of being airborne, through practice, then when bumps and moguls accidentally loft you, you'll have no concern and no fall to blame on a loss of balance. Note in the illustration the deep flexing of the knees and waist to absorb the shock of landing, and yet, throughout, the body remains very close to the basic stance for balance.

•Any skier worthy of the name must know how to handle two types of transitions of terrain which almost every descent throws in his path. The first is the *accelerating transition*—a sudden increase in the pitch of the slope which causes your skis to shoot forward, leaving you sitting in the snow, unless you know how to keep your balance at such moments. The second is the *decelerating transition*—a sudden upward swelling in terrain which slows down your skis, pitching you forward, unless you learn to handle the decelerating forces.

Recall that to maintain a balanced stance, keep your weight resting on the balls of both feet most of the time. Hence, when crossing over an accelerating transition—as when going from a gentle slope to a steeper one—avoid a loss of balance by increasing the amount of forward lean *before* you get to the new slope. Anticipate the change of pitch by moving your hips forward—always maintaining a slight bend at the waist—just as the ski tips begin to cross the crest of the transition (Figure 4-17).

It is equally important to anticipate the slowing down action of a decelerating transition by moving your weight backward just *before* the ski tips hit the change of slope. Caution—whenever you move your weight backward, be sure to keep a bend at the waist to avoid falling over backward (Figure 4-18).

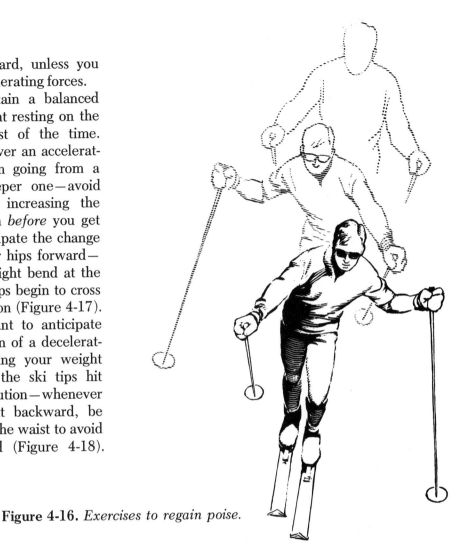

Figure 4-16. *Exercises to regain poise.*

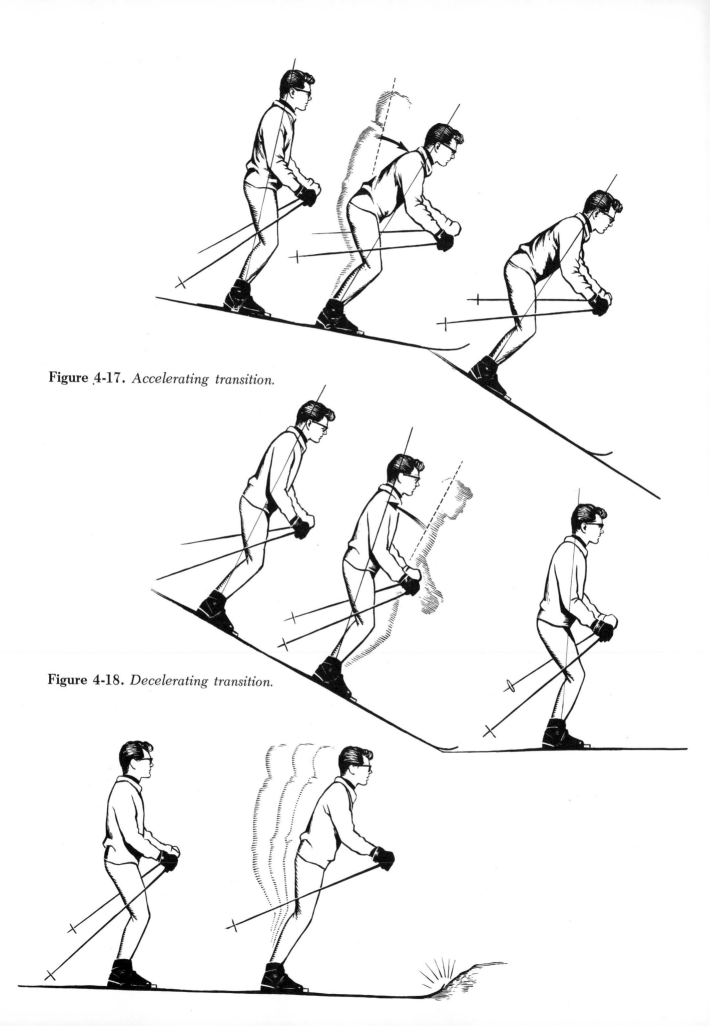

Figure 4-17. *Accelerating transition.*

Figure 4-18. *Decelerating transition.*

Figure 4-19. *Traversing.*

BASIC TRAVERSING

Whenever you are skiing in a straight line across a hill, you are traversing. Basically, the stance for this is similar to straight running except that you have to compensate for the slant of the hill, and the skis must ride on their uphill edge to prohibit any sideways skidding action.

On gentle slopes, or whenever the snow is soft on any slope, the stance for traversing is very similar to the basic balanced stance for schussing. That is, body bent slightly forward at knees, ankles, and waist, so that your weight rests lightly more on the balls of the feet than on the heels, and you remain active and alert, never allowing any muscle stiffening or fixed position to result. While traversing, since one foot

is higher up the slope than the other, the upper foot advances about a half boot length to allow both knees and ankles to bend an equal amount, a fact which will help you use both skis with equal efficiency once you begin to make christies. Your skis should be kept comfortably apart, at least four to eight inches, until you develop good edge control.

As you learn to traverse steeper and harder surfaced slopes, you will need to develop a good "feel" for your edges, and learn how to angulate—that is, to push the knees sideways, toward the slope, allowing the shoulders to become parallel to the pitch of the hill.

You can start to develop a good feel for your edges while merely standing still on a traverse, like this: Bend away

Figure 4-20. *Correct (below) and incorrect stance for traversing gentle slopes.*

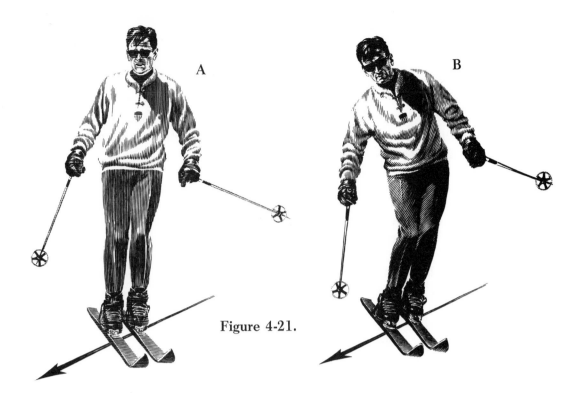

Figure 4-21.

from the slope at the waist, pushing your knees toward the mountainside to put yourself in a position as shown in Figure 4-21B. Then return to the first position. Repeat the exercise a dozen times. Then do an about face and do the whole sequence again. Once you begin to get a good feel for your edges while at a standstill, try the exercise while traversing and sideslipping. Work first one way and then the other to avoid onesidedness.

Finally, as you gain a precise feel for your edges by having practiced traversing for an accumulated period of several hours, you can begin to polish your style by bringing feet and legs close together. If you lose balance more easily with your feet kept close together, realize that your sense of lateral balance may not yet be highly enough developed. After all, the closer together your feet get, the more like walking a tight rope skiing becomes. It is usually best to postpone polishing the traversing stance until you have mastered several sideslipping skills.

Here are three good rules to remember about traversing:
1) Unless you are either an expert or working on a specific exercise, never carry more weight on your upper ski than on the lower. 2) The steeper and icier the slope becomes, the greater becomes the proportion of weight you should carry on the lower ski. 3) Never squeeze feet and legs together at the sacrifice of balance. If you start to lose balance with your feet together, then widen your stance somewhat, and lower your body position by bending slightly more at the knees and ankles.

In proper traversing, the upper ski should never be *pushed* ahead. It should be ahead because you stand on your skis with slightly more weight on the lower ski, both skis on their uphill edges, both ankles bent the same amount, both knees bent the same amount, and your weight on the front part of each foot. Practice traversing on gentle slopes, with your weight more or less equally distributed on the front of each foot. Bounce up and down as you traverse,

79

practice kicking up the heels of the skis (called a ruade—say "roo ahd"), learn to *feel* solidly supported by both skis at all times, and you'll soon find that your upper ski goes where it is supposed to without being pushed there. Caution: Start looking in the direction you are going. That will help keep you forward and give you better balance.

THE STEM TURN

Anytime you ski across a slope in one direction and then want to head back across, part of the difficulty which must be overcome is the change of edges. Snowplow turns don't present that problem. You start out with skis in a plow position, resting on their inside edges. Then you turn left and right and the skis always remain on the inside edges.

A stem turn, sometimes defined as a snowplow turn linking two traverses, does involve an edge change. Initially, when you are traversing with skis parallel, the skis rest on their uphill edges. You open into a stem position by swinging out the heel of the uphill ski. Do this correctly and the uphill ski has its edge changed so that now both skis rest on their inside edges. So there you are, actually in a snowplow . . . so make your snowplow turn. When the lower ski points in the direction of the new, desired traverse, close up the plow by bringing the upper ski alongside. Don't forget to change it from inside edge to uphill edge. Now you know why the stem turn is said to have, in the technical jargon of ski technique, a two-stage edge change. In Figure 4-22, you can see how the stem turn makes use of the snowplow turn to link up a traverse across a slope with a traverse in the opposite direction. During the traverse,

skis are kept parallel. During the turn, the snowplow position is maintained. Thus, the learner is confronted with two new problems as he progresses up the traditional sequence of ski school maneuvers. The first problem is how to open the skis into a snowplow; and the second, how to close the skis when the new traversing direction has been reached.

The first problem is resolved with a stem—a movement done with either the upper or lower leg, to move the tail of one ski apart from the other. In the American system of instruction, stemming with the upper leg and ski is advocated, as illustrated here. The second and third figures show how the lower ski maintains the direction of traverse, while the upper ski is slipped (or lifted) into a half snowplow. Actually, once the skier is ready to turn by centering his body between the two skis, he is in a small snowplow position. From there, he merely makes a snowplow turn, pushing the front of his inside ski of the intended turn toward the fall line and simultaneously thrusting out the heel.

The second problem encountered upon first tackling the stem turn—that of closing the skis—presents no difficulty. The trick is to wait until the outside ski of the turn—the lower one—points directly toward where you want to go. Then the edging of that ski is increased to establish the new traverse, and the upper ski is gradually allowed to run alongside the lower one. The last three figures illustrate this phase of the turn.

Like the snowplow turn, the stem turn is a source of controversy among instructors. Some say that plowing and stemming are habits which must be unlearned before going on to parallel christies. Therefore, why teach these movements to begin with? Other ski schools pass over the maneuver quickly, merely allowing students an opportunity to get the "feel" of opening and closing the skis. Still other ski schools will have students in advanced classes revert to stem turns. That's because at slow speeds, errors in edge control, in lack of ability to "carve" a christie, show up as if in slow motion, giving both instructor and student opportunity to eliminate the difficulty encountered at faster speeds. And still other ski schools, following a fifty-year old tradition, use this cornerstone of skiing as a slow-speed maneuver to develop many of the muscle habits needed for more advanced skiing.

Figure 4-22. *The Stem turn.*

TURNS—FROM STEERED TO SKIDDED

For ease in pigeon-holing the many kinds of turns possible, the following three categories serve nicely: static turns, steered turns, and skidded turns. Static turns (a misnomer) are the type taught in the beginners' walkie-talkie classes—step-around turns and kick turns. Steered turns are those which require only a small amount of momentum, a fair amount of shifting weight from one ski to the other, and a husky amount of twisting of the feet and legs—in other words, snowplow turns and stem turns. Skidded turns are the christies, stem and parallel, of which there are perhaps a hundred or more, depending upon how fussy the system of classification becomes.

Putting it simply, to do a christie—even a stem christiania—you merely start the skis into a skid, then control the skid. To turn gradually, let your skis skid slowly. To turn sharply, allow the skis to slew around quickly. This slewing and skidding is called sideslipping, and it accounts for as much as 90 percent of a parallel christie. To become a versatile skier for all types of snow, obviously you must develop precise control of the sideslip, and that's done through practice and understanding.

Sideslipping control is a matter of controlling the edges, in combination with where you place your weight. But it's also a matter of getting used to the sensation. What you will experience during your first few attempts at doing christies is something like the sensations felt in an automobile when its back end breaks loose into a skid. On skis, you must not tense up with this sensation. It's exactly what is part and parcel of the thrill and pleasure of the sport. Sideslip practice, and lots of it, is required to feel natural about skidding and to feel exactly where your edges are, and to know where they should be for every situation. Until that day comes, excuse your falls by saying, "I caught an edge." Meanwhile, bone up on the next chapter. It's all about sideslipping, edge control, and lateral balance—the stuff that lifts you from the leg-grinding steered turns to the spirit-soaring skidded christianas.

5

EDGE CONTROL
An Uncommon Skill

Master This, Conquer All

On the surface of things, and on good (i.e. easy) surfaces, skiing is an easy sport. All you have to do is slide down a mountain keeping your speed under control and avoiding obstacles by turning this way and that. But anyone who has skied for a time knows that it's more complicated than that. There are such matters to be concerned with as traversing, side-slipping, weight shifting, bump running, stemming, and varying snow conditions. As you become involved in the sport, and more determined to savor more of the pleasures to be had from skiing expertly, you find that the matter is far from uncomplicated. And if you talk to a number of instructors or read books and articles on technique in the magazines, you find that skiing—or skiing expertly—is not only complicated but also confusing. There are so many ways to make a turn and so many seemingly conflicting theories about what's right and what's wrong that, for the person for whom the right thought must precede the right action, the situation becomes almost impossible. But the confusion can be avoided if you keep in mind a framework to which all the details can be attached. As I see it, skiing—the down-mountain, Alpine variety—consists of three primary facets: schussing, traversing, and turning. Learning to ski consists of improving your own physical attributes while you develop the skills needed for schussing, traversing, and turning. The most important, fundamental skills basic to all skiing maneuvers are those which I call edge control. If you've ever ice skated and become aware of the need to control the edges of your skates, you'll easily see why, with skis which are five to seven times longer than skates, the need for edge control is keen.

Edge control—lateral balance, the skills for sideslipping—that's what this chapter is about. As a gauge of its importance, consider that when an instructor or racer speaks of someone having amazing edge control, he means that that skier is a master of the slopes. So then, prepare to fly down the slopes.

To have a feel for your edges means to know exactly how much to cant the skis toward the slope, or away from it. With skis edged, you traverse. With edges released, Figure 5-1, you will sideslip. The degree of movement between edged skis and released edges is subtle. It is grossly controlled by the position of the whole body, more precisely by the action of the knees, and

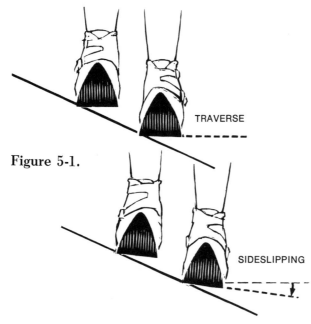

Figure 5-1.

TRAVERSE

SIDESLIPPING

by subtle lateral actions of the ankles. Since as much as ninety percent of most parallel christies is nothing more nor less than a controlled sideslip, you can see the importance of mastering this skill. More details on this topic can be found further in this chapter. Just as it is important to develop a good sense of balance in the forward-backward sense,

via plenty of practice at schussing on all types of terrain, you must master the hang of things in the side-to-side sense—via sideslipping.

If ever you are to ski like a hotshot, eventually you must have a pair of boots that support you like walls of lath and plaster, skis with the sharpest edges ever honed, and a sense of kinesthetics to wow an acrobat. Before that time, if you take off across a .hill trying to ski with the legs tucked primly and trimly together . . . well sir, you might as well try high-wiring it across Niagara. Meanwhile, build up your edge control—with feet apart.

FALL LINE EXERCISES

•Out on the slopes, the development of good edge control must begin very early. At the outset, you should not try to learn the "correct way"—the final form way—to herringbone, to snowplow, or snowplow turn. Rather than being goals in themselves, such maneuvers initially must be used merely as vehicles to help you achieve better balance,

Figure 5-2. *Skating the fall line.*

more confidence, improved coordination, great edge control—the real basics of skiing. Skating is a desirable exercise for developing these traits. Learn to skate the fall line as soon as possible. Of course, start off on very gentle, packed slopes, and as you get better, cut your edges into steeper pitches. Here are some of the things you'll need to know:

First, just as for ice skating, your upper body has to twist toward the direction in which you intend to thrust. Since this involves a considerable amount of arm motion, as the sequence of Figure 5-2 shows, it's advisable to hold the hands so that the knuckles face the snow at all times. Do so, and your poles will not become entangled with either you, the slope, or your skis.

Secondly, realize that you must always push off from each ski's inside edge. On gentle slopes, push off from the inside edge of one ski onto the outside edge of the other ski. On steeper slopes, push off onto the inside edge of the other ski.

Here's a step-by-step accounting of what's going on in the illustration:

1. Pick up the right ski and angle it away from the other one, while simultaneously twisting arms and shoulder toward the direction of the intended thrust.

2. Begin to lean to the right to get a firm purchase with the inside edge of the left ski.

3. Push off the edged ski, directing the thrust in line with the right ski.

4. Glide for several feet on the uphill edge of the right ski (for gentle slopes) while bringing the left leg and ski back under you. At the same time begin to twist the upper body to the left.

5. Here, the right knee is deeply bent, the arms and poles rotated to their maximum, and the left ski placed in position on its upper edge, ready to receive the force of the thrust. Note that the body has also leaned in the new direction, causing the right ski to roll from its outside edge to its inside one.

6. Thrust! Note that the upper body has already begun to twist to the right.

7. The thrusting leg is brought close to the standing one, permitting the body to keep its balanced stance.

If you are unable to control your edges while attempting to skate, consider whether or not your boots provide enough support. Seek the advice of a ski teacher on this matter.

Scooter Skating. Here's another skating exercise, with a practical application as well, which will help you develop edge control. The upper ski remains on the snow, while the lower ski is angled slightly downhill and used for pushing, very much as if riding a scooter. Practice traveling in both directions across the slope—with the hill to your left, then to your right. Scooter-skate across

a slope this way anytime you want to traverse without losing much altitude.

DEVELOPING EDGE CONTROL WHILE TRAVERSING

It's unwise to speak too much of "positions" for snowplowing or traversing or for whatever maneuver. The word implies a static, statue-like posture contrary to what is really needed. When you ski, your body must always undergo very subtle movements of adjustment to maintain balance and rhythm. Yet, for descriptive purposes, to help you get the idea about technique, it is convenient to refer to certain body positions, such as the traverse position described on the previous pages. However, when you ski, keep firmly in mind that you must never freeze into this position or that.

•Here's a tip to help you develop good balance, even with your feet close to each other, when traversing. The key lies in knowing how to angulate. By way of review: When traversing, the upper ski boot should be ahead of the lower one by about half its length. Then, the rest of the body must conform to this basic position of the feet. Consequently, the upper knee, hip, shoulder, and arm should be ahead of the corresponding downhill parts. Slightly more of your weight should rest on the lower ski.

If the slope is steep enough—more than 15 degrees—and you want to keep the legs together, then you must angulate. Here's how. Push the knees toward the hill to cause your edges to grip the slope firmly. At the same time, to counterbalance the push of the knees, bend sideways from the waist so that the shoulders are tipped more or less parallel to the slope. Some people find that the position feels less awkward if the lower hip is pulled back slightly. This total position is called angulation. Remember this: As a general rule, the more you edge your skis the more you angulate. Consequently, as you ski, angulation is never a fixed body position. You must remain flexible, always changing the amount of angulation to conform to the demands of the terrain.

•To develop rhythm and grace in body as well as in spirit, practice traversing, being conscious of what you are striving for. All the exercises previously presented for developing basic balance while schussing can be repeated while traversing. For example, while zinging your way across a slope, pick up one foot, or rise up and down, ski over bumps and down hollows, etc. Make a point of trying the exercises in Figure 5-4 too. If you do, you can cut down the learning time for parallel christies by nearly half.

•Here's another "pure" exercise— pure in the sense that it has little practical application—that's worth trying. It does, however, help develop an ability to control your edges more effectively. And it may help you to avoid a few rocky patches at some future time. Traverse a slope that is smoothly packed and pitched at about 20 degrees. Exaggerate the amount of angulation needed so that your skis become slightly over-edged, lowering your body position at the same time. Now spring up and sideways quickly, "de-angulating" as you do so, as the center illustration in Figure 5-5 shows. (De-angulating is simply a short way of saying, move your body back into a straight vertical line with your skis directly under you.) Spring just enough to move sideways

Figure 5-3. *Angulating with knees only (above) with exaggerated use of hips and shoulders (below).*

87

Figure 5-4.

through the air about four inches. Land on your edges—the same uphill edges from which you sprung—and continue the process several times in a row. Traverse as much or as little as you like between each hop.

•Occasionally, find a gentle smooth-packed slope, one on which you couldn't go faster than 10 miles per hour even if you schussed it. Shed your poles. Ski down the slope. Jump off any little bump or knoll you can find. Make some turns by using a series of hops, lifting the entire length of both skis off the snow. Try skating off the fall line, and into it. Break out of the mold of the overly organized ski class or of your overly cautious concern. Nothing could be better for your learning progress if you have reached a learning plateau or if you seem to be locked into a stagnant rut of repetitious maneuvers. Enjoy a little freedom of expression for a change, and the thrills of experimentation. Take time out to ski casually occasionally and you will make more than the usual amount of progress.

•Incidentally, when standing on a hillside in a ski school class, here's a sure-fire way to rest your ankles and ease the soreness caused by the continual edging necessary for control on hard-packed slopes. Simply stab the lower ski pole into the snow, preferably sinking it up to the basket. Hold the pole as you normally do. Stand with your lower ski and foot directly over the basket. Now, relax that lower ankle, allowing the boot to rest against the pole. Welcome relief will be yours.

SIDESLIPPING

In the sideslip, the skis are edged less, to the point where they begin to slip sideways more than they move forward. One of the skills to develop is the very subtle distinction between too much and not enough edge release The amount of release is different for each skier, each different pair of skis, and each snow condition. That's why, skiers speak of the need to develop a fine feel for the edges. Basically, you must feel that the skis remain on their uphill edges. When your skis are completely edged, or set, you traverse. When they are released slightly, you sideslip slowly. When they are released a lot, you sideslip quickly. And when you want to stop sideslipping, we say that you re-edge, or you set your edges.

When discussing sideslipping, instructors often speak of "flattening the skis," a phrase which isn't exactly correct. A good skier never actually flattens his skis to the snow when sideslipping (to do so would cause the downhill edges of the skis to catch, flipping him onto his ear); he merely "releases the edges" by moving his knees and ankles away from the slope until his skis skid sideways the desired amount. In addition, for effective sideslipping, the upper edges of both skis must remain in slight contact with the snow. Thus, the skis are never actually "flattened" to the snow. When your feet become too far apart, or even when only comfortably apart, some muscle energy of the legs must be used to keep the upper ski on its upper edge.

There are a number of types of sideslipping. Just what form your skid takes depends on how much you release your edges, in combination with how far forward or backward you apply your weight. Before getting into the details of this, here are the various types:

Lateral (or Fall Line) Sideslipping. You skid with your skis kept at right angles to the fall line.

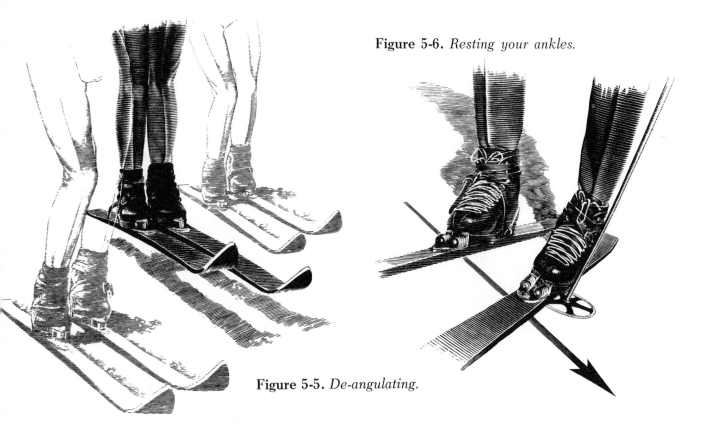

Figure 5-6. *Resting your ankles.*

Figure 5-5. *De-angulating.*

Figure 5-7. *Sideslipping.*

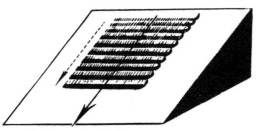

1. Lateral sideslipping.

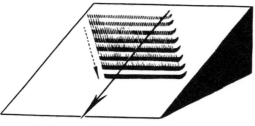

2. Forward diagonal sideslip.

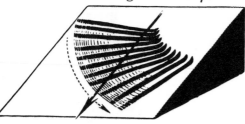

3. Backward diagonal sideslip.

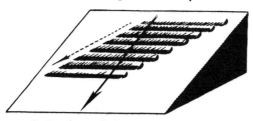

4. Forward curving sideslip.

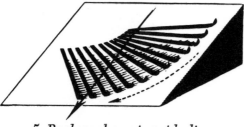

5. Backward curving sideslip.

Forward Diagonal Sideslip. You skid forward and sideways simultaneously so that you cross the slope on the bias.

Backward Diagonal Sideslip. Believe it or not, this is one of the easiest skids to do, and it is a great face-saver for those moments when you get stuck on a hill, too apprehensive to plunge into a good turn toward the fall line. You simply skid backwards, on the bias.

Forward Curving Sideslip. For this, you let the tails of the skis skid faster than the tips, so that you turn into the hill.

Backward Curving Sideslip. This one is just the opposite to the forward curving skid.

These various sideslips can be combined to make interesting and useful maneuvers, for practice and for practical application.

DIAGONAL SIDESLIPPING

The ideal slope on which to learn or practice sideslipping is shaped like this: It is gently convex, fairly steep—20 degrees or more—easily accessible, covered with firm, packed snow, and has a short vertical drop of perhaps ten feet. The steepness makes it easy to sideslip since so little edge release is required to start skidding. The short vertical makes the steepness less perturbing. Practice to the left and right.

Forward diagonal sideslipping is the most practical form to learn first. It is important to follow the correct sequence

Figure 5-8. *Ideal slope for sideslipping.*

Figure 5-9. *Forward diagonal sideslipping.*

of movements if your initial attempts are to be immediately successful. Proceed as follows:

1. Ski across a slope which approximates the ideal, choosing a traversing angle which allows you to slide forward at about 5 mph.

2. Once under way, move your hips forward to apply the pressure of your weight to the ball of each foot. You may lean forward enough to feel a slight upward strain against the heel unit of each binding.

3. While maintaining the position of increased forward lean, gradually and slowly move knees and ankles away from the slope to cause the edges to release. The instant the edges are sufficiently released, the skis will begin to sideslip.

4. As soon as the skid starts, let your body lean sideways, ever so slightly in the direction of the skid. Don't fight the skidding sensation by leaning uphill.

Two of the key words used above are gradually and slightly. If you don't heed them and release the edges too much or too fast, your skis will slip out from under you, making you get so much weight on the uphill ski you will fall into the hill. As you get used to the delicate balance between amount of edge release and amount of sideways lean, you will eventually be able to release the edges as quickly and as much as needed. But practice with a gradual and slight release, and plenty of it, is needed to develop the happy balance.

On your first few attempts, it is important to increase the amount of forward lean before releasing the edges, to make sure that when the skid starts, the heels of the skis will skid slightly faster than the fronts. This gives you the reassuring feeling that you are turning into the hill. With practice, you'll be able to combine the edge release with the forward lean or back-

91

ward lean, to produce other forms of sideslipping. To do that, you'll need to understand a few simple principles. I dubbed these the friction-gravity principles.

FRICTION-GRAVITY PRINCIPLES

Gravity, for our purpose, is the force which pulls you down the slope, either forward, sideways, or whichever way you happen to fall. Friction, as it refers to sideslipping, is the resistance of the edges to the pull of gravity. By varying the positioning of your body over the skis, either forward or backward, you can alter the place where friction is applied to your edges. You can also vary the amount of resistance your edges offer to the pull of gravity by the amount the edges are released. Now, to put these principles into more meaningful terms:

Situation 1. I've explained above how to do the forward diagonal sideslip. For that maneuver, you apply more friction to the front uphill edges and let gravity go to work on the tails. This maneuver can very easily be converted into a curving sideslip toward the hill by simply applying slightly more bite of the edges up front. Practice will teach you the right amount of forward pressure to apply combined with the right amount of edge release for each different pair of skis you use and for every different snow condition. When you've developed a fine feel for your edges and your weight placement, the subtle adjustments required will take place almost automatically.

Situation 2. Let's go back to the ideal practice slope. Suppose that once again you traverse the ideal hill, then move the hips forward, but, this time, release the edges to a considerable degree. What happens? In this situation, the tips of the skis begin to skid toward the fall line because there is practically no friction on either the front or back edges and the heavier, weighted end of the ski will drop into the fall line.

Situation 3. Once again, traverse the hill. This time, do not apply forward pressure. Instead, move your hips back slightly to load your heels and the tails of the skis. Now release the edges only a slight amount. What happens? The tips of the skis will seek the fall line because the front uphill edges offer less frictional resistance to the pull of gravity than the back edges.

Situation 4. Now, for another traverse, and as in the previous situation, apply backward pressure to the skis. This time, however, release the edges a considerable amount. Now the tails of the skis will begin to sideslip much faster than the tips. Once again, that part of the ski which is most weighted will swing down the fall line.

FRICTION–GRAVITY PRINCIPLES

Weight Placement	Edges Set	Slightly Released	Normally Released	Considerably Released
Well Forward	No Skid	Tails Skid	Diagonal Skid	Tips Skid
Normal	No Skid	Diagonal Skid	Diagonal Skid	Diagonal Skid
Slightly Backward	No Skid	Tips Skid	Diagonal Skid	Tails Skid

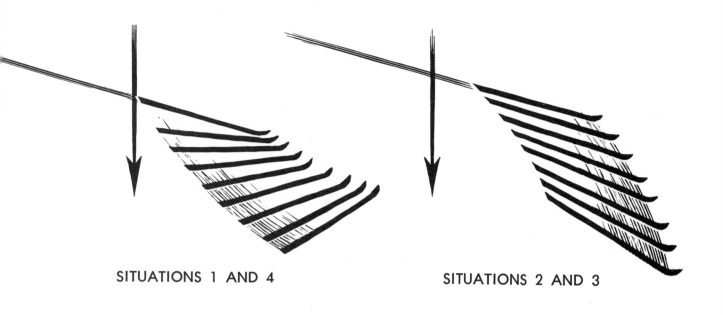

SITUATIONS 1 AND 4   SITUATIONS 2 AND 3

Figure 5-10. *Friction-gravity principles.*

SIDESLIPPING EXERCISES

•Fortunately learning to sideslip does not require much strength or much athletic ability. It does, however, require finesse. Subtlety is the key. Knees and ankles have to be moved away from the hill just the right amount. The action is complicated slightly by the fact that you have two skis to be concerned with, and the edges for each usually require differing amounts of release. As a general rule, the lower ski has to be released more than the upper because it carries more of your weight. You can perfect the subtle movements required with practice, of course, and here are two aids to developing the necessary control.

1. Stand across a short, steep, smooth-packed slope. Twist the upper body toward the valley and plant both poles — each on its own side — as if you were about to do a kickturn. Then begin to push yourself down the slope while simultaneously releasing your edges by moving knees and ankles away from the hill. Work more with the lower knee and ankle if needed. Be sure to practice while facing in each direction across the hill, and work on whichever side is difficult for you. (Figure 5-11.)

2. To develop the right feel for the right amount of edge release for the upper ski, stand across the same slope as shown in Figure 5-11. Move your upper ski up the slope about two feet, while keeping the lower ski edged and stationary. Now, pull the upper leg and foot toward the lower one, keeping the upper edge of the upper ski in contact with the snow. Have the feeling that you are smoothing down the slope with the outside edge of your upper foot. When doing a curving sideslip, think of your upper little toe as smoothing out the slope. This little mental trick will help you to prevent catching the inside edge of that upper ski, provided

93

Figure 5-11.

you practice in both directions and really get the feel for the edge. (Figure 5-12.)

Lateral Sideslipping. When you stand across the hill so that you slide neither forward nor backward—instructors say, stand across the fall line—and you release your edges, you should begin to sideslip with your skis remaining at right angles to the fall line. You are then sideslipping laterally.

Lateral sideslipping isn't the easiest type for most people, partially because you have no speed at the outset to make the initiation of the skid easier, partially because almost all skis are stiffer in the tail than in the forebody, and partially because bindings are not always mounted so that the ball of the foot rests directly over the center of the supporting surface of the skis. Yet,

because of these complications, the maneuver is indispensable for learning the handling characteristics of each pair of skis you use. Experience and practice teach you just where to carry your weight, either slightly more forward or backward, to get maximum performance out of any given pair of skis.

Lateral sideslipping has another practical use: When you find yourself on a steep narrow trail or gully with little room to traverse and too much pitch for you to dare to wedeln, then sideslip laterally. Figure 5-13 shows how to avoid some of the pitfalls often associated with this type of sideslipping. Note that the lower pole is tucked up under the lower arm to prevent it from accidentally sticking in the snow below, which would cause you to trip over it and end up with snow jammed into your lower ear. Note too, that the upper pole is allowed to drag on the snow, serving alternately as an outrigger for balance and as a prod to help push you down the slope when the skis begin to hang up because of an accumulation of snow along the lower edges. Also note where to look. That's downhill, where you are going. And since you are going sideways, try to lean ever so slightly sideways, toward the valley, so that your body never gets behind the movement of the skis. Do yourself a favor. Practice lateral sideslipping every now and then, facing both to the left and to the right of the hill, and especially, work on your weakest side. After all, a parallel christie is as much as 90 percent sideslip. Special note—unless your sense of balance and edge control are quite good, don't try to hold your legs and feet together. Instead just keep the skis parallel.

Polishing Your Edge Control. To adjust the radius of a turn, it is necessary to release your edges a considerable amount. You can move your knees only a certain distance away from the slope before you begin to jeopardize your stability. When this point is about to be reached you can further decrease the angle your edges form with the slope by forcing your lower ankle to bend sideways an extra amount (Figure 5-14). This takes subtle muscle control, and it is well worth the effort to learn because it gives your skiing an extra measure of precision. Many experts have become so good at this, and do it so automatically and so subtly, they don't realize they do it.

•An exercise called forward and backward sideslipping is invaluable to the

Figure 5-12.

skier for learning the effect of the friction-gravity principles—for understanding how the forward or backward placement of your weight combined with the amount of edge release will affect your parallel christies. The exercise has its practical application, as when you want to maneuver around a mogul, stump, or obstacle on a steep slope without having to plunge into the fall line. Proceed as follows: Traverse the proper slope, lean forward, and release your edges to produce a curving sideslip. Once the tail section of the skis slips lower than the tips, re-edge the skis. You will begin to slide backwards. Watch where you are going by looking back on your downhill side. After a few feet of backward traversing, move your weight to your heels and release the edges the needed amount to allow your skis once

Figure 5-13.

Figure 5-14.

again to curve into the hill. When the tips have skidded lower than the tails, set the edges and allow yourself to traverse forward again. Repeat as often as you like, with the hill to your left, then to your right.

PREPARING FOR THE UPHILL CHRISTIE

•Long before you learn the intricacies of heelpushing your way around a christie into the hill, you should learn how to make a curving sideslip by the "friction-gravity" method. Here's how it works: Imagine you are traversing a smoothly packed slope pitched at 20 degrees or more. You increase your forward lean by moving knees, hips and shoulders slightly forward. That takes some of your weight off the back uphill edges and places it on the front uphill edges. Therefore, the instant you begin to ease off on your edges by moving your knees and ankles away from the slope, gravity will affect the back ends and cause them to skid faster than the front of the skis. The extra friction on the front uphill edges causes them to drag somewhat, acting as a sort of movable pivot for the skis. Hence, they turn without your applying any turning force. Once you master this incisive little act, you can then amplify the turning action by using heel push combined with either rotation or counter-rotation.

HOW TO SET YOUR EDGES
•There are two good ways to set your edges. Here's one: Traverse a good sideslipping slope in an exaggerated position of angulation with the skis edged more than necessary to hold the traverse. Stand up to decrease angulation and cause either a lateral or forward diagonal skid to result. After skidding for a few feet, drop down quickly into the original position, pushing your knees up the slope as you do so. When your weight suddenly drops to the edged skis, your skidding will stop abruptly. The other way to learn to set your edges: Once again, traverse a good sideslipping slope. This time, drop into a low position and release the edges. Skid for a few feet, then quickly push the knees into the hill and stand up into a normal, traversing position. Repeat both exercises until you develop the correct timing for the movements— i.e., your edges should be set at the end of the down movement or at the start of the up movement.

Figure 5-15. *Setting your edges.*

TYPICAL EDGE CONTROL PROBLEMS AND SOME SOLUTIONS

As mentioned in earlier, the development of good edge control begins with boots that provide adequate lateral support for your ankles and with skis and edges that will respond to subtle manipulation.

The handling characteristics of your otherwise excellent skis can easily be seriously altered by some minor defect in the condition of your edges or the bottom of the ski. If the plastic has eroded away, leaving the edges exposed like a couple of steel rails, then the skis will tend to go straight. They'll be very difficult to make sideslip. They won't respond to the usual maneuvers to make them carve. If you bang your edge against a rock, or something harder, you could easily create a small burr on the edge—a sliver of steel which sticks out from the edge. A burr hanging down from the edges, say, up near the shoulder, could cause a ski to dart and drag quite unpleasantly on hard packed snow. Fortunately, a few minutes' judicious use of a file can correct almost all bottom irregularities and restore your skis to top shape.

Just exactly how your skis will respond to where you place your weight and how much you release your edges will vary with the mounted position of your bindings. Assume that the normal mounting position allows the ball of each foot to rest over the center of the running surface of each ski. When your foot is ahead of this position, you may have to ski with your weight pressing slightly more on the heels than you would expect. With the foot resting behind the normal position, you may find that you must ski with more forward lean than you'd normally expect. The point being made in the foregoing is this: Don't be reluctant to put the blame on your equipment if your performance is somehow thwarted. And, inasmuch as this is basically about edge control, there is no better way to feel out the faults of your equipment than by sideslipping.

Good edge control may start with good equipment, but it ends with the skier who must do the right thing at the right time. And since most christies consist of as much as 90 percent sideslipping, then quite a case builds up in favor of your learning to control your edges by practicing sideslipping. A number of things can go wrong when you do try to sideslip. Here are most of the problems you might encounter, and their solutions.

DIFFICULT TO START THE SKID: Possible causes—1) Railed edges. 2) Too much camber. 3) Skis too stiff flexurally for your weight. Solutions—File edges flush to plastic sole or get new skis.

TIPS SEEK FALL LINE: Possible causes—1) Your weight is too far back. 2) Edges released too much. 3) Bindings too far back. The solutions are self-evident.

TAILS SKID TOO FAST: Possible causes—1) Bindings too far forward. 2) Weight too far forward. 3) Skis too flexible. 4) Skis without enough camber. 5) Edges too dull. Solutions—1) and 2) self-evident; 3) and 4) use different skis; 5) sharpen the edges.

YOU FALL DOWNHILL: Possible causes—1) You released the edges too much. 2) You tripped over the downhill pole. Solutions are self-evident.

YOU FALL UPHILL: Possible causes —1) You released the edges too quickly. 2) You failed to lean sideways ever so slightly in order to keep up with your skis. Solutions are self-evident.

DOWNHILL SKI SLIPS AWAY: Possible cause—Too much weight on the uphill ski, because you are fighting the skidding sensation by leaning toward the uphill side. Solution—Push the lower knee more forward and lean sideways toward the downhill side so that your shoulders become parallel with the slope.

DOWNHILL SKI PERSISTS IN STEMMING: Possible causes—1) Warped tail of downhill ski. 2) Bindings too far forward. 3) Burred edge on uphill edge of downhill ski. 4) Most likely, you have practiced snowplowing and snowplow turning too much. Solutions—1) Replace skis. 2) Position bindings properly. 3) File off the burr. 4) Take lessons to kick the habit.

UPHILL SKI DRAGS: Possible causes—1) Squeezing legs and boots together. 2) Insufficient strength of muscles along inside of uphill leg. 3) Releasing the edge of the upper ski too much. Solutions—Practice. Also, if your uphill foot is excessively pronated, you might require arch supports or a wedging device to cant the boot sole. Seek the advice of an instructor who has witnessed your problem.

EASIER TO DO FACING ONE WAY THAN THE OTHER: Possible cause—If skis and boots are not defective, you lack the needed muscular control of the ankle which is on the downhill side. You may need a wedge under that boot. Seek advice from an instructor who has observed your problem.

SKIS CROSS IN BACK: Possible causes—1) Too much weight on lower ski. 2) Warped upper ski, or a burred edge. 3) Weak leg muscles. 4) Squeezing your boots together. The solutions should be self-evident.

SKIS CROSS IN FRONT: Possible cause—Your uphill foot is not advanced enough. It should be about a half boot-length ahead of the lower one.

THE UPHILL CHRISTIE

Skidded turns of the legs rely less on the steering action than they do on the skier's wise manipulation of external forces such as friction and gravity to provide much of the turning impetus. By creating more friction on the uphill front edges of his skis as he traverses a slope, the skier allows gravity to pull the heels of the skis downward. A skidding turn away from the valley, toward the mountain, results. And that maneuver—a turn away from the fall line with skis parallel—is called an uphill christie. Perhaps no single maneuver, other than the complete downhill christie itself, is more improtant to a skier's development of confidence and skill on the mountainside. The skier can now cross steep slopes, slowing down at will by turning uphill. The easy, pleasant, sidesliding action is the skier's first introduction to the special treats of skiing, the parallel christies. An uphill christie is really the last portion of such a turn. Once a learning skier knows that he can finish a christie—the kind where he at first seems to have to plunge down toward the valley—he is much less hesitant to start one.

Just as with the snowplow, instructors the world over have used the uphill christie as a basic turn to which they can attach numerous body movements which will be needed as the skier becomes more of an expert. Some schools of thought have it that the turn should be initiated with an upward movement to unweight the skis. Others insist that a downward motion should be used to do the initiating. One school may demand that the body twist in the direction of the turn, another that the body rotate counter to the direction of the turn. And other schools will insist that you must use heel push to force the skis around.

There's no question about it, the uphill christie is handy, for instructors as well as students. And there is also no doubt about it, if you wish to become a thoroughly accomplished skier, you should be able to make an uphill christie using any and all of the motions tacked onto the basic turn.

•The version illustrated in Figure 5-16 is very similar to the standardized approach advocated by adherents of the American Technique. Follow the action, figure by figure: Prepare for the turn by increasing the bite of your edges into the hill and lowering your body position. When ready to turn, rise up into what is best described as a neutral position and move your hips forward to make sure that your weight is definitely transferred to the ball of each foot. The up-movement should partially straighten the legs, so that the knees move away from the slope causing a decrease in the bite of the edges. Thus, the skis

should begin to slip sideways. Since you have applied more weight to the front of the skis, that is, more friction to the uphill front edges of the skis, gravity will most affect the tails, causing them to skid faster than the fronts. The combined effect of these forces is that you turn into the slope.

Once the initial skid has resulted, you may increase in several ways the speed at which your skis turn. You may simply push the knees forward more and gradually tilt them toward the slope, causing the front edges to bite even more and the tails to skid even faster. Or, you may actively push your heels downward and sideward, allowing your upper body to compensate for this twisting action by rotating slightly in the direction opposite to your turn. Or, finally, you may simply keep your body comfortably aligned with your skis, with the lower arm slowly reaching forward to prepare the pole for inserting at the instant you may want to turn downhill—if, that is, you've acquired enough confidence to hazard the attempt.

Figure 5-16. *The uphill christie.*

6

CHRISTIES
The Whole Turn Concept

Learn This, Understand All

Unquestionably, one of skiing's great attractions is speed. Feeling the wind in your face. Moving out. And just as unquestionably, the greatest satisfaction of the sport is in controlling speed by turning—by christieing.

But turning by what technique? The counter-rotation of the Austrians and the Americans? Or the rotation method of the French? Should you shift your weight or keep it evenly divided between both skis? And what about angulation? Should you or shouldn't you use it?

Complete answers to such questions cannot be given on a thumbnail. Suffice it to say for now that an expert skier, in order to cope with the many challenges of skiing, knows when to use each of these techniques. And as for the learning skier, he should first learn to make parallel christies via the method which comes most naturally to him. Meanwhile, there is the task of understanding the many variations of christies. Not just the uphill christies, which will be dealt with at length in the section on edge control, but the complete turn, the so-called downhill christie. The *Whole Turn Concept* provides a framework for understanding advanced skiing and it brings new meaning and results

to your search for the most pleasure from skiing.

What is the whole turn concept? This is it. Everytime you make a downhill christie you must:

A. Get your weight off the skis.

B. Turn the skis while they are unweighted.

C. Change your edges and the leading ski while the skis are unweighted.

D. Shift your weight as needed.

E. Sideslip as desired.

Always keep this simple framework in mind. Memorize it. It will enormously simplify the confusing array of techniques and turns which you'll encounter. Now let's take a look at a *complete* parallel christie. Complete, because the skier initially moves in one direction and ends up moving in the opposite direction. In Figure 6-1A, the skier merely traverses the slope, his skis resting on the left edges. Figures 6-1B and C represent the Preparation Phase for a christie, where the skier lowers his body position and prepares to plant his inside pole. Figures 6-1 D and E represent the Initiation Phase, where the skier springs (or lifts) upward to momentarily take the weight off his skis. During this critical moment, he must apply a turning force to his skis,

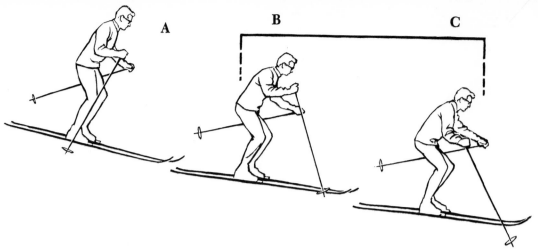

Figure 6-1. *The parallel christie.*

and, if needed, shift his weight to the outside ski of the turn, as well as roll his skis so that he changes the set of edges upon which the skis rest. Figures 6-1F through K indicate the Sideslipping Phase of the christie, where the skier adjusts his weight forward or backward and releases his edges more or less, to control the amount of curving sideslip just as if he were performing an uphill christie.

THE WHOLE TURN CONCEPT—PART A:
THE SIDESLIPPING PHASE OF ANY CHRISTIE

Just consider for a minute, that gravity, for our purposes, is the force which pulls you down the slope, either for-

ward, sideways, or whichever way you happen to fall. Friction, as it refers to sideslipping, is the resistance of the edges to the pull of gravity. By varying the positioning of your body over the skis, either forward or backward, you can alter the place where friction is applied to your edges. You can also vary the amount of resistance your edges offer to the pull of gravity by the amount the edges are released as explained in the *friction-gravity principles.* I've discussed them at length elsewhere (see page 92). An uphill christie is really the end part of a full downhill christie, and, therefore, I will not dwell on this phase of the downhill christie. Now, see Chapter 8 for the other whole turn components, after taking a look at several basic christies in the next one.

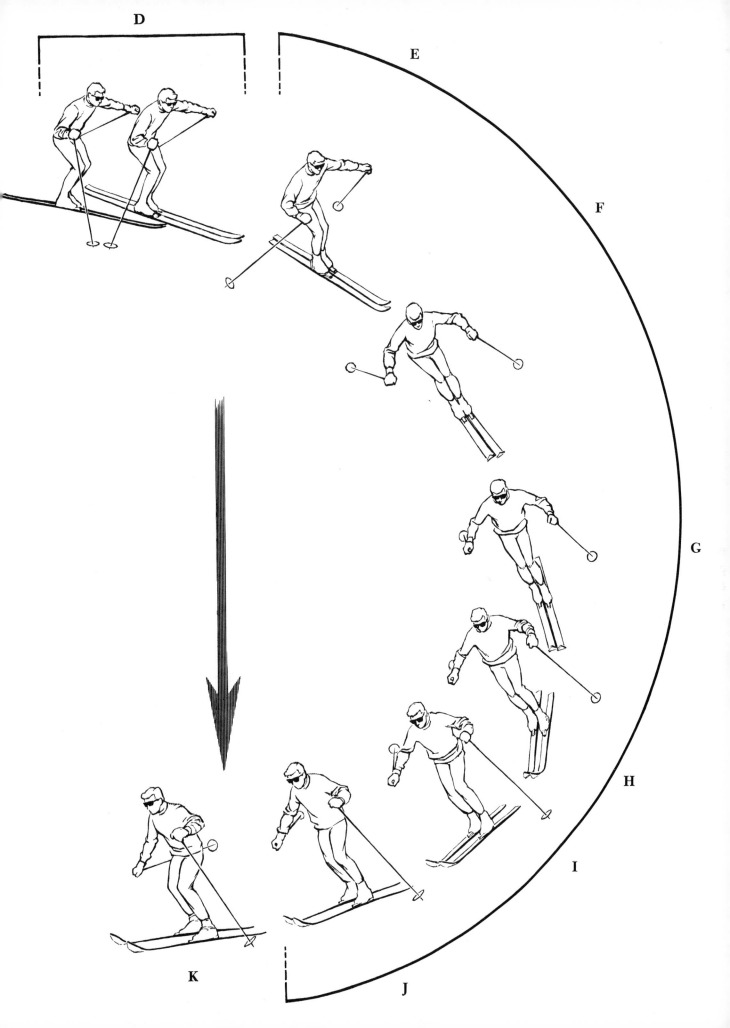

D

E

F

G

H

I

J

K

7

CHRISTIES
The Basic Ones

Do These, Be an Expert

THE STEM CHRISTIE

The stem christie is very often the intermediate skier's first real introduction to the excitement of making fairly fast turns down the mountainside. This christie is often confused in skier's minds with the stem turn because of the similarity of the words. But the movements are not really similar. True, both start from a traverse and end with one. But with a stem turn, the skis are held in a snowplow throughout the turn, whereas in a stem christie, no sooner is one ski stemmed then the skis are brought parallel to one another and the turn is completed with a curving sideslip. No sideslipping is present in a stem turn.

The stem christie is the maneuver which, sixty years ago, first opened the door to the satisfying thrills of controlled speed on skis. Credit is generally given to Hannes Schneider, the father of the ski school system of teaching, for developing the stem christie into a cornerstone of skiing. By 1910, Schneider had perfected his basic version of the stem christie, and it became one of the important goals of his teaching system—the Alpine System, as he preferred to call it, the Arlberg System as it became generally known.

Schneider developed his system at St. Anton, in the Arlberg province of Austria.

The word christie is a contraction of Christiania, the old name for Oslo, the capital of Norway. The word appears to have crept into usage because jumpers from Oslo (in the 1870's) brought their runs to a halt with what was then a unique turn. The other turn of the day was called the Telemark, after the region from which other competitors came. In those days, however, the Christiania was done by pushing the inside ski forward, putting your weight on the heel of your inside foot, and sort of steering and "guts-ing" your way around. Norwegians brought the turn and its name down to central Europe around the turn of the century where it gradually became known as the *schere christiania*—the scissor christie. However, the stem christie did not come into being until 1909, when Hannes Schneider, determined to find a way to make turning on skis possible at speeds faster than the Telemark permitted, invented it. Through the years, he perfected it and developed his entire teaching system toward it as a final goal.

To perform the type of stem christie

advocated by the American Technique and illustrated in Figure 7-1 proceed as follows: Choose a smooth, packed slope, preferably having the configuration of that in the diagram at the bottom of the next page. Traverse the slope to pick up speed—to about ten miles per hour. Stem the uphill ski by lifting it or sliding it into position and lower your body as shown. Keep the lower ski edged, with most of your weight on it, until the instant you are ready (third figure) to spring up and turn the skis (fourth figure). As you come up, push off the lower ski toward the stemmed ski to start it skidding. Then bring the lower ski parallel to the stemmed ski. The two skis should be parallel before heading down the fall line. From there, the turn continues as for an uphill christie.

A stem christie, in many respects, is a speeded-up and movement-compressed version of the stem turn (see pages 80-81). Edge change and lead change begin as the upper ski is stemmed. However, the idea of a stem christie is to get rid of the plow position as soon as possible and get the skis back into a side-by-side orientation. Not necessarily any closer than eight inches, mind you, but parallel nonetheless. The more proficient you are the sooner you will bring the lower ski parallel to the outside one, and the sooner is the edge change completed. In the upper drawing, note that the skis are parallel, with edges changed, before they reach the fall line. Now, both skis can skid around the turn, with you controlling the edges to vary the turn's radius. Though it is not evident in Figure 7-1, because of the angle of view, the inside ski assumes a slight lead over the outside one as soon as the skis become parallel.

The lead change takes place normally, as the christie continues.

There are many versions of the stem christie. Either the uphill ski or the downhill ski can be stemmed, though current usage almost universally favors the uphill ski. All varieties make use of an upward body movement to unweight the skis. All of them, at least in their polished forms, require that the skis be parallel before reaching the fall line. All require some form of turning power, though this is where the biggest differences in execution lie. The American Technique and the Austrian System use a shifting of weight from one ski toward the other, with an attendant heel-push and counter-rotation of the upper body. The French Method utilizes a simple twisting of the whole body in the direction of the intended turn. Whatever form you use, one thing is clear. Once you can make a stem christie in either direction, left and right, you are well on the way to tasting the full pleasures of down-mountain skiing. That will occur when you can ski parallel.

THE PARALLEL CHRISTIES
So you're a parallel skier. You've learned how to keep your skis parallel—more or less—in a schuss, in a traverse, in a sideslip, and even throughout your turns. That makes you an expert, doesn't it?

Well, not exactly. You start down a slope feeling like a hotshot, you make a few nice turns, and suddenly you find yourself almost out of control, looking desperately for a parking place. The real expert, meantime, has started out with the same swooping turns you made, but as the terrain changes from open

Figure 7-1. *The stem christie.*

gentle slope to steep slope to narrow, mogully trail, and back out to the flats, he adjusts his style to the mountain— always in control, always rhythmical, seemingly effortless.

What is the basic difference between the two skiers? The key lies in the different ways they use their edges. The first skier has learned how to start into a skid with his skis parallel but, beyond that, he relies almost on brute force to change direction or speed. No matter what the terrain, he makes the same kind of movements. Particularly on steep slopes, he picks up momentum steadily, each turn leading into a more uncontrolled skid and traverse. Inevitably, he gets into trouble.

The second skier recognizes that there are four quite different kinds of parallel turns for packed surfaces, and that each is best suited for certain kinds of situations. Above all, he has learned that control of speed and direction is pri-

marily a matter of control of the edges. He has learned that the edges are the masters of the skis, and, therefore, he has learned to master his edges.

The first of the four important, or advanced, turns is the basic parallel christie which we discussed in broad detail in Chapter 6. Unfortunately, the beginning parallel skier usually learns this on a wide gentle slope. He may not match the picture of grace that his instructor paints with those effortless long-arc turns, but he gets the feeling of making an honest-to-goodness parallel turn, and suddenly he feels like an expert. Yes, this is the same turn as that which the true expert uses for wide slopes, but there is a big difference.

That difference begins with the distance the skis are displaced when they are unweighted. The less skilled skier swings or hops them quite far to the fall line, or even beyond it. Thus, for much of the circumference of the turn,

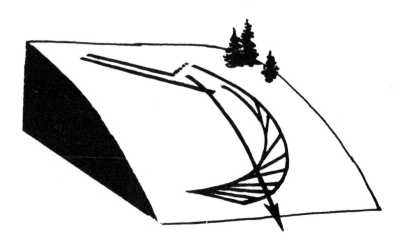

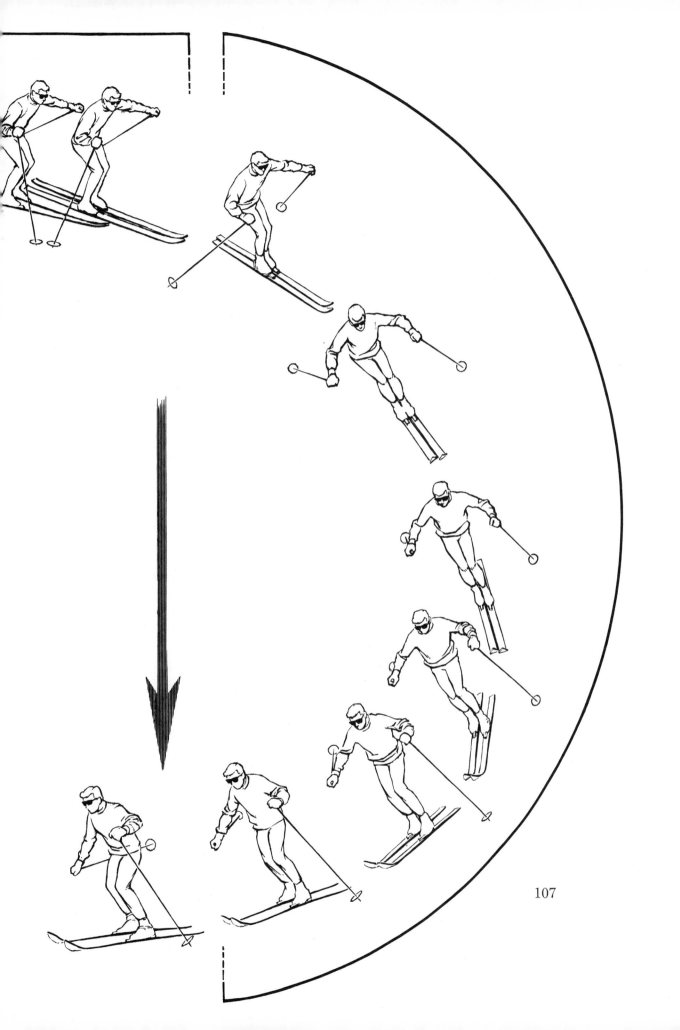

his edges play no role, and there is no precision in the direction the turn takes and very little controlled braking effect. The expert, on the other hand, has his edges in contact with the snow almost constantly—except for the actual brief moment of the edge change. As a consequence, his skis bite during almost the entire turn. Pressure on the edges is exerted by the angulated position of the body.

When properly executed, the basic parallel christie permits the skier to link turns without accelerating. It is ideal for wide open slopes where there is room for thirty feet or so of traverse between each turn. When the angle of traverse gets steep or narrow, or both,—say 25 degrees or over—another type of turn is called for—the check christie.

THE BASIC PARALLEL CHRISTIE

Until 1932, parallel christies were performed by only a very few of the world's top skiers. And the "parallel-ness" of their turns was the subject of a great credibility gap. Many a pro, even the late great Hannes Schneider, did not believe that the "pure" christiania was possible. Somehow, they thought, there just had to be a minute stem at the start of the turn. Today, however, no one disputes the existence of a pure parallel christie. In fact, the most athletic type of person, properly equipped, can learn the basic turn in as little as a day or two. Not to perfection, of course, but at least enough to revert to stemming and snow-plowing only on the necessary occasions.

Once you master even just one of the numerous forms of parallel christies, you've got the basic structure of the sport quite well built. All that's left is to add the trim, the finish. You can make that as elaborate as you want.

The basic parallel christie—called parallel because both skis are turned simultaneously without any stemming at all—requires the five points of the whole turn concept previously discussed; that is:

1. Get your weight off the skis (unweighting action).
2. Apply a turning force to start the skis into a skid while they are unweighted.
3. Change the edges and the lead ski during the process of unweighting.
4. Shift your weight as needed.
5. Sideslip, as desired, to control the radius of the christie.

As we've already seen, the unweighting action can come from a jump, or an upward springing action where the skis are not actually lifted off the snow. Or it can come from a sudden rapid lowering of the body. Or from a sort of horse-kick action which we called the *ruade*. Or from a combination of these or from a variety of subtle actions such as those used in the racing turns called jet christies. Both series of illustrations included here show up-unweighted types of christies.

The edges of the skis must be changed as you go from one parallel christie to the next. This involves rolling the skis from their uphill edges to the inside edges of the new turn. This can be done by either banking or a change in angulation. Banking requires leaning the whole body toward the center of the turn, rolling the edges as you bank. Change in angulation requires moving the knees and lower legs from their into-the-hill position away from the hill and pressing them toward the center of the new turn.

The turning force for triggering a parallel christie can come from a number of sources. From the feet. From the lower

legs. From the entire legs. From the hips. From the entire body, or even from the arms and poles alone. Whatever the source of turning power, it must be applied to the skis at the instant they are unweighted and during the edge-changing process.

In Figure 7-2, the parallel christie is initiated by what French instructors call *projection circulaire*. That phrase refers to a combination of up-weighting and banking. Turning force is applied by the upper body which twists toward the intended direction. This rotational force is called anticipation, because it usually precedes—or anticipates—the turning of the skis.

Illustrated in Figure 7-3 is the Austrian or American way of applying turning power, where the source of the force originates primarily in the lower body. The heels of the skis are picked up off the snow to unweight them; the legs then thrust the skis toward the outside of the intended turn causing them to skid.

Once the turn has been started and the skid established, all that remains is to control the edges. For example, more friction of the edges up front will let the backs of the skis slip faster, making a tighter turn possible.

Figure 7-2. *The French way.*

THE CHECK CHRISTIE

This is the *check turn*, so called because the skier checks his speed *before* initiating the turn. A good skier employs this turn whenever he feels he is picking up too much speed as he enters a turn. Like the basic parallel christie, it's a long radius turn with traverse, so that a fairly wide slope is required. It could be used on a fairly gentle slope, too—say one that had become rather crowded

109

and where a definite slowdown was indicated.

As the skier approaches the point where he is going to make his turn, his body is upright, in a traverse position. Instead of holding his edge until he up-unweights, however, he momentarily releases just prior to the down-up movement, allowing the tails of the skis to slide downhill. The body then begins to lower while the knees and ankles are moved back toward the mountain, to prepare for the setting of the edges. They are set with a quick up motion and the edges are changed. The turn is carved as in the basic parallel turn.

As the name of this turn implies, the main difference between it and the basic parallel turn is the definite check made before the turn starts. This check not only moderates speed, it creates a firm platform from which the edge change and unweighting can be initiated with precision. The check also takes care of speed build-up before a dangerous situation develops. The amount of check to be used, of course, depends on your speed and the condition of the slope. When moguls are present, the check is always made on the shoulder of the mogul around which you are going to turn. Again, the check is made with a short, quick down motion with knees and ankles pressed into the hill. This sets the edges, slows down the skis, and builds a platform before your controlled plunge into the fall line.

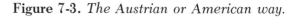

Figure 7-3. *The Austrian or American way.*

Figure 7-4. *The up-unweighted parallel christie.*

THE FALL LINE CHRISTIES

I have mentioned the fall line throughout the book and even defined it in Chapter 2. Let's take a minute or two and really fully understand what is meant by the fall line. First of all, this imaginary line has nothing to do with the act of falling, although skiers often "bottom up" there. Loosely speaking, the fall line has been defined as the path of direct descent, of least resistance of maximum velocity, of maximum slope. Somewhat more precisely, it has been pegged as the path which a ball would follow when dropped at any given point on the slope. However, because most slopes consist of many segments—dips and rolls such as those presented by moguls—most slopes have many fall lines.

Practically speaking, the fall line serves as a very handy point of reference, essential for intelligent discussion about ski technique. For example, the act of traversing a slope is spoken of by instructors as skiing across the fall line. Similarly, when a turn is made toward the valley, the act is called turning into the fall line. You are said to have reached the fall line once your skis are headed directly downhill on that particular section of slope on which you are turning. (When schussing, as when a ball runs freely down a slope, you are skiing directly down the general, or overall, fall line of the slope.) As your turn continues, you go off the fall line into a traverse.

As with the definition for fall line, the definition for fall-line christies is more pragmatic than it is specific. These turns consist of a series of linked parallel christies in which traversing and pronounced checking is virtually eliminated (Figure 7-5). Thus, they provide only partial control over speed. Their virtue lies in their use for avoiding obstacles, people or otherwise, and in providing pleasurable movements to do on skis.

SHORTSWING

Suppose there is no room to traverse for several ski lengths between turns as, for example, on a steep, narrow slope. In that case, *shortswing!* This maneuver is actually a series of closely linked check christies. Speed is controlled by the width of the arc made by the ski tails as they are swung back and forth across the fall line: the wider the arc, the slower the speed. Also, the bite of the edges at the start of each turn is used to brake speed.

In the execution of the shortswing, the shoulders face more or less square to the fall line at all times. In the sequence illustration (Figure 7-5), the backbone remains approximately parallel to the bones of the lower leg. When the body is lowered in preparation to set the edges and to suddenly spring upward, note that all forward-bending hinges of the body (i.e., ankles, waist, knees) bend an equal amount. Though not visible from this artist's angle, the same holds true when the body is raised. This accordian-like folding of the body must be done quickly and without causing excessive body weight to go to the rear. Also, since the object of the shortswing is to link christies while eliminating traversing, the end of one christie must immediately become the beginning of the next. In other words, at the end of the down motion, the edges are set to stop the previous turn and to start the takeoff.

Shortswing is a rhythmical succession of unweighting, foot swivelling and heel pushing with most of the action confined to the legs.

Figure 7-5. *Fall-line christies.*

WEDELN

On gentler slopes where you don't need to control your speed, you might not want to set your edges. The turns to use then are called wedeln christies.

Wedeln (say VAY duhln), as the Austrians have dubbed it and the Americans have followed—*godille* (go-DEE) as the French call it—fits into the category of fall-line christies. So does the type of parallel christie called mambo, in which the upper body twists in the direction of the intended turn long before (relatively speaking) the feet are turned, and then twists in the opposite direction once the feet and skis do swing around. For all fall-line christies except the mambo variety, the upper body remains relatively square (at right angles) to the fall line, as illustrated. Turning is done by the legs which either swivel the skis around directly underfoot or thrust the heels of the skis from one side of the fall line to the other. Since the amount of turning is less in these types of christies than for those parallel christies which involve traversing, the amount of turning force, the amount and duration of unweighting, and the amount of edge change are all correspondingly reduced. And because these turns are linked quickly together, the development of rhythm and quick reflexes becomes correspondingly more important.

The position and movements of the body for wedelning are much the same as in the shortswing: shoulders square to the fall line, upper body quiet, up and down motion with the legs but with little amplitude. Ideally, the skis remain in contact with the snow as they are brought back and forth across the fall line. The edges are changed while the skis are unweighted, the width of arc controlled during the down motion, mostly by the cut of the skis. The faster you wish to go, the less effort you put into the unweighting and turning power movements. There is relatively little edging throughout the turn, and virtually no check at the completion of one turn and the start of the next.

SUMMARY

While hotshot skiers employ many other christies—mambo, wedeln, jet christie, Reuel, airplane turn, avalement, Killy, etc.—the recreational skier can be classified as an "expert" if he can handle the four important turns—the basic parallel christie, the check christie, the shortswing and the wedeln—with ease. Remember that these four turns *can* be made on any kind of terrain. They are simply most appropriate in the situations we have indicated. Try the basic parallel turn on a steep, narrow trail and you could find yourself skiing off into the woods or picking up speed at a breakneck pace. Use the shortswing on a flat, wide section and you will be needlessly expending energy. Controlled parallel skiing requires not only that you learn these four turns, but that you use them intelligently. You are well on the way to becoming a well-rounded skier, ready to enjoy the delicious subtleties of mastering all types of snow, all kinds of slopes.

114

8

CHRISTIES
Their Components

Know These, Be a Knowledgeable Expert

UNDERSTANDING UNWEIGHTING

An important part of every christie involves the deliberate attempt to unload or unweight your skis. While the skis are unweighted, the task of turning them and rocking from one set of edges to the other becomes vastly simplified.

There are a number of ways to unweight. Of these, the most universally used and taught is the "lift" or as it is called in the Austrian and American systems, up-unweighting. This method is easy to do, inasmuch as it resembles the movements used to spring up into the air. It also provides a relatively long period of time during which the apparent weight of the skier is at a minimum, a factor which allows more time for the learner to start his skis turning and to change his edges. The illustrated chart (Figure 8-1) shows what happens to your apparent weight as you displace the body vertically. The shaded area beneath each figure represents the approximate alteration of pressure exerted against the snow. The scales are an adjunct and merely make the apparent change in weight more graphic.

Here are the steps of *down-unweighting:*

1. While standing in a normal balanced stance position, the skier's normal weight and apparent weight are identical.

2. As soon as the skier begins to lower his body position quickly, he appears to be losing weight. The apparent loss in weight—the unweighting—lasts for a very short time and continues only as long as the body continues its quick downward folding.

3. While actually skiing, seldom does the body fold up so completely, but it can if a longer than normal period of unweighting is needed. The unweighting continues just as long as the body continues to lower, but for only as long as the downward folding action occurs at a fast pace—actually faster than the speed at which gravity pulls the body downward.

Here are the steps of *up-unweighting:*

4. Once the body has stopped its downward movement, a sudden increase in apparent weight occurs.

5. After the initial upward thrust has begun, the apparent weight will begin to decrease. It will continue to decrease provided the initiating upward thrust has been quick and powerful.

6. When skiing, the body seldom becomes more erect than illustrated in the drawing. This should be the term-

inal position for up-unweighting. It is now that the apparent weight is minimal. In fact, if you spring up powerfully enough to jump, your apparent weight will be nil.

7. If you should stop all vertical movement at the peak of the body's extension, as in the previous figure, your apparent weight would quickly increase to normal. In actual practice, during an up-unweighted christie, the body is immediately lowered slightly upon attaining maximum extension, thus prolonging the period of unweighting for a scant, but important tenth of a second or so.

It's important to realize that the apparent loss in weight takes place while the body is in motion. Once you stop the movement there is an apparent and momentary increase in weight, a factor which the expert skier uses to good advantage by setting his edges at this moment, when that action is appropriate. If you observe how your body apparently gains or loses weight when you move up and down by using ordinary bathroom scales, you'll note that what counts is not so much how much you move up and down, but how quickly you do so. You'll also observe how short-lived the unweighted phase actually is. That explains why the timing for the initiation phase of a christie is so critical, and so tough to perfect.

Ways to Unweight. Illustrated in

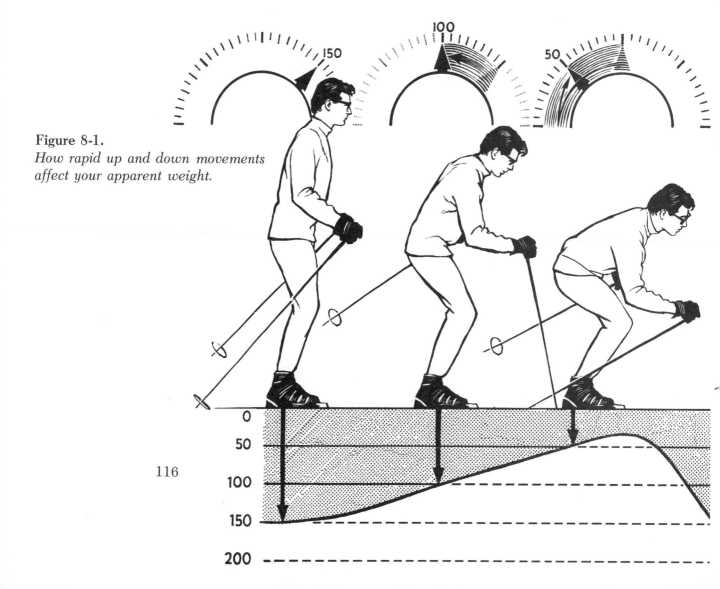

Figure 8-1.
How rapid up and down movements affect your apparent weight.

116

Figure 8-2 are five ways to unweight:

1. *Uphill Stem.* The most common way taught. Unweighting is effected simply by raising the upper ski off the snow, placing it at an angle to the original direction, changing its edge, weighting it, then bringing the lower, unweighted ski alongside.

2. *The Lift.* Most useful form of unweighting, providing a relatively long period of apparent weightlessness.

3. *The Quickdrop.* Here the body is lowered quickly. Period of weightlessness is very short. Useful for racing turns and skiing the moguls. Often referred to as down-unweighting.

4. *The Ruade.* The heels are quickly retracted toward the seat as the upper body is lowered slightly. Useful for slow-speed, short-radius christies on steep slopes.

5. *The Hop.* As the body reaches the peak of an up-unweighting movement, the heels are retracted slightly. Excellent for learning parallel christies at medium speeds on intermediate slopes.

UNWEIGHTING AND THE UPHILL CHRISTIE

Strictly speaking no unweighting movements are necessary for the performance of an uphill christie. As described in Chapter 5, the turn can be executed easily by a simple release of the edges accompanied by varying amounts of forward lean. However, be-

117

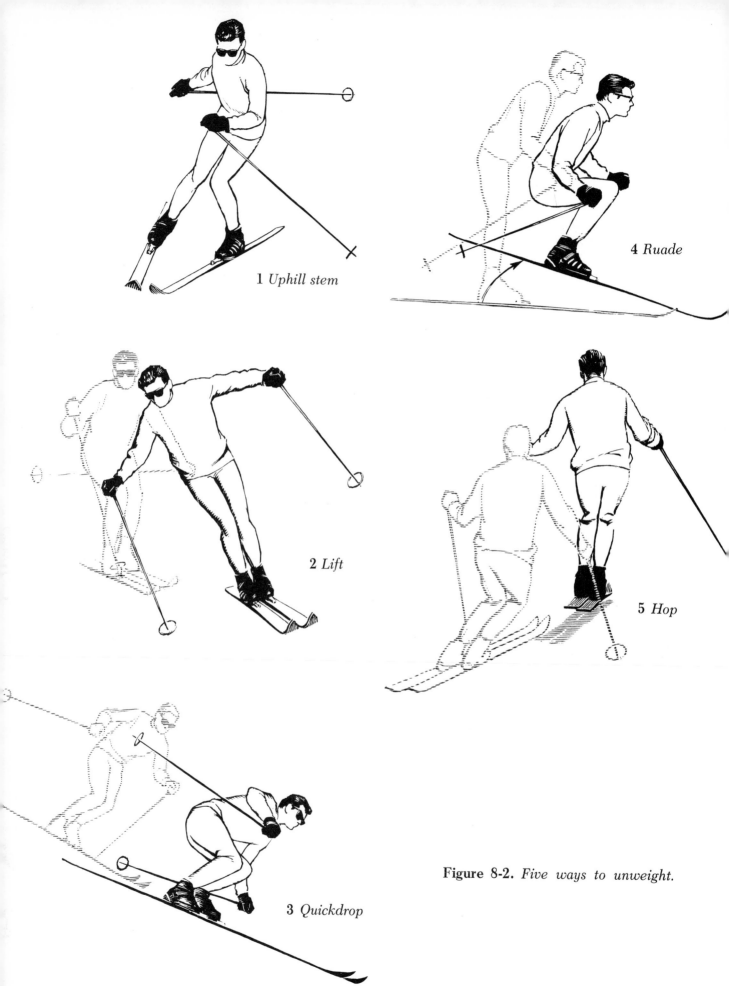

1 *Uphill stem*

2 *Lift*

3 *Quickdrop*

4 *Ruade*

5 *Hop*

Figure 8-2. *Five ways to unweight.*

cause an uphill christie can have appended to it both the movements for unweighting and pole-planting, thereby making it very close to a downhill christie, it is frequently taught as illustrated (Figure 8-3), with the use of up-unweighting.

The first figure represents the skier as he approaches his turn while traversing. The second figure shows him lowering his body position. This movement is done slowly since its purpose is not to unweight the skis but merely to prepare the body for a quick upward spring. That spring takes place explosively the instant the pole is planted. After the spring has started, the skis become partially unloaded, making it easy to release the edges the desired amount. The body is immediately lowered once it reaches its high point—an action which prolongs the period during which the skis are unweighted. The body may continue to lower as the turn progresses—an action which prevents any sudden increase in downward pressure.

The accomplished skier coordinates his downward movement: The moment his body is lowered as much as is wanted coincides with the instant he re-edges

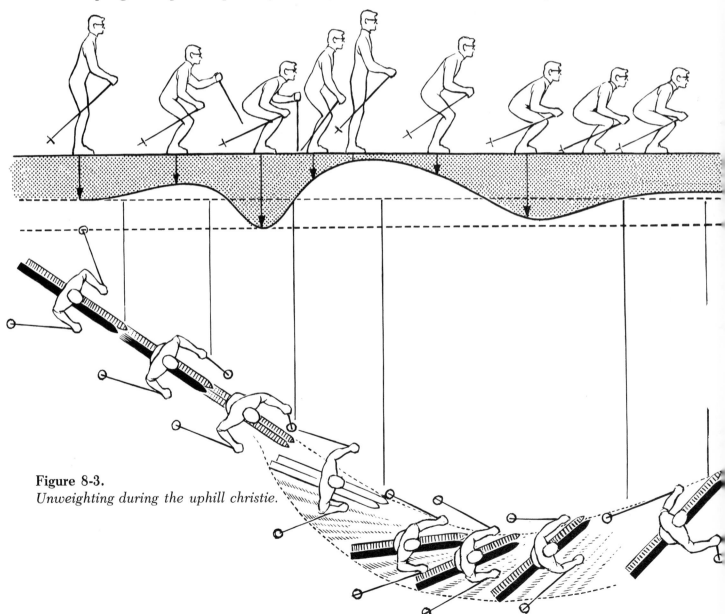

Figure 8-3.
Unweighting during the uphill christie.

his skis to bring the skidding to a halt. At that moment, since his apparent weight will increase, his edges will be pressed more effectively into the snow.

UNWEIGHTING AND THE DOWNHILL CHRISTIE

Before we get into the actual technique of downhill, or parallel christies, let's look at the effects of unweighting on turning as shown in Figure 8-4. When this drawing is compared with Figure 8-3, the similarity between a downhill parallel christie and an uphill christie becomes obvious. Note that in both, the apparent weight decreases as the skier prepares to plant his pole to trigger the turn. Triggering—the initiation phase— takes place during the period when the skis are most unweighted, when the turning force must be applied and the skis rocked over to their other set of edges. From then on the turn is just like the uphill christie.

Recall the Whole Turn Concept: For every downhill christie you must get your weight off the skis. Therefore, the movements illustrated at the top of Figure 8-4 can be replaced with those for down-unweighting, for a ruade, a hop, or a stem. The timing for the turns remains the same: When the skis are unweighted the edges are changed and the turning impulse unleashed.

THE WHOLE TURN CONCEPT PART B: TURNING POWER

How do you start your christies? Do you use rotation? Counter-rotation? Will a shift of weight do the trick? Or is heel thrust the answer? There is probably no topic in modern skiing more confusing and controversial. It's confusing because there are almost as many ways to start a turn as there are varieties of snowflakes. It's also confusing because certain systems of ski teaching— so-called techniques, like the Austrian, the American, the French, or the Natur Teknik—have each adopted arbitrary approaches to the problem and then proclaimed its own approach to be *the* way, the only right way, to ski. Well, you are now reading one ski instructor who doesn't subscribe to the one-way-only approach. Start your turns in the way that comes most natural to you. Master that style, then add the refinements and variations necessary to mold your turns to every snow and slope situation.

This section is about turning power. It tells of the different ways used to get your christies going.

TURNING POWER FROM THE SKIS

The shape of a ski has a great deal to do with its ability to turn. No doubt you've noticed that it is widest up-front, where the forebody begins its upturn. That widest point is called the shoulder. The sides of the ski become narrowest back at the waist. Then they flare out again toward the tail.

The Drag Effect of the Wide Shoulder. If you visualize the ski on the snow, moving sideways rather than forward, it is easy to see that because of the greater width at the shoulder, the tails will tend to skid faster, producing a curving sideslip. This drag effect has its influence on almost every sliding turn made.

The Sidecut Effect of a Modern Alpine Ski. The other way that the ski provides turning power is more complicated. Try this, or else visualize the procedure: Cut a smooth curve out of a 3 x 5 inch card or piece of paper,

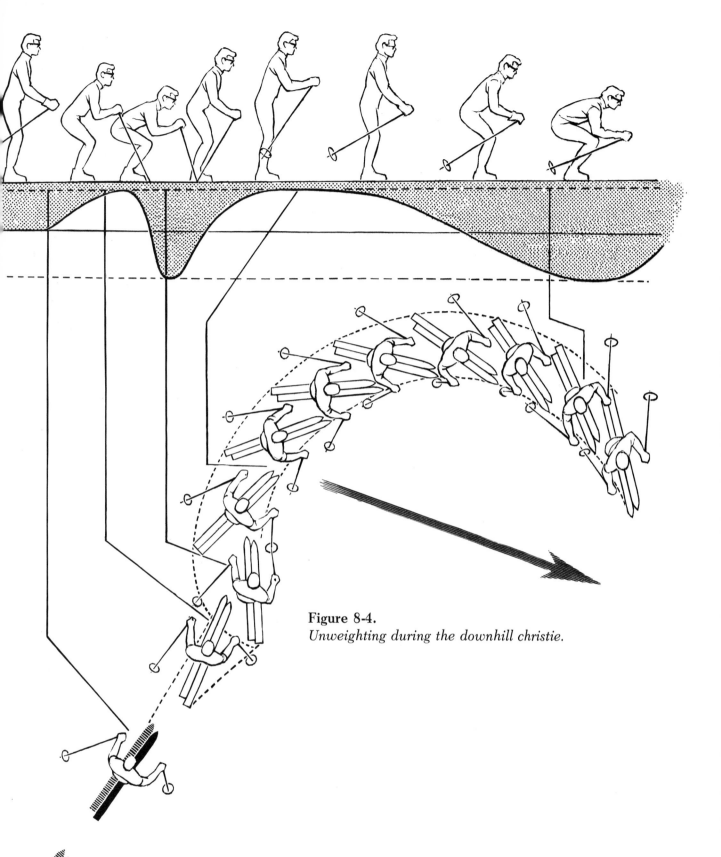

Figure 8-4.
Unweighting during the downhill christie.

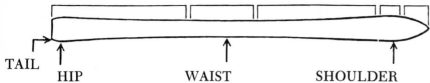

TAIL SECTION   MID-SECTION   FOREBODY   SHOVEL

TIP

TAIL   HIP   WAIST   SHOULDER

Figure 8-5A.

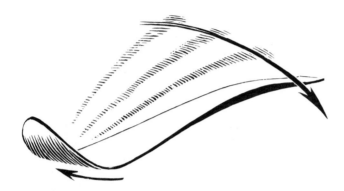

Figure 8-5B. *The drag effect of the wide shoulder.*

Figure 8-5C.

as shown (Figure 8-6). The exaggerated cut represents the sidecut of a ski. Now, hold the edge of the cut card against a flat desk top (Figure 8-6B). Note that a ski resting on the slope would touch only at shoulder and hip.

Now press down obliquely on the card (Figure 8-6C) and note the way the card bends into an arc. The same thing happens to a ski when it is put on edge, forcing the ski to follow an arcing track. When a ski does that, it is *carving* a turn. It is a powerful turning force.

TURNING POWER FROM WEIGHT TRANSFER AND WEIGHT SHIFT

Almost all movements you make have a direct and subtle effect on where your weight rests on your feet and where it presses on your skis. In Chapter 5, we emphasized the effect which a transfer of weight, either forward or backward, has on sideslip (friction-gravity principle). There is also a turning effect on the skis when you transfer weight from one ski to the other, as in the snowplow turn. The effect is even more noticeable when your skis are soft and can flex deeply—then the ski to which you transfer the weight tends to carve its own way around, as described above. To get the most turning effect out of a weight transfer, wait until the outside ski of the turn passes over the fall line before applying more weight to it.

When an instructor says, "shift your weight," he usually refers to an action somewhat like that used to aid a snowplow turn. But the movements are more pronounced and done faster and often combined with an unweighting movement. And what's more, the body is displaced sideways, giving an added impulse to the turn. This type of weight

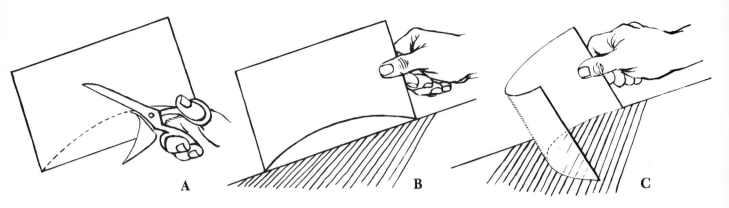

Figure 8-6. *The sidecut effect of a modern ski.*

shift is often used to initiate a stem christie, and might more appropriately be called a body thrust, since the quick sideways displacement of the body provides the angular momentum to launch you into the turn.

TURNING POWER . . .
DISPLACEMENT OF THE SKIS

The angular displacement of the skis begins very early in the learning progression of skiing. A beginner soon learns the step-around turn, of which there are two versions. In the first, the heels of the skis are left on the snow to serve as pivots while the shovel of one ski is stepped away from the other, making a fan pattern on the snow. In the other, the heels are stepped around with the shovels serving as pivots. For these simple changes of direction the turning power is supplied by the muscles of the legs. Later on, the static turns give way to the first of the kinetic turns—a simple skating step into the hill—used to come to a stop from a traverse and especially as an edge control and balance exercise.

Still later, when ready for it, you learn the snowplow and stem turns with their attendant complexities of weight shift, weight transfer, steering with feet, knees, legs and sometimes the hips —all components of turning power. The action of the skis in these turns is more involved than is usually admitted. The tail of the outside ski must be heel thrust around while the front of the inside ski is being tip thrust around.

The displacement of the ski in a stem christie is more complex. First, the uphill ski is stemmed. The stemmed ski can be further displaced by weight shift, or by weight transfer, or by a thrust of the legs, or by knee crank, then the other ski brought alongside as the turn progresses (Figure 8-7). Or, once the ski has been stemmed, both skis can be unweighted and turning power simultaneously applied to them, making the turn from that point on similar to a parallel christie (Figure 8-7B).

There are three basic ways to displace the skis to initiate parallel christies, plus various combinations of the three. The usual approach, though not necessarily the best, is to hop the skis off the snow and to displace the tails of the skis uphill (Figure 8-8A) using the thrusting power of the legs. When both skis are unweighted simultaneously, both ends can be swivelled around their middles (Figure 8-8B). When it is

123

Figure 8-7.

Figure 8-8.

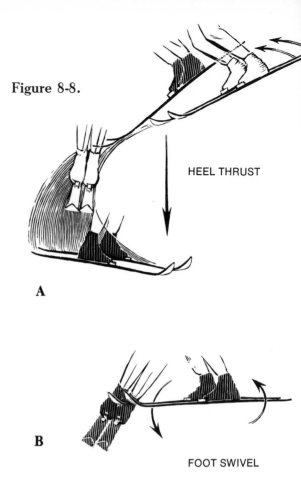

HEEL THRUST

A

STEM CHRISTIE

A

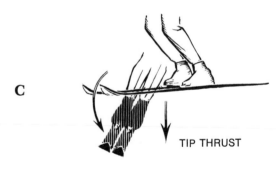

B

FOOT SWIVEL

B

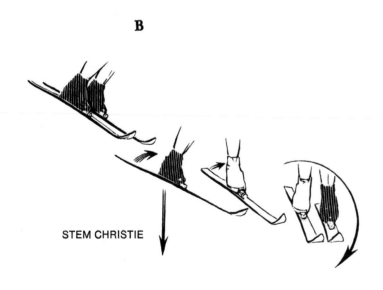

STEM CHRISTIE

C

TIP THRUST

COMBINED DISPLACEMENT

D

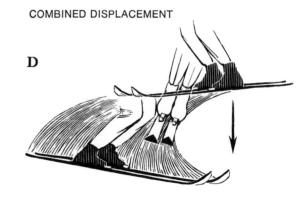

urgent to displace the skis into the turn the tips can be thrust downhill (Figure 8-8C). These ways can also be combined for the greatest efficiency. For instance, the skis can be swivelled around underfoot to initiate the christie, then the tails thrust to the outside of the turn to tighten up on the radius (Figure 8-8D). Which of these ways is best depends entirely upon the condition of slope and snow. And that's something you'll learn from experience. It's part of skiing's constant, exciting challenge. More on christies will be found in this chapter and in Chapter 9.

TURNING POWER . . .
IT'S IN THE FEET AND LEGS

The feet, particularly for an expert skier, are a subtle but important source of turning power. They can be partially rotated to the left or right, just enough to change the direction of the skis so that other forms of turning power can be applied to complete the turn. Actually, the rotary force comes from the muscles of the lower leg—muscles which are not normally used and which must be strengthened and educated through practice. Furthermore, the lower legs and feet cannot twist alone unless the knee is bent at least 45 degrees. This partially explains why so many racers and deep-snow skiers assume a low, almost sitting stance. You can develop an awareness for this source of turning power, as follows: Sit in a chair with only your heels touching the floor, as shown in Figure 8-9. Swivel the toes to the left and to the right for a form of tip thrust. Now, raise the heels and with the ball of each foot on the floor swivel the heels back and forth for a form of heel thrust.

The contemporary hotdog skier gets most of his turning power from the legs. Try this: Sit on the very edge of a table, or better, support yourself on the backs of two chairs as shown in the illustration. Now, thrust your heels from one side to the other, turning your feet to point toward the center of the intended turn (the same direction that the knees point). Definitely allow the legs to rotate in the hip sockets. This action is sometimes referred to as knee crank because in a very real sense you crank the knees from one side to the other. The turning force developed in this fashion is very powerful, especially when the body is in a slightly lowered position. The force also gets stronger as the knees bend more. With the advent of quicker turning skis, and rigid-soled and stiff-sided boots, this type of rotary force is becoming *the* way to power your parallel christies.

TURNING POWER . . . IT'S
IN THE ARMS, THE SHOULDERS,
THE TORSO

The use of the upper body as a source of turning power has become less important in recent years. Yet, an accomplished skier will often—knowingly or not—resort to the aid of a pole swing, or arm swing, or even to a rotation of the hips or shoulders in the direction of the turn. The movements of a christie used to be compared to a whack at a golf ball or tennis ball—a matter of windup, swing, and follow-through. The action was called rotation.

Whenever rotation or swing is used, an interesting muscle phenomenon called blocking takes place. Without it you could twist your body and swing your arms all day and your feet would still not turn (Figure 8-10). But if you block, or tense, the rotary muscles of

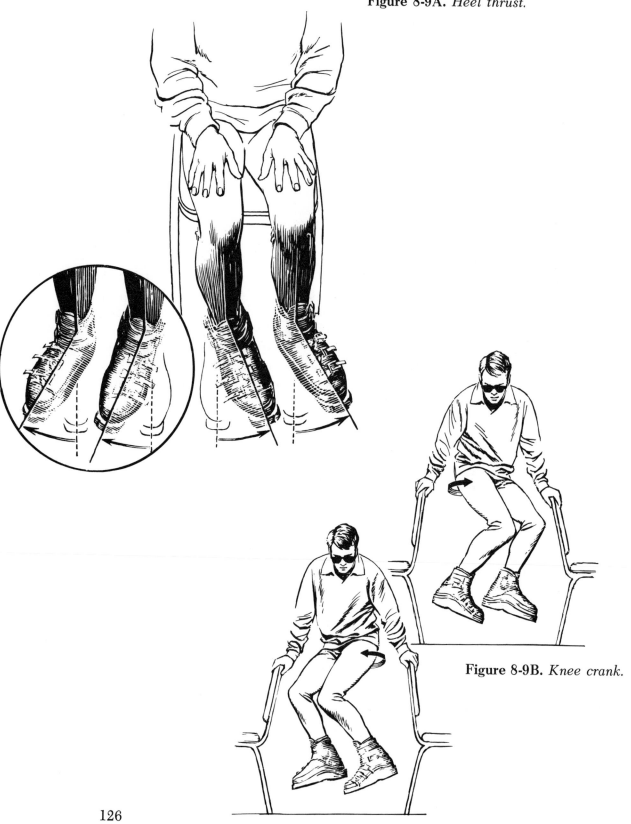

Figure 8-9A. *Heel thrust.*

Figure 8-9B. *Knee crank.*

126

Figure 8-10. *Without blocking, your feet and skis remain stationary.*

the legs, you can make the feet twist with your hips and shoulders.

Blocking happens automatically if you unweight at the correct moment. Prove it to yourself in this fashion: Stand on the floor. Keeping your feet in place, rotate your hips and shoulders in one direction, while lowering your body position. Then unwind quickly and spring up at the same time so that at the instant your body is back to a normal position your feet come off the floor. Your whole body, feet included, will turn. The illusion is that the twisting action stops while you are in the air. In reality, blocking allows the whole body to turn as a unit.

Finding the existing vocabulary of skiing to be too limiting for accurate description, I've often had to coin phrases. One is arm swing, another, pole swing, both being movements frequently used by all good skiers to assist their parallel christies. Figure 8-11 shows how the wrist can be turned to "windup" the ski pole in preparation to swinging it quickly and forcefully so that its tip describes a section of a circle behind and to the side of the body. Note how the wrist and arm muscles are blocked when the pole has been swung approximately parallel to the skis. If the body is unweighted at that instant, it will be displaced as shown. The blocking action transmits the angular momentum developed by the swing to the whole body. Careful observation of good skiers will reveal to you many subtle variations of pole and arm swing used to provide a source of turning power.

TURNING POWER FROM OTHER SOURCES

If rotation is described as the twisting of the body in the direction of a turn,

Figure 8-11. *Ski pole windup.*

then counter-rotation is the opposite. Actually, counter-rotation has been the subject of much pseudo-scientific piano-stool analogizing and theorizing, with the conclusions purporting to prove indisputably that it is the only effective turning force. Nonsense. Suffice it to say that it has its place, for example, as when christie-ing off the fall line (Figure 8-12A) where the legs and heels are quickly thrust to the side. The mass of the upper body, when twisted slightly counter to the leg thrust, then acts as a counter balance for the hasty lower body action and avoids an upset.

Figure 8-12B shows how you can move your upper body downhill, into an effective position from which to swivel the feet or thrust the legs for a very quick type of wedeln. The initiating

action for this movement is a form of anticipation.

Figure 8-12C illustrates another type of turning force where the body fully anticipates the turn before the skis begin to turn toward the new direction. Blocking takes place here, when the twisting force of the pole, arm, and shoulder, coincides with the moment when the skis have been placed flat to the snow by banking the whole body into the turn.

Figure 8-12D shows part of a sequence of a mambo christie. Here the turning force comes from the hips. Note that the body rotates around as far as it can, before the edges are changed and the skis unweighted. Hence, mambo is sometimes said to require very "late blocking."

128

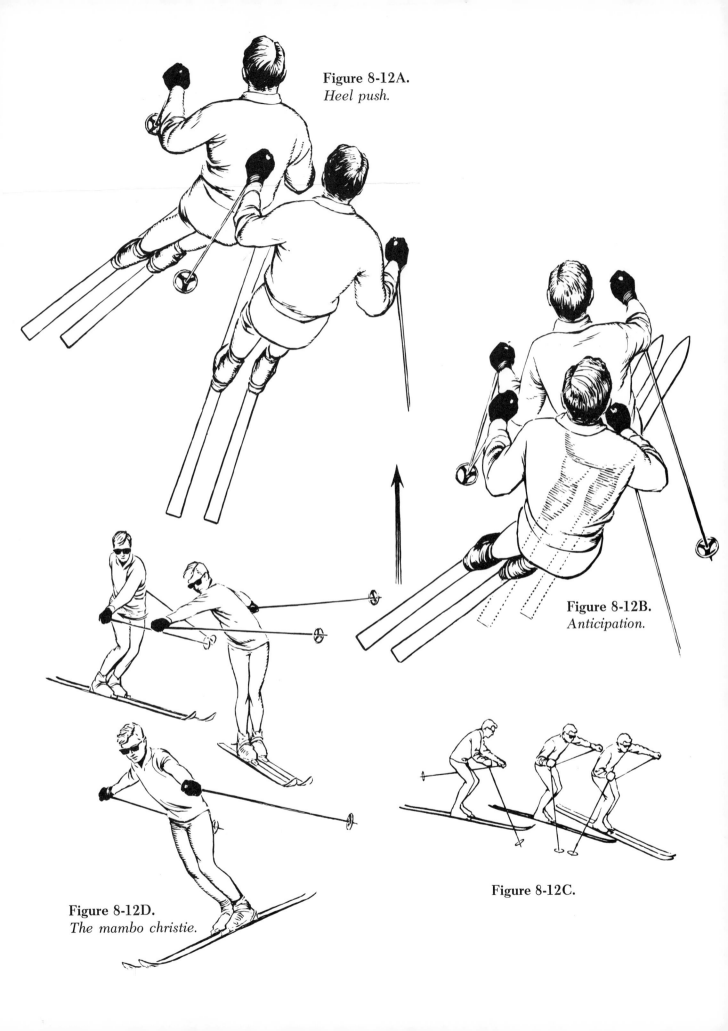

Figure 8-12A.
Heel push.

Figure 8-12B.
Anticipation.

Figure 8-12C.

Figure 8-12D.
The mambo christie.

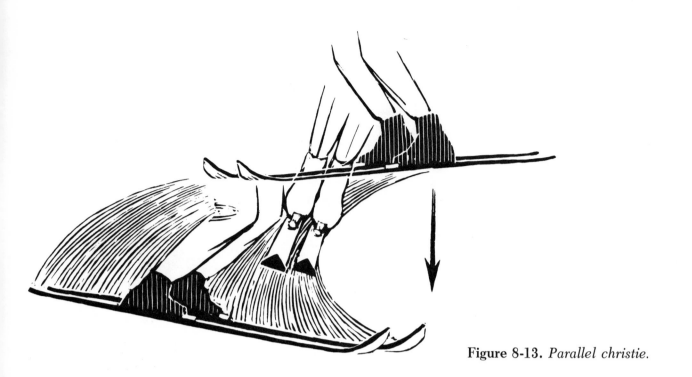

Figure 8-13. *Parallel christie.*

Figure 8-14.
Edge change by banking.

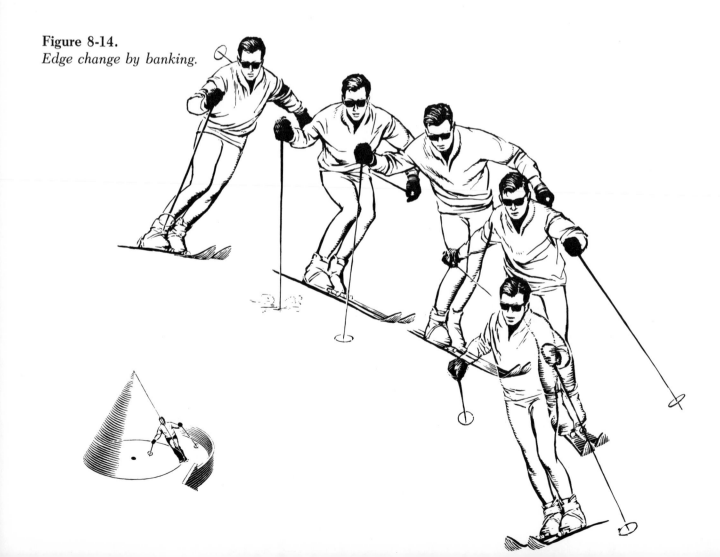

THE WHOLE TURN CONCEPT—PART C: EDGE AND LEAD CHANGE

In Figure 8-13, you see a close-in view of what goes on during a parallel christie, down there where the edges meet the snow. What I'm trying to bring into focus are two misunderstood actions of christies. One of them, the act of changing the edges, is often ignored by people who maintain that the edge change happens automatically—a suspect word when used in an analytical context. Sure, edge change happens automatically, *if* you do everything right with your upper body. That *if* is a big joker. What happens if you haven't yet learned to do everything right? You get snow in your neck, that's what happens, and you don't learn as fast when you don't know what you are trying to do.

The other action to be considered here is, of course, lead change—the change in position of the leading ski—and it should occur simultaneously with the change of the edges.

In the first set of feet and skis in Figure 8-13, note that both skis rest on their uphill edges, to the skier's right—and the uphill ski is slightly advanced. All is in order. In the next set, the skier has unweighted and begun to swing his skis into the new direction. Note that the skis no longer rest on either set of edges. Edge change has begun. Also note that the ski tips are now even, with neither one being ahead of the other, which means that the inside ski of the turn has already begun to assume its leading position. In the final set, edge change is virtually complete. The skis now rest on their other set of edges, those on the skier's left. Also note that what was the leading ski, the right one, has simultaneously changed its position,

and the inside ski of the turn has crept into the lead (see Figure 9-10).

EDGE CHANGE BY BANKING

Anytime an object moves in a curve, centrifugal force is developed. As an occupant in a car cornering a flat curve, you feel that force pushing you to the outside of the curve. It also pushes the car sideways, but the friction of the tires on the road prevents the car from going into a skid. A runner, when rounding a turn, leans into his turn to overcome the outward thrust. Similarly, a bicyclist leans into his turns, and an airplane banks its way through space. And so does a parallel skier. He leans into his turn to overcome centrifugal force and to cant his skis onto their inside edges for a firm frictional support on the snow to prevent him from going into a wild skid. Lean too much—that's called leaning into the hill—and you will fall to the inside of your turn. You will know when you are exceeding the limits of merely leaning into the turn when you sense more weight on the inside ski than on the outside one. When this happens, you should immediately correct the situation. How? Well, that's a book in itself.

This leaning movement of the whole body is called banking. To visualize the process, think of it as leaning against the side of a giant inverted cone with your skis describing the circumference of its base. Banking is used to change edges, but it isn't the only way, as you'll read on the next couple of pages. But it is very efficient on smooth slopes, in powder or mush, at fast speeds, and for long radius turns. Follow the skier in Figure 8-14 as he banks around the big cone, leaning to his left. The second drawing in the sequence shows that

banking toward the next big cone —
to his right — has begun. The pole has
been planted, the edges set, and the up-
unweighting started. The skis are still
on their uphill edges. The third drawing shows how the body has continued
to lean into the new turn and the skis
have rolled over, flat to the slope. At
this moment, they are virtually weightless and turning power takes its immediate effect. By the fourth drawing, you
can see that the body has continued to
bank and the edges have now changed.
As the turn and banking continue, the
new edges take an increasingly positive
grip on the snow.

It takes time to learn the subtle art
of banking just the right amount at the
right time. Instructors have many exercises to help you develop the delicate
balance. Even at that, collecting snow
with the inside ear is part of the game
for anyone.

Figure 8-15.
*Edge change by de-angulating and re-
angulating.*

EDGE CHANGE BY ANGULATION

When performing christies on hard
snows, it is frequently necessary to
push the knees a considerable amount
into the turn to force the edges to hold
the skis on course. The tighter you make
the radius of the christie and the faster
you go, the more you must counteract
the outward-thrusting force which develops. But there is a limit to how much
you can control your edges by banking
the whole body into the turn. If you
go beyond that limit, you'll tumble into
the hill because the skis will slip sideways out from under you. The solution
is to bank into the turn primarily with
the lower body while bending sideways

132

from the waist toward the outside of the turn. When you do this you are angulating.

There are as yet no generally accepted words in the jargon of ski technique to express the way edges are changed by the use of angulation, so I'm inventing two verbs for the purpose—de-angulate and re-angulate. In the first drawing in Figure 8-15, the skier is angulating his way around a tight turn to the right. The second figure shows the body an instant after the edges have been set and the pole planted. He has just begun to move his knees back under the body, to de-angulate. This starts the edge change. In the third figure, the de-angulation process is completed. Now the body is in an almost natural position over the skis which are flat on the slopes. They have also been up-unweighted and can swivel easily as the turning power of the legs is applied. While the skis turn, the body re-angulates—fourth figure—and the edge change is now complete. From here on, you can now either carve or skid the turn, varying the radius at will. This process of changing the edges by changing angulation is quick and works excellently for almost all kinds of snows at speeds above fifteen to twenty miles per hour.

FAST EDGE CHANGE

On mogulled or crowded slopes, the need often arises to get a turn underway very quickly. At such times, a quick change of edges is necessary. Basically, do this by moving the knees rapidly from the uphill side of the skis to the downhill side, rocking the skis over to the new set of edges. It's a matter of rapid-fire action—from angulation, to de-angulation, to re-angulation.

But that's only part of the action. The other part involves the use of a kind of banking. I haven't yet discovered a verb to cover the total motion of the situation, but if I were to follow the Teutonic tradition in ski technique, it would take a strung-together phrase something like this: Anticipated shoulder-thrusting, hip-banking, knee-cranking action. A close study of Figure 8-16 along with the following explanation, should clear up that involved phrase: "A" shows the finish of a turn to the left. The edges are about to be set and the pole planted. In "B," both those actions take place. Notice that the shoulders have already begun to move downhill, in the direction of the fall line. In "C," the outside shoulder of the turn, the left one, has already anticipated the new direction by moving toward it. Hips and shoulders have banked even further toward the cone of the new turn. The edge change has progressed sufficiently to allow the unweighted skis to swivel into the turn. In "D," the knees have cranked the skis around and they are now on their new edges. The body is banked into this quickly started turn and the re-angulation process is just about to begin. In "E," re-angulation, with the skis carving fiercely.

THE WHOLE TURN CONCEPT— PUTTING IT ALL TOGETHER

Timing is the *when*—the precise instant to make the right movement. When do you change the edges? When do you unweight? When do you apply turning power? Variations in timing are almost infinite. They are influenced by snow conditions, pitch of slope, speed, terrain, the type of christie desired, the nature of the skis, boots, etc. —enough factors to frustrate a com-

Figure 8-16. *Fast edge change.*

E

D

C

B

A

puter. Experience, however, teaches you to feel what's right, to develop that sense of rhythm—that keen, almost intuitive judgement which a hotshot skier has acquired. And which, incidentally, a good instructor can teach fairly quickly.

Without going into elaborate details best left for on-the-slope discussions, here are some clues to help you tie together edge change, turning power, and unweighting—three aspects of the whole turn concept:

Heel Thrust (Figure 8-17A). The heels of the skis cannot be displaced into a christie until either the edge change has progressed to the point where the skis are flat on the snow, or until the skis have been freed from the snow by a hop or a ruade. Consequently, heel thrust is a slow starting motive power, despite its reliability.

Foot Swivel (Figure 8-17B). The timing of unweighting and edge change is the same as for heel thrust, since the tails of the skis must also move uphill with this type of turning power. However, a crest of a small bump can be used as a pivotal point, eliminating the need for much unweighting. This foot swivelling action gets you into a christie faster than a displacement of the heels alone, bump or no bump.

Tip Thrust (Figure 8-17C). This strenuous action gets the skis into a christie very quickly. The turning power can be applied even before edge change begins, since the fronts of the skis are swung downhill and have no slope resistance to overcome. This fast action is used by skiers who have mastered the exotic techniques for mogul taming.

Variations on these basic themes are considerable. Remember that a previous

Figure 8-17.

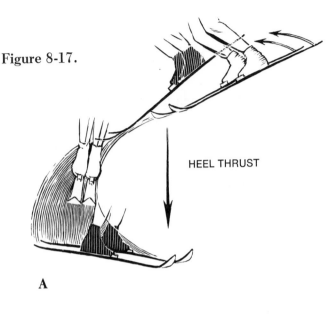

HEEL THRUST

A

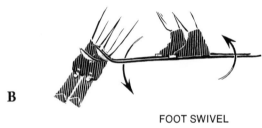

B

FOOT SWIVEL

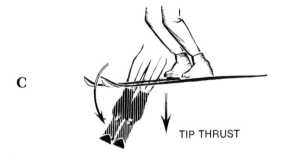

C

TIP THRUST

135

section on unweighting discussed five ways to lighten the load on the skis, that another section revealed multiple sources of turning power, and that this section showed three ways to change the edges. And what about lead change? Well, if you do everything else right, it takes place—excuse the word—automatically, naturally.

Once you have learned a crude, basic, parallel christie on easy, packed slopes, improvement along the lines of your natural bent—your own style—comes remarkably fast. All that remains is the additional polish on the details of technique—subtle edge control, variations in pole planting, handling different challenges of terrain effectively, and of course, the development of timing, feeling, coordination, judgement of speed-distance relationships . . . all those things which keep skiing a challenging sport during a lifetime of healthful recreation. Long may you enjoy it, and improve.

9
CHRISTIES
Self-Help on the Slopes
Be Perfect, Through Practice

UPHILL CHRISTIE SELF-HELPERS
•To get the feel of controlling your upper ski while doing an uphill christie, try smoothing out the slope with your upper little toe. Here's how. While standing on a traverse assume an exaggerated position of angulation as demonstrated in Figure 9-1. Hold that pose, but step uphill as if to sidestep. Now draw the upper ski toward the lower one, keeping it on its upper edge. Repeat a dozen times or so. You'll soon become aware of the feeling you're smoothing the slope with the uphill side of your foot. That's part of the feeling you should have when sideslipping. Now try an uphill christie, practicing in both directions. Since your weight should be forward when in motion as you turn into the hill, now have the feeling your upper little toe is smoothing out the slope. A note of caution: At this stage in your skiing progress, never feel more weight on the upper little toe than on the lower big toe. That is, concentrate on feeling the pressure needed on your upper little toe, and the lower big toe. Once you can definitely feel the uphill front edges of both skis carving for you, you can begin to ski with, at first, just the thighs touching. Then gradually get the feet

close together. A good skier has his feet together, not because he presses them together, but because he uses his edges correctly.
•If your attempts to christie into the hill look like the illustration on the left in Figure 9-3, and you'd like to look like the skier on the right, then learn about what I call the "friction-gravity" principles (see page 92) and how they work to do much of the turning for you. That's right; to learn to turn into the hill you must do certain things which let the skis turn for you. The "wrong" skier in the illustration has tried to twist his body in the desired direction in an effort to turn his skis. Brute strength has failed, where gentle finesse might have availed.

Here's how to use finesse. Traverse a smooth packed slope of 15 or more degrees. Increase the amount of forward lean so that your weight very definitely rests on the ball of each foot. This will apply more *friction* to your front uphill edges. Then gradually and slowly release your edges by decreasing angulation and bending the lower ankle ever so slightly away from the slope, all the while maintaining the forward lean. This decreases the friction on the back edges enough to let *gravity* pull

137

Figure 9-1.

Figure 9-2. *Stemming the lower ski.*

the tails of your skis down the slope. As a result, you will turn without having to exert any turning force. Once you master this action, then add as much heel-push or rotation as you may need in order to turn fast. Note how the "right" skier has subtly bent out his lower ankle to release the inside edge of the lower ski—an action really necessary for slow-to-medium speed skiing, but less so for fast skiing.

STEM CHRISTIE SELF-HELPS
•When making a stem christie the change of lead (when traversing, the upper ski should always lead) must begin at the same time the ski is stemmed. Practice traversing an easy, packed slope while continuously opening and closing the upper ski. Look to see that once the ski has been stemmed, the ski tips are even, with neither one ahead of the other. If your skis are crossing because you are squeezing your boots together, then practice skiing with the feet a couple of inches apart. Occasionally, a stem christie is done by stemming the lower ski, a maneuver which works well on smooth, packed slopes. Figure 9-2 shows the correct position when the lower ski is stemmed. The dotted line shows where the body was centered during the traverse. Note how it has now moved down with the lower ski to allow the upper one to have its edge changed and remain centered. Simultaneously, the lower ski has moved forward to begin the change of lead. So what do we have? A position very much like that achieved with the up-stem—a small snowplow from which to launch into a stem christie.
•Here's a good exercise to help you lose the stem habit. It works best on mogul-free, packed powder slopes

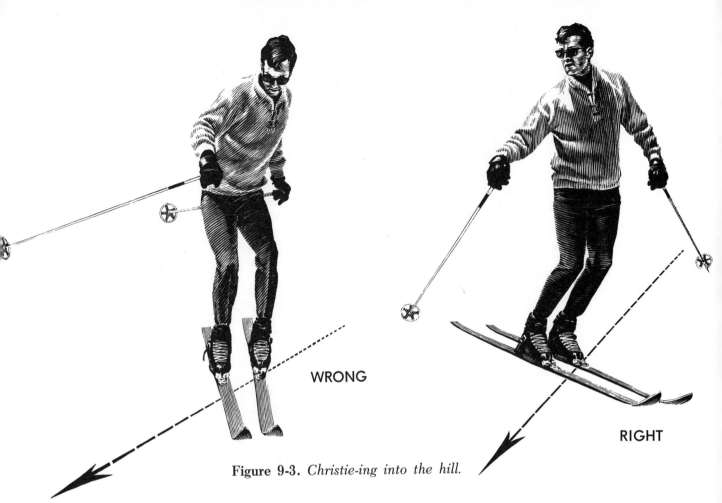

WRONG

RIGHT

Figure 9-3. *Christie-ing into the hill.*

slanted at about 15 degrees. You prepare for a usual stem christie with an uphill stem, down-motion, and pole-plant. When you spring up to unweight, instead of concentrating on a shift of weight from downhill ski to uphill, try to unweight both skis at the same time. Make a slight hopping motion directly from the stemmed position. While the tails of both skis are unweighted, turn them toward the fall line, as shown in the middle drawing of Figure 9-4. Land softly by absorbing the shock with a deep bending of the knees and ankles, and press more on the outside ski. The skis should land almost flat to the snow, only slightly tilted onto the new set of edges. Now let yourself slip around as for a normal stem christie. During the first few attempts, start off skiing down the fall line in a snowplow, and don't be con-

cerned with feeling awkward. As you catch on to the movements, start from a shallow traverse, then stem and hop into the fall line. As you improve gradually reduce the stem opening, bringing the legs closer together with each stem and hop. Gradually quit stemming, hopping directly into one turn from the end of the previous one. Be sure to practice this exercise in both directions.

•If you have difficulty in pushing around the heel or heels of your skis the desired amount needed to complete a turn, the problem generally takes place as you initiate the turn, and not at its conclusion, as you may think. There is too much counter-rotation (reversed-shoulder action) as you stem the upper ski. To correct, don't deliberately pull the upper shoulder as you stem the upper ski. Instead let the reversed-shoulder action (if any occurs) happen

139

Figure 9-4. *Losing the stem habit.*

naturally at this point. By so doing, your upper body will not have used up its potential reversing action, necessary for heel pushing to complete a stem christie.

•To make parallel christies easier and more certain, even at slow speeds, take advantage of the humps, bumps, and moguls found on almost all packed slopes, the way experts do. The idea is to use the crest of each hummock as a pivot point around which—propeller-fashion—you can swivel both ends of the skis. The amount which the skis must be displaced to start the turning and edge change is perhaps no more than 15 degrees. At first, practice at a standstill, atop a suitable snowy knob. Then approach the knob with a slight amount of speed, timing your movements so that you apply a turning force to the feet at the instant the crest of the knob is directly underfoot. The pole

should be planted no closer than at the crest, and preferably, just below it as in Figure 9-5. Gradually increase the speed as your sense of timing improves. You may almost completely eliminate any unweighting motions once you have mastered this technique of swivelling on the hummocks.

PARALLEL CHRISTIE SELF-HELPS
•Many skiers in the transitional stage between stem christies and the parallel varieties have difficulty in that their uphill ski stems slightly before starting a parallel turn. If you're in this category, you must first unlearn your stem habit and begin the development of the "parallel habit" of initiating christies. Here's how:
1) Choose a smooth-packed, very gentle slope on which you have no fear and on which you can make a good stem christie. 2) Learn to initiate each turn from

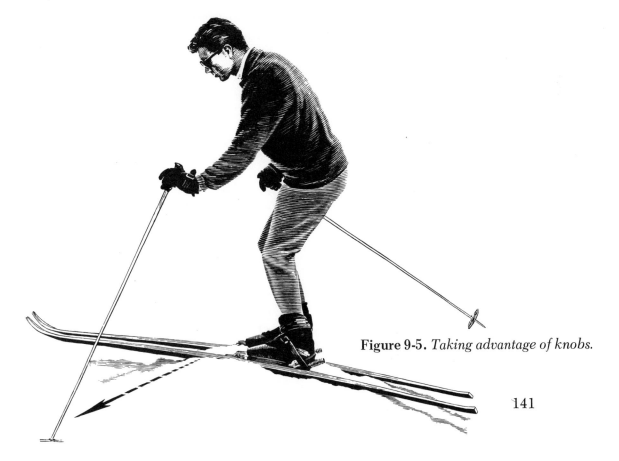

Figure 9-5. *Taking advantage of knobs.*

141

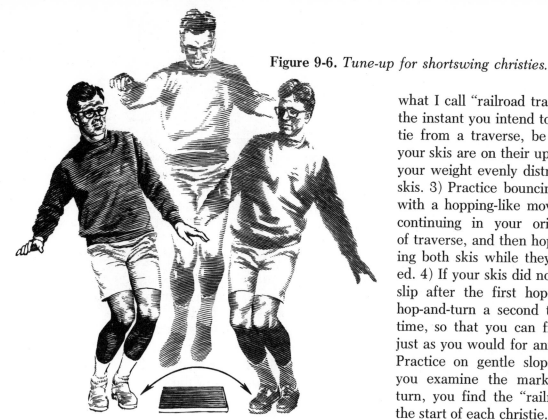

Figure 9-6. *Tune-up for shortswing christies.*

what I call "railroad tracks," that is, at the instant you intend to start the christie from a traverse, be sure that *both* your skis are on their uphill edges, with your weight evenly distributed on both skis. 3) Practice bouncing off *both* skis with a hopping-like movement at first, continuing in your original direction of traverse, and then hopping and turning both skis while they are unweighted. 4) If your skis did not begin to sideslip after the first hop-and-turn, then hop-and-turn a second time or a third time, so that you can finish your turn just as you would for any stem christie. Practice on gentle slopes until, when you examine the mark left for each turn, you find the "railroad tracks" at the start of each christie. Only after you have mastered this basic elementary parallel christie on very gentle slopes should you attempt them on progressively steeper slopes.

Most experts agree that parallel christies are easiest to do when you first build yourself a platform from which to spring. Stated differently: To do parallel christies successfully you must learn to use your skis, both of them, like a single, solid platform, and then spring upwards into your turn. The word *platform* is used because you must weight both skis equally for at least a split-second, giving you the sensation that your skis really are a firm, very stable foundation. That split-second is just at the time when you have lowered your body position in preparation for springing upward and forward. Once you have unweighted *from both skis,* it is easy to turn both of them at the same time, thereby making a true parallel christie.

•To tune-up for shortswing christies at home, place a book or small pillow on the floor. Stand on one side of it, as in

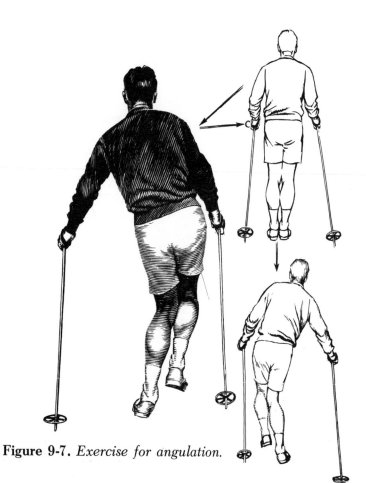

Figure 9-7. *Exercise for angulation.*

Figure 9-8. *Preparing for spring.*

Figure 9-6, with the feet angled slightly toward it. Jump from one side of the pillow to the other side, turning your feet in mid-air so that when you land they will still be slightly angled toward it. The object is to jump as often as possible, just barely skimming over the top of the object, with as little disturbance to your upper body as possible. Jump as fast as you can without losing balance for at least five times in each series attempted. Try five or more series daily. Test for minimal disturbance by holding a glass partially filled with water as you jump. Don't spill any.

•To improve your use of angulation, try the home tune-up exercise shown in Figure 9-7. Here's how it is done: Start by standing normally, feet together. On a count of ONE, raise your right knee and foot off the floor. At the same time, push your left knee forward and to the right, leaning the upper body to the left (angulate). Your weight should now rest along the inside edge of your left shoe. On TWO, return to a normal position (de-angulate). On THREE, raise your left knee and foot from the floor. At the same time, push the right knee forward and to the left, leaning the upper body to the right (re-angulate). Your weight should now rest along the inside edge of your right shoe. On FOUR, return to a normal position. Repeat, to the count of 1-2-3-4, 2-2-3-4, etc., about twenty-five times daily.

For the maximum benefit from this exercise, emphasize the sideways push of the knees and not the bend at the waist. If you have trouble balancing, leave the toe of the raised foot in contact with the floor.

•Actually, if there is any one predominant weakness on the part of the aspir-

Figure 9-9. *One foot leads too much.*

FALL LINE

ing parallel skier, it is his (or her) inability to realize how helpful the act of up-unweighting can be. Time after time an instructor will tell a student to lower the body position as one turn finishes so that a good lifting movement can be used to help initiate the next turn. And just as often the student makes a barely noticeable "down" motion in preparation. Of course the ensuing "up" movement will be weak and ineffective, and the resulting turn either not very parallel or not a turn at all.

If this is your problem then take a good look at just how the skier in Figure 9-8 lowers his body position to prepare for a powerful upward spring. Note the deep ankle bend, the deep knee bend, and the deep waist bend. The skier is now in a position from which to uncoil swiftly upward and into the turn, making the task of changing edges and turning both skis relatively easy. Once you have mastered all the subtle movements of initiating a parallel christie with a pronounced "sink and spring," then you can gradually lessen the amount to a minimum of effort. But not before.

•When attempting a parallel christie, you may catch yourself turning with one foot leading the other a great deal, as shown in Figure 9-9. The inside ski, of course, has to lead during a parallel christie, but the amount should be only about a half boot-length. If the difference is more than that, then something has gone wrong and you will have trouble maintaining balance, controlling the skis, and making closely linked turns.

What has gone wrong is that you undoubtedly shoved the inside foot forward as you initiated the turn. You should not have to do this unless poor balance

makes the action necessary. Under normal circumstances, the change of lead during a parallel christie should be *automatic*. Here's why: The inside ski, being closer to the center of the turn, has a shorter circumference to travel than the outside one. Therefore, since both skis are travelling at the same speed the inside one gradually assumes the lead position as the turn progresses.

Here is a clue to the timing involved: Once the skis are canted on to their inside edges (of their turn), the inside ski must have gained no more than a slight lead over the outside one.

Let me forewarn you about the word *automatic* in a previous paragraph. Its synonym in ski technique is the word natural. Lead change will not happen naturally—automatically—if you squeeze your boots together; if you pick up your inside ski at any time during the christie; if you shift your weight markedly from the lower ski to outside ski at the outset of the turn. In those instances, you must deliberately shuffle the feet to take care of the dynamics which would otherwise take place. Shuffling the feet is not wrong, provided it is not exaggerated. In fact, with some skis, on certain snows, you must change the lead deliberately and quickly. Relatively thin, undamped, torsion-resistant skis usually require such deliberate action to prevent the tips from crossing. Often, the inside ski must take a slight lead by the time the skis have been rolled flat to the snow during the edge-change action. In contrast, during normal lead change the inside ski assumes a slight lead only as the skis are rolled onto their new set of edges.

•Here is an exercise which will help beginning parallel christie students develop tremendous confidence. Called the *hockey stop* because of its similarity

Figure 9-10. *Hockey stop.*

to a quick stop done on ice skates, the exercise teaches you how to make an emergency stop. Careful planning is necessary to learn the hockey stop (Figure 9-10). Choose a smooth packed slope pitched at from 10 to 15 degrees, where no obstacles are present to cause unnecessary concern. Place a slalom pole in the snow about 10 feet below the place which you select to make your stop, first making sure you will be able to pick up sufficient speed to make a christie. Lacking a slalom pole, choose some distant tree or other stationary object to head towards but one which is well beyond your intended stopping place.

Ski down the fall line toward the slalom pole (or the distant tree) without using your ski poles for the first few attempts. To make that quick stop, exaggerate all movements when sliding at christie speed, bend down low in preparation, then suddenly spring up while simultaneously swivelling both skis directly under your feet. That is, turn both ends of the skis around the middle, propeller-fashion. Immediately as the skis are turned, sink down again into a low position. Throughout the maneuver, *keep watching the slalom pole or its facsimile and keep the chest facing in its original direction.* If you do this you will develop a powerful counter-rotation and comma position which will allow you to stop on a dime when the emergency arises. After a few successful attempts without poles, repeat the exercise using them. After a few more tries, you should no longer have to watch the slalom-pole.

•The ability of a skier to slither between moguls, trees, or knots of people is directly related to the ability to link together parallel christies. A marked difference may exist between the move-

145

ments made for a sudden emergency stop, such as that described in the hockey stop, or the methods used to teach a person how to make a parallel christie, and those used for linking together two or more turns. In the former situations a student must often be made to exaggerate the counter-rotation movement of the arms and shoulders. In so doing he may develop a habit of letting the outside arm and shoulder lag behind the body. This presents no great problem if the student intends to pull his turn to a stop or to follow a traverse across the slope after the turn. But it does definitely hamper his ability to make a quick change of direction linked to his last turn. Why? Simply because the outside arm and shoulder must be brought forward to plant the ski pole for the next turn. The further back that arm or shoulder lags as a turn progresses, the more time will be consumed in bringing it forward to prepare for the next turn. Hence the slower the skier will be to link together his turns.

To link turns together quickly once the first turn has started, keep that outside arm and shoulder coming forward and around so that they are always in a position to effect an immediate pole plant. A good rule to remember when linking turns together quickly is this: Always be able to glimpse both hands in front of you.

•If you're unable to link together two or more parallel christies, the reason generally is because your skis are not edged into the turn; they are too flat. The result: You cannot finish one turn correctly, nor can you mold your body into the comma position from which to *set the edges* and swing into a smooth, linked christie. Practice these edge-setting exercises: A) Traverse a smooth-packed, 20-degree-plus slope. Stand rather high on your skis and release the edges. B) Allow yourself to sideslip laterally for a few feet. C) Drop down into a low position of angulation (comma) while gradually pushing knees and ankles toward the slope (re-edging the skis). D) At the moment the lowest position is reached, make sure the edges have re-gripped the snow, then forcefully resume an upright position. The resulting downward thrust will cause sideslipping to cease immediately, while at the same time the up movement will provide the unweighting for your next sideslip attempt. It is this control over the edges which you lack when trying to link parallel christies. E) Repeat the exercise a dozen or so times while traversing both left and right. For an additional corrective exercise, ask your instructor to teach you "parallel garlands."

•Let's take a look at garlands. They are incomplete turns. You ski across a slope, leaving a festoon-like track (see Figure 9-11) by alternately turning downhill from a traverse (not quite reaching the fall line), and, instead of completing the turn, turning back into the hill so that you're heading very much in the same direction as your first traverse. The process can be repeated over and over again, two, three, or as many times as there is room on a particular slope.

There are two basic types of garlands:

Figure 9-11. *Garlands.*

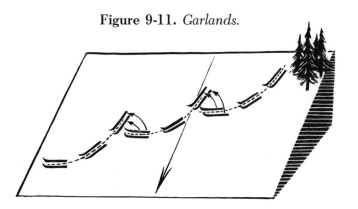

stem, and parallel. In the first type you stem your uphill ski, turn toward the fall line, then turn back toward the slope, while bringing your skis together to make an uphill christie so that you continue in the same direction as your original traverse. Then repeat the whole process. For parallel garlands, you simply do not stem.

It's very important, by the way, that whenever the edges are changed, there should be no chatter from your skis as they begin to skid around. Sometimes, chatter comes from poor quality skis. More often it comes from poor technique. If you swing the tails of your skis too much past the fall line and then try to edge sharply, instead of producing a smoothly carved turn, your skis will chatter and start to jump and even cross one another. You lose speed control, and soon you have to find a place to stop if you are to avoid serious trouble. Practice with garlands will help you to eliminate any tendency you might have to overpower or over-turn your skis. If you persist in using too much strength to start the turn, here's another exercise to help you lick the problem: Begin an uphill christie as in Figure 9-12A. Bring the skid to an end, Figure 9-12B, by setting your edges and planting the pole. Now, as you spring up to unweight the skis, Figure 9-12C, be conscious of the amount of twist you apply to the feet, be it a result of either rotation or counter-rotation. You can heighten your consciousness of the turning power used by realizing the point of the exercise: That is, do not hop the skis beyond the fall line. (See Figure 9-12D.) For full benefit from the exercise, you must continue moving in the same general direction as that in which you started, by making another uphill christie as in Figures 9-12E and F. Then repeat the entire

sequence. The drawing on pages 148–149 will help make the whole sequence clear.

For easiest results, choose a smooth packed slope, about 20 degrees in steepness, with plenty of room to traverse and hop, preferably at least four times. Vary frequently the amount you displace the tails of the skis. Work going to the left and to the right. Practice of this kind will teach you the exact amount of turning power needed to start a good parallel christie so that neither chattering nor over-turning will occur.

•Some skiers are faced with the inability to vary the radius of longer christies. Fortunately this can be easily solved by cutting down greatly on the amount of counter-rotation and angulation which you use to initiate your turns. Better yet, learn to use "anticipation," a sort of rotation without preparation, for starting a parallel turn. For maximum efficiency in being able to vary the radius of a christie, or to change direction suddenly, your body should be in as normal a position as possible during the fall line phase of the turn. This way, you can suddenly heel-push and counter-rotate to sharpen the radius of your turn, or you can "anticipate" right into the next one.

Many variations of the parallel christie are possible, not just in the skidding phase of the turn, but in its initiation phase. The four basic components outlined in the Whole Turn Concept can be combined to form wedeln, shortswing, long- or short-radius christies, reversed-shoulder turns, airplane turns, and so on.

•During your first year or two of skiing, a prime consideration for maintaining good balance during any christie is that your weight remains well forward on the ball of each foot during most of the turn. If you should suffer a moment of

timidity just at the instant you turn into the fall line, you may push your feet into the turn ahead of your body. This action automatically puts your weight on the back of your skis and forces your skis out from under you. Only experts, with the very latest in high-backed, raised-heel boots, can successfully cope with such a situation.

Realize this: As you turn from a traverse into the fall line—your direction of travel gets steeper. Therefore, as your body rises upward to unweight at the start of a christie, at the same time you must make a conscious effort to increase the amount of forward lean by moving your hips and shoulders forward-and-down the hill. This conscious effort will keep your feet slightly behind you, providing optimum balance.

•It's also not difficult to see that the ability to move the feet quickly is a prerequisite for being able to wedeln well. You can develop this ability by using the exercise illustrated in Figure 9-13. Choose a flat spot covered with packed snow. Place both poles in front of you in a position similar to mine, as shown. Then, keeping the ski tips and the points of the poles in place, hop the tails of the skis back and forth several times, chang-

ing from one set of edges to the other. Repeat this exercise as often as you can, perhaps six times a day at first. Strive mainly to displace the legs and skis with little up-and-down movement of the upper body. Look ahead, keeping your head steady as you exercise. Strive to hop faster each day. As you acquire strength and speed you will develop the ability to wedeln faster—that is, to change from one direction to another faster.

•Up to this point in the book, we have not stressed form too greatly. Sure, it's good form—elegant form, as the Austrians refer to it—to ski down with legs together, boots seemingly glued side by side, as if wearing one-legged ski pants, as illustrated in Figure 7-5. Achieving this kind of elegance is not a mere matter of squeezing the legs together and holding them there. It results from being able to use the edges precisely, shifting weight subtly from one ski to the other or backward and forward. To attempt the one-legged look too soon is to try to walk a tightrope before you can walk normally. Your arms will tend to flail the air in an attempt to compensate for the unstable foundation. Your skiing will improve much faster if you concen-

148

Figure 9-12. *Exercise for turning power.*

149

Figure 9-13. *Exercise for wedeln.*

trate first on having your feet and legs apart enough to insure that your balance is not jeopardized in the slightest. When balance and edge control become refined, and when you can simultaneously start both skis into a turn, you can then begin to pull your legs and feet together. Becoming a truly elegant skier is a case of developing the proper functions before polishing the final forms, of developing stability before style, not vice versa.

•I'm not implying that it shouldn't be the goal of every recreational skier to be able to wedeln and shortswing down a slope without having any daylight show between the legs. What I am saying, however, is: Don't expect to be able to do this until you can wedeln with your legs apart, since you must have precise control over the edges of both skis in order to have that locked-up leg look. Before you can expect to do this, however, you must learn to traverse and sideslip with good, quite precise, edge control. As your ability to do this im-

proves, then you can try to keep the legs together. Okay, that you can do. Now place a glove, a handkerchief, or other such object between the knees and practice the wedeln (Figure 9-14). You'll soon learn how to squeeze the knees together without forcibly squeezing the feet together, making your turns as if you were in one-legged ski pants.

•To make shortswing christies effectively, you must, of course, be able to set your edges firmly and suddenly, ending each turn abruptly before swinging into the next turn. Hence you must be able to time the pole-plant properly. When you wedeln, you must blend the end of one turn smoothly into the next. Pole-planting is not necessary if you don't set the edges hard. To help you develop a good sense of rhythm hold the poles as illustrated in Figure 9-15 and try wedelning down a smooth-packed slope. The poles should swing from one side of your skis to the other, remaining parallel both to your shoulders and the slope as they swing.

150

Figure 9-14. *Wedeln practice.*

Figure 9-15.
ercise to develop rhythm for wedeln.

10

POLE PLANTING
A Necessary Skill

Polish, for Precision

In previous chapters I've made several references to the phrase "pole plant." By this I mean the act of inserting the point of your pole into the snow, then using that pole as a pivot during the initiation of a christie. The pole referred to is always the one toward the inside of the turn which you intend to make. Exactly where should you plant the pole? And just as important, when and why should you plant it? There are no pat answers to these questions, but there are certain guiding rules.

The beginner needs poles to help maintain stability, to use as crutches or emergency props on occasion. He needs them to get up from a fall, to climb up, to turn around, and so on. He does not need them for turning while in motion. In fact, beginners—once they get to this stage—often learn much faster without poles. Pole planting is not a significant aspect of correct turning until the christie stage. Sometimes it gets to be significant sooner—whenever your instructor believes you are ready for the complications of hand (pole) and foot (ski) coordination. However, the pole plant is not absolutely necessary even for a parallel turn until you have some command over the intricacies of edge setting. Then your poles become highly

important tools in the precise initiation of precise turns.

Why? Here are the primary reasons:

1. To set up a kinesthetic cue so that you know just when to rise up into your turn, and when to begin turning the skis toward the fall line. The pole plant, thereby, becomes an instrument for timing your turns—a sort of "turn and bank indicator."

2. To assist with the rising movement of the body, thereby helping to get more weight off the skis faster and easier; in other words, as an aid to unweighting.

3. To use as a guiding prop, both to help guide you into the turn and to absorb part of the surge of momentum felt in the upper body when you suddenly jam the edges of the skis into the snow. This kind of edge setting immediately slows down the feet, but the shoulders inevitably continue in the direction that they were moving—somewhere downhill. You must temper the momentum of the upper body by soaking it up in the muscles of the arm and shoulder which push against the pole, although hot shots might let the skis be launched into the air, using the pole to help steer around in mid-air.

As important as it is, pole planting is not yet a completely understood art.

152

Even the hottest of the hot sometimes have trouble with the art. Perhaps you have seen a great skier, after a beautiful run, come a-cropper in deep powder when he swings to a sudden stop. Why? Because even though he may properly plant his pole, it simply sinks into the bottomless powder with the rest of the skier following right after it, victimized by unabsorbed momentum.

HOW TO POLE PLANT

The pole can be planted in a number of different ways. Arms held in close to the body. Arms out. Wrist in line with the forearm. Wrist out. And there are several other variations. Most are not particularly pertinent to technique. What is pertinent is this: Whenever the pole is planted (with some exceptions) the muscles of the arm, shoulder, and chest must actively resist the strong tendency created by the forces of motion

to shove your arm and shoulder back, eventually pushing you over backwards.

The double-pole plant illustration (Figure 10-1) shows how to develop a good feeling for pole planting, and the timing required for unweighting. Schuss or traverse a very gentle slope. Lower your body, and move the poles forward as shown. The instant the points are positioned low, up front, drive them into the snow. Simultaneously spring upwards with the legs, making your weight rest on the poles. Study the illustration to see how the hands and arms move forward throughout.

The single-pole plant (Figure 10-2) is an exercise to learn timing and action for a pole plant like that used for making christies. The center figure shows that the arm has resisted the backward thrust it receives upon insertion of the pole. Practice only at slow speeds.

Proper timing for the movements is

Figure 10-1. *Double pole plant.*

Figure 10-2. *Single pole plant.*

Figure 10-3. *The hand does not move behind the body.*

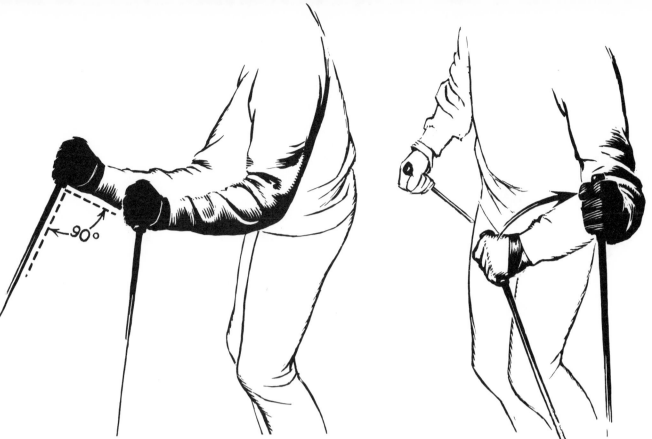

Figure 10-4. *The pole and forearm makes a 90° angle.*

Figure 10-5.

important. Plant the pole at the exact instant your body stops its preparatory downward-hinging movement and starts its upward spring to unweight. Always plant your pole so that, in relation to your intended direction, the hand is in front of you. If the hand, wrist, forearm, and upper arm are all in line with the pole at the moment of planting, your muscles will work most efficiently. It's also good practice to keep the angle the pole makes with the forearm close to a right angle. If the elbow is seldom bent more than a right angle, the pole will usually point safely downward.

Study Figure 10-3 and note how the elbow, and particularly the hand, is not permitted to move behind the side of the body. In fact, once the insertion shock has been absorbed—third figure—the hand is deliberately pushed forward to put the pole at an angle favorable to its quick extraction from the snow. The detail in Figure 10-5, shows how the fore-

arm is moved quickly, to effect a pole plant which accompanies a pronounced edge set.

Here are some *don'ts* of pole planting that you should remember:

1. *Don't* bend your elbow deeply as you prepare to plant, since this movement swings the basket of the pole ludicrously high. After all, you are not preparing to stab a bull. Figure 10-6.

2. *Don't* angle the pole inward to plant it close to the lower ski. This affectation does not provide the bracing support needed for a solid set of the edges. Nor should you swing the forearm backward out of line with the pole and rest of your arm—in a sort of open-palm position—unless you are strong enough to withstand the insertion shock. (Figure 10-7).

3. *Don't* plant the pole too near the tip if you intend to make a short-radius christie—you can't swing the fronts of the skis into the turn until your feet

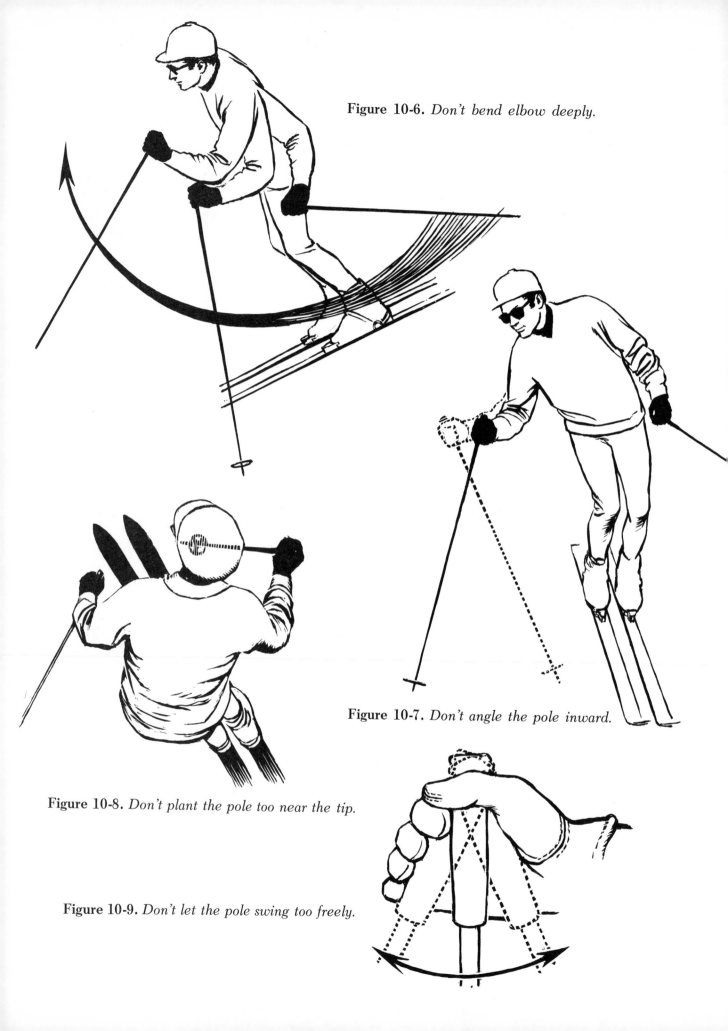

Figure 10-6. *Don't bend elbow deeply.*

Figure 10-7. *Don't angle the pole inward.*

Figure 10-8. *Don't plant the pole too near the tip.*

Figure 10-9. *Don't let the pole swing too freely.*

pass the place of insertion and you lose valuable time and ground. Figure 10-8.

4. *Don't* let the pole swing too freely, in a sort of pendulum action, by gripping it improperly. Your pole must work as an integral extension of your arm, not as an independent agent. Figure 10-9.

WHERE TO POLE PLANT

The most difficult question to answer precisely regarding pole planting is the *where* of the movements. A number of variable factors considerably complicate the topic. Such things as these exert an influence: your speed at any given moment; the turning radius desired; how quickly you intend to swing into the fall line; your skill and strength; the firmness of your edge set; and the length of your poles. To resolve all of these factors, you must use your own athletic ingenuity and intuition. However, you can do this more easily if you understand the basic principles discussed here.

Keep this general rule in mind: Plant the pole so that a line drawn from your lower ski boot to the point of insertion indicates the fall line at that moment. Figure 10-10 should make this concept clear. Also keep in mind: There is no specific pole-plant spot right for all skiers. The spots indicated in the illustrations should be thought of as the center of zones that have a one-foot diameter. The factors listed above determine the specific pole-plant spots within these zones.

To further clarify the topic, I've broken down the numerous kinds of christies into three categories—long-radius christies, short-radius christies, and stop christies. Each type makes use of a different pole-planting zone.

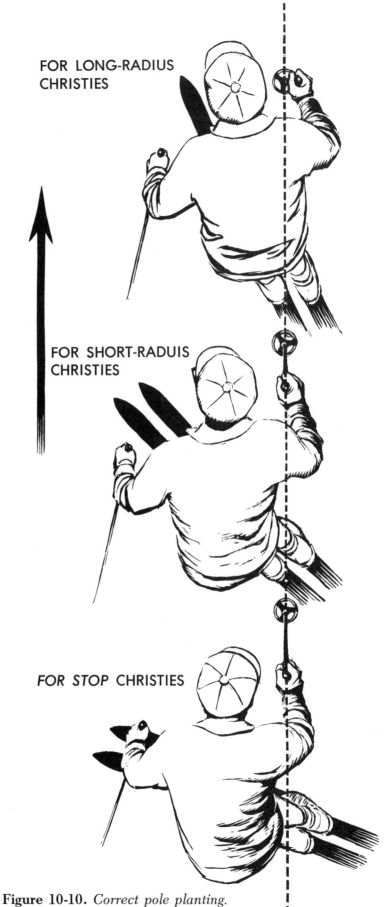

FOR LONG-RADIUS CHRISTIES

FOR SHORT-RADUIS CHRISTIES

FOR STOP CHRISTIES

Figure 10-10. *Correct pole planting.*

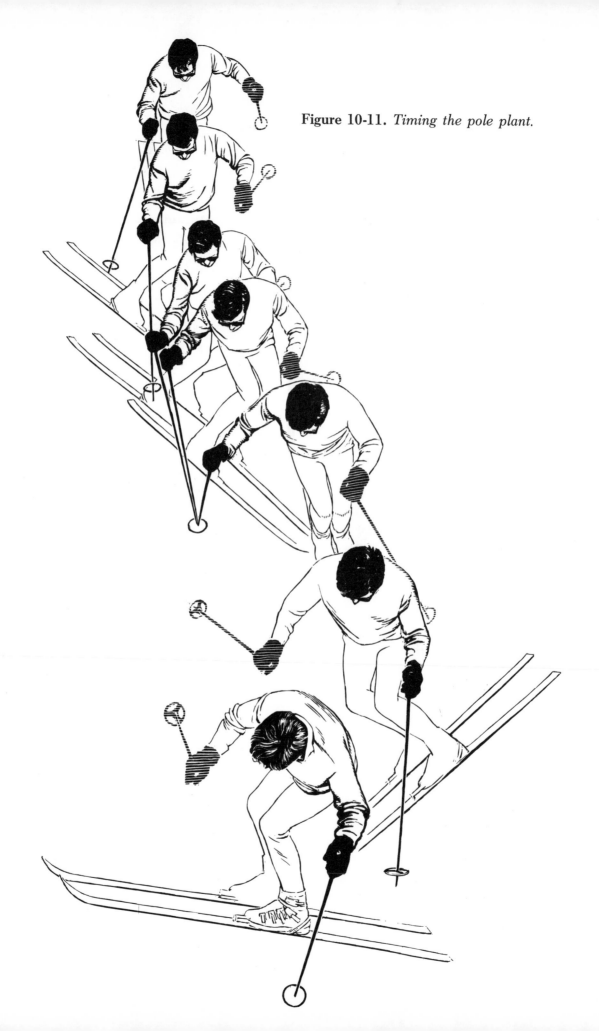

Figure 10-11. *Timing the pole plant.*

Long-Radius Christies. These turns are done on smooth terrain at fast speeds, and are seldom preceded by a checking or hard setting of the edges. Since there is no hurry to thrust the skis into the turn, plant the pole a few inches in back of and about a foot from the tip of the lower ski.

Short-Radius Christies. The object is to get the skis into the turn quickly by swinging their fronts around immediately after the edges have been set. Hence, the pole is planted further back, near the middle of the ski's forebody. Since a short-radius turn is usually preceded by a firm setting of the edges, a considerable amount of shoulder thrust will develop. Plant the pole off more to the side to enable the arm and shoulder to absorb that thrust more easily and to give room for the fronts of the skis to be shoved into the turn.

Stop Christies. When you come to a stop, plant the pole down the fall line, up to four feet from your lower boot. This wide plant is needed to prevent your shoulders from being thrown to the outside of the turn as you jam your skis on their edges, terminating the sliding movement.

WHEN TO POLE PLANT

The right moment to pole plant is when the new turn is actually launched or triggered. That moment should be the same for each turn—the moment the entire running edge of the skis takes a firm grip on the snow. It's the instant when you reach the bottom of the "down" phase of a "down-up-and-turn" christie and as you start on the "up" phase. Look at Figure 10-11 and you'll see angulation, de-angulation, and re-angulation used to change the edges. Less visible is the unweighting action,

though it is quite apparent in the last three figures, where down-unweighting is used to heel push the skis around for a quick stop. Visible here, through inference, is the strong shoulder-to-slope linkage, where the strength of the arm and shoulder—and the pole—absorb and modify the momentum of the upper body which develops at the instant the edges are set. And that instant is when you reach the bottom of the "down" phase of a "down-up-down" christie, and as you start on the "up" phase. It's the moment when the new christie is actually launched or triggered. And that moment is the same for practically all types of parallel christies, regardless of *why* the pole is planted. You plant the pole when you set your edges, and you time the plant to coincide with the instant you cause the entire running edge of the skis to take a firm grip on the snow.

•Here's an exercise to help you develop a sense of timing and rhythm for a good pole plant, up-unweighting, and turning of the skis. Needed: a small scatter rug and a heavy piece of furniture to push against, such as a credenza. A projecting corner of a room will serve equally well.

Stand on the scatter rug (Figure 10-12) with it bunched up between the feet, and face the credenza. On ONE, lower your body position while turning the feet to the left. Keep your shoulders more or less parallel to the credenza at all times. On TWO, with your right hand on the credenza, push (pole-plant) against it while raising your body and turning the feet back so that once again you face it squarely. On THREE, lower your body again, this time turning the feet to the right. On FOUR, when you have lowered sufficiently, push off the credenza with your left hand, returning to the original starting position. Repeat the whole sequence at least twenty times. Develop rhythm as you count out the movements, 1-2-3-4, 2-2-3-4, etc., and a sense of timing by "pole-planting" against the credenza on the second and fourth count of each sequence.

ADVANCED POLE PLANTING TECHNIQUES

The advanced maneuver shown in Figure 10-13 is one of the modern jet (or *avalement*) christies, so-called because the skier allows his feet and skis to shoot ahead of him as he starts the turn. This jetting action partially replaces conventional up- or down-unweighting movements. Here the pole plant is prolonged to aid in taking the weight off the skis, facilitating the initiation of this turn. Here's how:

The pole is planted firmly, angled forward more than normally, while the body is in a very low position from having absorbed the distrubances of a previous mogul. The arm and shoulder stiffen in an attempt to slow down the upper body while the feet and skis are allowed to slide forward. In the process, the skis become unweighted, and the skier banks into his new turn to change the edges. He hangs onto the slope via his pole until the edge change is complete. Normally, the pole would have been extracted before this. The retarding action and the turning leverage he gets from his pole allows the knees and feet to crank the skis into the turn easily. The legs are partially straightened once the turn is started, and the rising action of the body helps to flex the skis, causing them to carve more efficiently. During the initiation phase of this turn, the pole-planting arm is allowed to move

Figure 10-12.

Exercise to develop timing and rhythm.

Figure 10-13. *Jet christie.*

Figure 10-14. *Preparing for the next turn.*

161

back further than is usual. Note, however, that once you reach the fall line, the arm is back to its normal position.

When skiing the steep or slithering between huge moguls, quick pole action is essential to keep your speed under control. It's a matter of: Plant the pole, unweight, swivel into your turn, and *zap* —that fast—plant the other pole. To use your poles as fast as needed, always keep the arms and hands ahead of your shoulders, with the poles ready for quick planting. Trouble is, the hill itself or an intervening mogul can inhibit the speed at which you can bring around the outside arm and pole, ready-ing them for the next pole-plant. The basket can simply get hung up on the slope. But, forewarned is fore-armed. Even as you come off the fall line, begin to prepare for the next turn by bringing forward your inside arm and pole. Keep the palm facing downwards toward the slope and move the pole itself, raising it up and extending it partially forward, as illustrated in Figure 10-14. This prevents it from getting hung up on the slope. Sure, getting the uphill pole cocked at-the-ready in this fashion will feel awkward at first. But practice makes perfect. And perfect control is skiing's ultimate thrill.

11

CARVING
The Ultimate Goal

Strive for This Soul-Satisfying Skill

Like wedeln a decade ago, carving is catching on—everyone is talking about the incredible control carving gives on ice and in heavy crud, the excitement and zap it adds to skiing. It's as though skiing is discovering itself all over again.

Actually, carving isn't really new. The hotshots, the racers in particular, have been talking about carving for years. Some of the elements that go into a carved turn were described four or five years ago in what was then called the round turn; and our better powder skiers have probably been carving for years without suspecting they were doing anything significant.

What is a carved turn? It's simply a turn in which the skis do not skid, a turn without heel push. And that is more complicated than it sounds. Try this: Find yourself a big, wide open slope which you can handle with ease. Start down the fall line with the skis parallel. When you are moving about five or six miles an hour, gingerly tip the skis on their edges—either to the left or to the right. The skis should cut a long, slicing arc in the snow—a crude but carved turn.

What made your skis turn? Two elements in the skis' design went to work:

the outline shape of the skis, wider at the tips than at the tails; and the side cut, the radii that are cut into the sides of the skis. Merely by being tipped onto, let's say, their left edges, the skis veer to the left because of their curved sides. And once firmly on their edges, the skis will keep curving around in an arc with a radius roughly approximating that of the sidecut. Slalom-type skis will cut arcs with the shortest radius, downhill-type skis the longest. That's not all there is to it, but we will get to the rest shortly.

I hope you followed the directions about using a big, wide-open slope you could handle easily. If you really allowed nature to take its course, you probably ran out of hill before you turned very far. But before you hit the panic button, you may have experienced some of the thrills of carving, the feeling as though your skis were turning on railroad tracks, the power of acceleration even though your skis were not pointing down the fall line, and, perhaps, a tingle of G's as the edges took hold.

How do you carve a turn of more practical dimensions? Obviously, there's something more to such turns than merely putting the skis on edge. Equipment is going to play a major role in your

163

Figure 11-1. *Carving.*

carving adventures, and you're going to have to make some adjustments in your technique.

EQUIPMENT FOR CARVING

The reason that carving remained in the realm of exotica until a couple of seasons ago is that there wasn't much equipment around to enable the garden variety of good skier to indulge. He would carve a good turn occasionally, but when he attempted to repeat the experience, the magic inevitably evaporated. The skis would hook, skid, or not respond at all. SKIING's ski test team puzzled over the elusive quality of carving at their annual Mammoth Mountain sessions. After much brain-storming, here is what they found:

Bindings—There must be a very positive link between boots and skis. If the boots wobble or rock in the bindings, the skier will not be able to maintain the constant pressure on the edges that is required for carving. If the skis can chatter because of an imperfect connection, the precision of the carved turn is lost, or the skis will not carve at all.

Boots—It is possible to make skis carve with ordinary boots, but it's difficult and puts a tremendous burden on the skis. For all practical purposes, the average skier in average condition cannot carve consistently unless he has boots with the high back, locked hinge, and raised heel features. The effect of these three features is twofold: They fix the ankle in such a position that the skier has at least some leverage and muscle power to recover from the more extreme positions that are involved in some carving maneuvers; and they enable him to put pressure on almost any point of the running surfaces of the skis. In addition, the boots should also have good lateral support; that is, the skier should be able to stand on the edges of the soles of the boots without having to use muscle power to keep the boots from going flat on the floor. However, lateral movement should not be so restricted that the skier can't make fine adjustments in the edging of the skis by rolling his feet from side to side.

Skis—The combination of characteristics that make skis good carvers can be devilishly complicated and is very much an individual matter depending to a large extent on the skier's weight and normal skiing speed. Generally speaking, the skier who is just coming to carving after turning by more traditional methods will need skis somewhat softer than the ones he is accustomed to, although this rule of thumb can be misleading. A soft ski is not necessarily a good carver. Other ski characteristics that have to be taken into account are the flex pattern of the ski (the relative stiffness from tip to tail), its torsional stiffness, its damping ability, and the amount and shape of the sidecut. Unfortunately, these factors cannot be measured easily, and even if this were possible, there is no handy formula that sums up the complex relationship between them and comes up with an ideal carving ski for a given skier. SKIING's annual ski tests are a reasonably good guide, providing it is understood that the tests were conducted by 145 to 170-pound men who normally move along at relatively high speeds. We have determined that almost every pair of skis has a segment in its performance spectrum at which it will carve. In some skis this segment is wide, or located in a more suitable speed range for a given skier. We have also determined that different techniques are required to produce a carving response with different skis. In any event, it will take a bit of shopping around and trial-and-error testing of your own to find the ideal carving ski for yourself. You'll probably have an easier time of it if you can use 210's or 205's.

Probably the best approach to the problem is to try to make your present skis carve by using the fundamentals described in the remainder of the chapter. If you can't get reasonably tight-radius carved turns, or can get them only be resorting to extreme measures, borrow or rent somewhat softer skis until you find a pair with which you are comfortable.

BASICS FOR CARVING

Carving as a distinctive way of making turns is so new, there is no widely accepted ski school methodology for learning it. The few ski schools that give lessons in the art generally consider it an advanced form—something for after parallel. However, there appears to be a growing tendency to relate carving more directly to fore-and-aft and side-to-side balance and edge play and, with more carving skis becoming available, to somewhat deemphasize the ability to handle great amounts of speed. Sensitivity to what is happening to the skis and the ability to respond correctly

Figure 11-2.

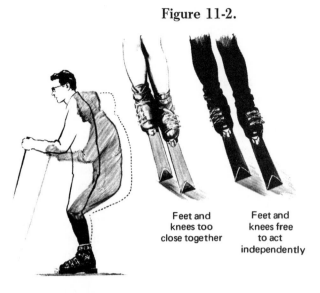

Feet and knees too close together

Feet and knees free to act independently

Normal and carving stances

Figure 11-3.

are probably more important than highly developed skills as such. You can try to carve at almost any time after you have acquired a working knowledge of edge control and balance, providing you try it on a smooth slope that's within your schussing capabilities.

FEET AND KNEES APART

If you, want to make your skis carve over a great range of speeds, and conditions, you will have to do a great deal of independent leg and ankle work. For that, the skis, boots, and knees should be slightly apart, two or three inches at least. The left of Figure 11-2 shows how a closed stance could inhibit ankle movement; the second (right) shows a more suitable position. The latter has the additional/advantage of providing more solid side-to-side balance when countering the centrifugal forces generated by carved turns. Initially, you may find a wide-track stance more helpful in acquiring leg independence.

166

BACKWARD AND FORWARD BALANCE

Good balance is essential for all types of turns and all types of skiing, but it's absolutely critical in carved turns. The locked-hinge, raised-heel boots will help you maintain the proper basic stance on the skis and provide support as you shift your balance point. However, this in itself is not enough: The carved turn requires constant and subtle shifting of your weight along the skis to maintain the carve and to control its radius. This is done by a certain amount of backward and forward ankle flexing and by shifting the body weight from a position over the ball of the foot to a point where it's resting on the heels. In Figure 11-3 the solidly outlined figure shows the traditional skiing stance. The shaded figure shows the carver's normal stance, and the dashed outline-figure the amount he may have to sit back during the late phases of the carved turn.

POSITIVE EDGE CONTROL

One of the major problems for the potential carver is that his edge control tends to be passive rather than active when turns are started with a hop and

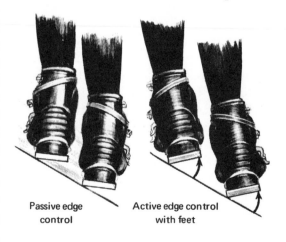

Passive edge control

Active edge control with feet

Figure 11-4.

steered with a skid. Most skiers rely on boot support to keep their skis edged and then control their edges by moving their knees away or toward the hill.

This kind of edge control is far too gross for carving, which requires subtle adjustments in edging throughout the turn. Only the feet can provide this kind of edge control, which is accomplished by rolling the feet slightly from side to side. Some carvers refer to this action as pulling up the outside edges in a turn since invariably the edging must be gradually increased as the turn progresses. (This is why there must be some lateral play in the tops of the boots.)

The differential edging exercise described on page 70 is good practice for this kind of edge control. You should also practice various sideslipping and traversing maneuvers with foot edge control only before applying it in a carved turn.

As noted, you can make your skis carve by simply rolling them on to their edges and letting them cut the arc that comes natural to them. Or by using a bit more speed, and thus generating more momentum, you can make the skis flex a little more, thus carving a tighter turn. But for safety's sake, neither approach is practical on anything but the easiest slopes.

INITIATING THE CARVE

There is no great difficulty getting the skis to carve during the opening phases of the turn. If the turn is initiated from a traverse, the skis will carve as soon as the edges make firm contact with the snow after the edge change since the skis will not skid uphill unless forced to do so. The difficulties start as the skis approach the fall line and increase as the turn continues. Fortunately, the centrifugal force that wants to send the skis

Figure 11-5. *Carving by edging.*

167

into a skid can also be utilized to flex the skis.

CARVING BY EDGING

As the skis start to turn, the skier counters the centrifugal force by banking or angulating. This countering force directs your weight directly down over the center of the skis and causes them to flex into an arc which has a radius much shorter than that of the skis' sidecut. If, once the carve is established, the skier does no more, the increase in speed as the skis pass through the fall line will generate more centrifugal force and ultimately cause the skis to skid. In fact, the skier may abet this skidding tendency by actively pushing his heels to the outside of the turn. However, if he counters the centrifugal force by increasing the edging, the result will be greater pressure on the skis, causing them to flex even more, which enables the skis to keep carving in a tightening radius. This is carving's first rule: To keep carving, gradually increase the edging.

CARVING BY STOMPING

"Get your weight on the outside ski," is the rallying cry of every ski instructor. By doing just that—with a vengeance—you can get a carving response from skis that are recalcitrant in this respect for one reason or another.

In the accompanying illustration, that's just what's happening. The skis were not coming around with the desired skidless precision. By quickly picking up the inner ski to emphatically shift the weight to the outside ski—stomping is just what it feels like—the ski is forced to flex deeply. That lays a good round curve of edge against the snow and enables the ski to zoom around on a far tighter track than would seem possible with less drastic treatment.

CARVING BY ROCKING

You maintain the natural carving radius of your skis by what some carvers call differential flexing, but what is better described as rocking because the point of deepest flex in the skis is moved from front to back or vice versa by shifting the weight along the length of the ski by rocking slightly at the knees and ankles. To maintain the carve without making any changes in your normal edging, you can hold the radius by gradually rocking back on your skis so that your weight eventually rests on your heels. This rocking need not be extreme. In fact, it's usually quite subtle since some of today's skis are extremely carve-sensitive and the special boots are excellent transmitters of the leverage you can exert. This is why you must be able to rely on your boots for support.

COMBINING THE THREE WAYS

In carving your way down the mountain, you don't only stomp, or carve, or edge. Usually, you use a combination of techniques, although it's a good idea to master each separately first. Actually, what will determine your particular approach is the equipment you use. Carving is probably more equipment dependent than any skiing development in recent years. Also keep in mind that carving is still a developing art. I'll bring you more on carving as this art is further defined . . . in my next book.

Figure 11-6. *Carving by stomping.*

Figure 11-7. *Carving by rocking.*

12

TERRAIN AND SNOW
The Never-Ending Variables

Be Forewarned, Be Forearmed

TRANSITIONS

In Chapter 4, I discussed gentle transitions in detail. At that time, I stated that there were two basic types of transitions: decelerating and accelerating. The former I defined as a sudden upward swelling in terrain that will slow down your skis, pitching you forward, unless you learn to handle the decelerating forces. An accelerating transition, on the other hand, is a sudden increase in the pitch of the slope that will cause your skis to shoot forward.

An accelerating transition with a pronounced increase in pitch can be handled with a ruade (Figure 12-1). As we learned when we were using the ruade to unweight, it is akin to a hop, except that the upper body is hardly disturbed during the kick. To ruade, first lower the body position. Then, as you quickly spring up, once the legs are almost straight, as in the second drawing, quickly fold your heels toward your hips, keeping the tips on the snow. Just as quickly, return the skis to the snow. To time these movements correctly, start the springing action as the tips reach the crest. Through practice, learn to pull up the heels only enough

to raise the skis parallel to the new pitch.

Maintain balance through a pronounced decelerating transition by using a telemark lunge (Figure 12-2). Immediately before reaching the up-turning slope, shove one foot forward about boot length, while keeping your weight on the heel of the other foot. Absorb the decelerating shock of the transition by letting your weight be forced forward onto the forward foot. Then return to a normal balanced stance.

Severe hummocks can be crossed, as illustrated in Figure 12-3A, with both poles being planted near the tips at the moment the feet cross over the crest. Thus the poles act as stabilizers. On the other hand, when severe hollows must be crossed (Figure 12-3B), both poles are planted near the tips at the instant the feet pass the lowest point. Use the poles, and arms, as shock absorbers.

CONTINUOUS TRANSITIONS

Bumps and rolls consist of both accelerating and decelerating transitions. The down side of a bump or roll accelerates you. The up side slows you down. Skiing through these rapid

170

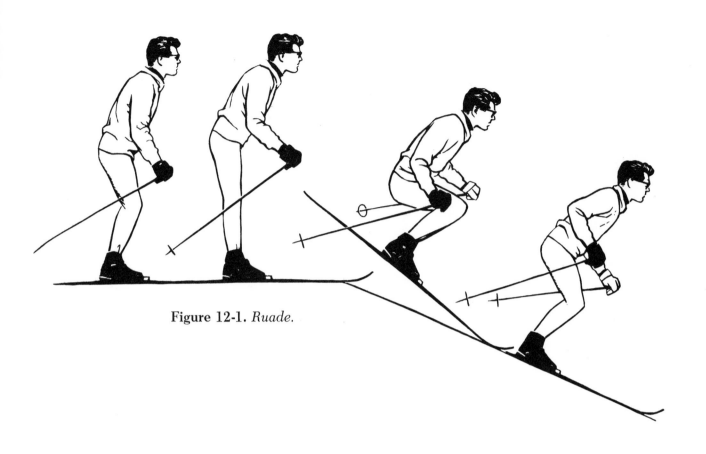

Figure 12-1. *Ruade.*

Figure 12-2. *Telemark lunge.*

changes of pitch is exciting. To maintain balance requires practice. Look for places to give yourself the chance to master these undulations, using the movements discussed here. Put yourself, for instance, in the boots of the skier in Figure 12-4 — as he crosses a breakover. First, move forward in anticipation of the increase in pitch. Then resume a normal balanced stance as you proceed down the slope. Next, prepare for the slowing down action of the up slope by taking a position of *rucklage*. (Say *rook LAH guh*. It's German for "backward lean.") When the transition has been absorbed, resume a normal stance going up the roll, and prepare to repeat the movements. Practice is required

to learn to time your movements with the speed at which you travel.

Practice is also needed to travel across a series of small bumps and hollows, such as a series of moguls (Figure 12-5). Here, try to keep your center of mass — a region located close to the belt buckle — traveling in a straight line down the slope. Use the upper body to counterbalance the legs, which must flex deeply at the knees and ankles, like piston-action shock absorbers. As you practice, think of the head and hips as always traveling in the same smooth plane, while the feet rise and fall, "filling in" the hollows between the high points.

When skiing the moguls, it's important to remember to turn early. If you do,

Figure 12-3A. *Crossing a hummock.*

Figure 12-3B. *Crossing a hollow.*

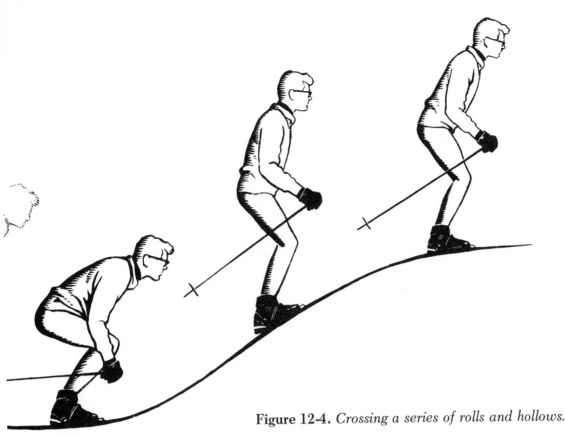

Figure 12-4. *Crossing a series of rolls and hollows.*

each mogul will help you turn. If you don't, it will fight you. Try to plant your pole, the inside one of the intended turn, about one foot before the high spot of the bump (see page 162). Then start your turn right then. But don't overpower your skis. If you do, they will turn across the trough with the tails riding up over the next mogul, making the skis very difficult to control.

Another thing you must do: Look far enough ahead. As soon as you get one turn started you must look ahead immediately to plan your next turning spot. If you are slow about this you will not be able to plant your pole soon enough for the next turn. You must train yourself to plan at least one turn ahead of yourself. Even more, if you can. It is best to know before you start the turn where you will want to be at the end of it.

When an accelerating transition is pronounced, and you've enough speed, you may become airborne. The sensation is most enjoyable, once you develop the skills to maintain balance. The leap in Figure 12-6 is a gelande-sprung. (Say *geh LAHNDEH shproong.* It's German for "terrain jump.") Put yourself into the action, going from left to right. Prepare for take-off by crouching. Plant both poles, up near the ski tips, and at the crest of the transition. Spring slightly forward and upward, stiffening your arms and shoulders. Use your poles to brace against, not for pushing off. The latter is to invite imbalance in the air. While airborne, don't upset your balance with wild arm waving. For an extra sensation of height, fold calves to thighs, allowing the tips to drop enough to bring the skis parallel to your landing slope. Extend the legs as you drop down, then flex deeply to absorb the shock of landing. Arms and poles, too, may be used to soak up landing forces. To gain con-

173

Figure 12-5. *Crossing a series of moguls.*

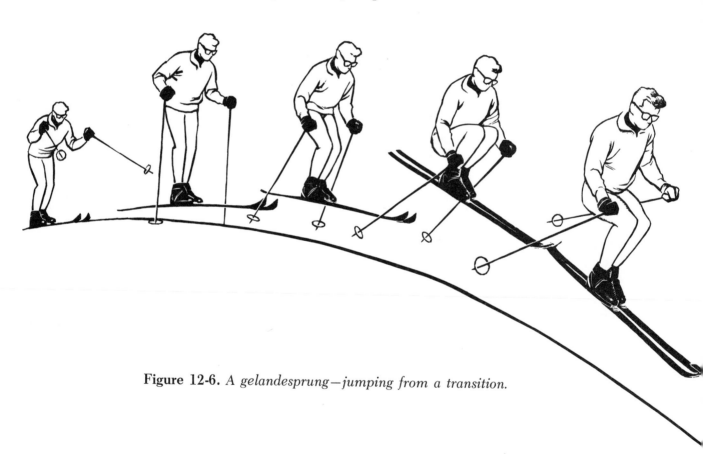

Figure 12-6. *A gelandesprung—jumping from a transition.*

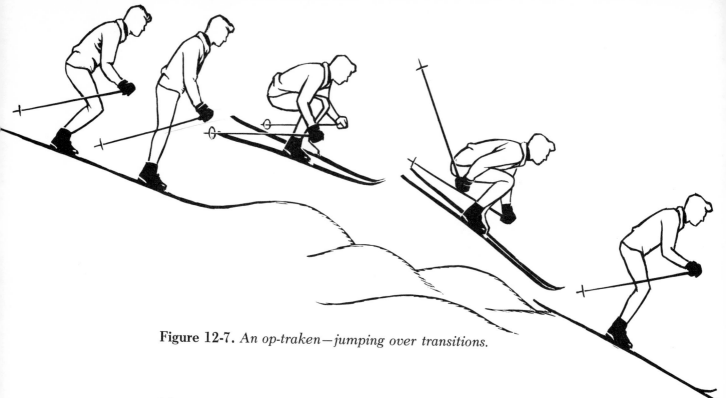

Figure 12-7. *An op-traken—jumping over transitions.*

fidence and balance make your first jumps off small bumps that have a smooth packed slope—not a flat—to land on.

Some bumps are so rough that it's better to fly over them than ski across them. That's when the *op-traken* (Say *OP trahken*. It's Norwegian for "pre-jump.") comes in handy. The sequence illustrates the movements clearly. Analyze them and apply the action to your own skiing by practicing over small transitions, then bigger ones.

SKIING ON VARIOUS SNOWS

Skiing is easy—on packed slopes. But when the slope becomes icy or is covered with deep powder snow, you'll have to adapt your technique to that particular snow condition. Here are some tips that will help you when these conditions occur.

SKIING ON ICE

There's a certain kind of snow that forms on ski slopes after repeated thaws, rains, re-freezes, heavy goings-over by skiers, and much wind action over its surface, which is not-so-endearingly called loud powder or boiler plate. Very few skiers ever feel completely at ease on this white asphalt and those few who do have built up their confidence and skill through five to ten years' experience.

You can do several things to improve your performance on hard surfaces. The most important is to be sure your steel edges are properly sharp every time you tackle the hard slopes. Skis with dull or improperly sharpened edges will not provide any sense of security, not even when traversing. Nor will dull edges permit you to make a christie with more than a semblance of control over either speed or direction.

Insofar as ice and technique are concerned, you must use proper and sufficient angulation and you must learn to initiate each christie with the minimum amount of turning force required. Most skiers who are inept on ice use too much turning force, be it anticipation or counter-rotation, which causes the skis to skid

176

out of control for several feet until enough speed has been lost, thus enabling them to proceed on a shaky, speed accumulating traverse to the next turn.

Too many skiers have the idea that it's essential to edge a lot to keep from sliding off the hill. It just isn't so. Too much edging on ice merely causes your skis to be pushed out from under you. The trick to skiing ice well is to use the edges very subtly.

When turning on ice or hard pack, remember that your turns may have a longer radius, so be sure to allow plenty of room to make them. Whenever possible, try to traverse between each turn. And when traversing, place the majority of your weight on the downhill ski so that this ski will have sufficient power to cut into hard surface. To test for proper weight distribution lift the uphill ski and balance yourself on the downhill ski. This downhill weighting can usually be accomplished best by leaning the upper body away from the hill while pressing the knees into the hill.

If only patches of ice exist, after you have passed over the patch—when you feel the edges grip again or when you no longer hear the sound of ice—set your edges to dissipate the extra speed you have picked up and then resume normal edging, depending on the kind of turn you plan to make.

If the situation appears bad enough, revert to the very basic, low speed techniques—stem christies and even snowplows. Take the gentler routes and ski with the narrow snowplow maneuver illustrated in Figure 12-8. The trick to maintaining your balance on this noisy snow is to keep the skis canted ever so slightly on their inside edges,

Figure 12-8. *Skiing on ice or hard pack.*

177

the fronts turned slightly toward each other. The edging keeps your skis under control. Remember that once you feel you've lost control of your skis, of course, you lose confidence. And once you lose confidence, loss of control continues. The net result—you hate skiing hard snow conditions.

DEEP-POWDER SKIING

Skiing in deep powder snow, as opposed to five to six inches of powder, is difficult, but once accomplished, it offers you the great thrill of moving down an untracked slope. To many skiers, this is the true essence of the sport. But, when skiing in deep powder, there is a different relationship between the skis and the snow. Often there is no longer a hard base under the skis. And unless you have special skis for the really deep stuff you must keep your weight resting somewhat on your heels, so the tips will "float" near the surface.

Skis for deep powder should have a flexible forebody, permitting them to plane close to the snow's surface, making them easier to turn.

As a rule, longer skis are best since they have more running surface. If the forebody of your skis are too stiff, the skis may dive deeper into the powder, making balance difficult.

Incidentally, the length of the ski poles is a personal preference. Shorter ones don't drag on the snow as much; longer ones find the solid base under the snow more easily.

It is important to develop a good body position for deep-powder skiing. You should be squarely over your skis with supple ankles and knees acting as springs and allowing you to rock back and forth on your skis, according to variations of terrain. Keep your body relaxed but ever-ready for action. In deep snow both skis ought to be equally weighted to prevent an unweighted ski from being pressed upward, which would cause poor balance and thus increase the danger of spills.

In deep snow, stemming or keeping the skis apart is a grave mistake. Both skis must cut through the snow as if they were one single board. Turns in the deep can be banked more, since the snow tends to form a slight embankment under the skis. Turning power comes mostly from the feet and legs, allowing you to ski with an economy of motion. If you change your direction in deep snow, increased speed is very helpful. Therefore, ski close to the fall line. The slope itself should be steep. A gentle slope, even on the fall line, won't give you enough speed to swing through the deep powder.

OTHER TIPS

Here are a few important suggestions that you should keep in mind when skiing difficult slopes:

Flat Light. This is a condition in which lack of shadows on the uniform whiteness of the snow makes it difficult to tell the size and location of the bumps and, under more extreme circumstances, the steepness of the slope. Flat light is encountered on cloudy or snowy days or in late afternoon after the sun has gone down.

Even knowledgeable skiers find skiing on open slopes in flat light an eerie experience. Rather than give up for the day, they look for runs with trees on them. The dark trees on the white snow provide a point of reference, which makes it easier to judge the steepness of the slope and also to determine the best place to turn. Of course, the use of amber, orange, or yellow goggles helps to accent what little shadows may exist.

Reading the Trail. One of the reasons a good skier looks good is because he takes a constant "reading" of the slope. Looking far ahead, he spots the hazards in plenty of time to either determine exactly how he will ski them or how to ski around them. Even the simplest trails have places which will throw the best of skiers off balance. The trick is to recognize the bad spots. Big, sharp-edged bumps are especially hazardous. Slow down or come to a complete stop at the edge of the trail and survey the situation. Booming into bad moguls or a blind spot is asking for trouble, and you may find yourself bouncing around and picking up speed with no place to turn or stop.

13

ACROBATICS
Stunts, Simple and Hard
Transcend the Ordinary

By definition, stunts are things of little practical use. But simply because they don't help you make turns in the conventional sense, don't miss the opportunity to add them to your skiing repertoire. While some don't have much practical application, they're not useless either. Stunts are great confidence builders; practicing them helps to improve timing and coordination; and sometimes they help you squirm your way out of tacky situations. But most of all, they're great fun to do. They add a dash of zap to your skiing and they're great for entertaining yourself and others while you're waiting for that slow friend to catch up. So when that day comes when the snow's no good, the terrain uninteresting, or you're just plain bored wiggling your way downhill, get in a session of stunt practice.

Although stunts look difficult, they really are not. What they do require is practice—and a sense of humor. Be prepared to laugh at yourself as your initial attempts end in an embarrassing tangle. The key ingredient for success in stunts is decisiveness in execution. Once you start a stunt, give it everything you have, go all the way; if you

try to ease your way into the maneuver, you're inviting failure.

ONE-POLE JUMP TURNS

Here's a rather easy stunt. Remember the hop you made when you first learned to ski parallel? The one-pole jump turn basics are very similar to those of hops, except that one-polers are made with a lot more gusto. To really come off the snow, you first have to get quite low on your skis as you approach the turn. Plant your pole close to the tip of your downhill ski, and be sure to keep your hand low so that you can get a real lift when you start bracing against the pole. Once you're in the air, you can tuck your knees for longer flight. The trick in this stunt is to coordinate perfectly the unweighting action with the pole plant. If you can do that, you'll soar two or three feet above the snow, which is a good place to be when you're turning in the crud or if an old log just out of winter hibernation should be in your way.

HANNES JUMP

The Hannes jump is named after Hannes Schneider, who popularized it back in the 1920's. It can be done from a standing start, but it's easier if you've

Figure 13-1. *One-pole jump turn.*

Figure 13-2. *Hannes jump.*

181

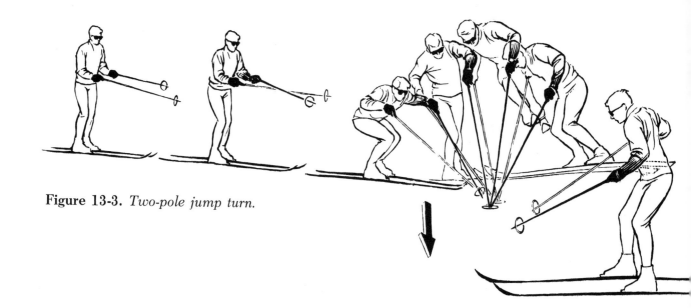

Figure 13-3. *Two-pole jump turn.*

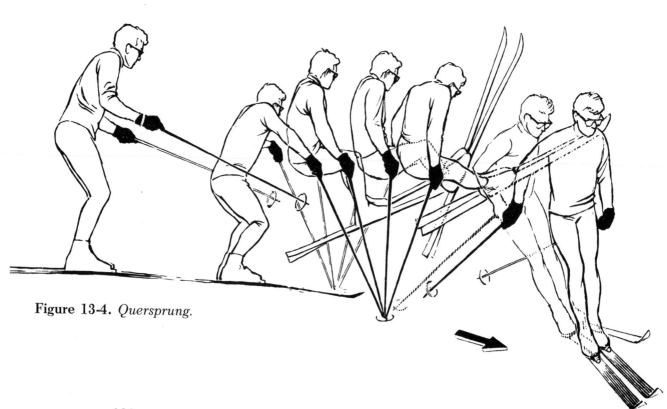

Figure 13-4. *Quersprung.*

allowed yourself to pick up a little momentum first. In Figure 13-2, note that I'm crouched very low on my skis at the moment when I plant my poles, and also that I'm anticipated in the direction of the turn. My uphill pole is near the tip of my ski, and this, in turn, allows the tails of the skis to swing clear of the poles as my skis turn in the air. Note also, the outside pole is withdrawn once I reach maximum altitude. This adds to the turning impetus.

TWO-POLE JUMP TURN

Here's another stunt which has practical application in dangerous breakable crust. The Austrians call it an *umsprung*, which is to say about-turn. Its purpose is to go from traverse to traverse without the skis being in the snow during the turning phase. The basic principles of other jump turns apply—body crouched low on the skis during the initiation, poles up near the tips of the skis at the moment of planting—but there are some differences. To prevent breaking the poles while you're pivoting, the outside pole of the intended turn is crossed *over* the other pole. Also, both poles are planted on the *inside* of the intended turn. When the poles are planted, spring up and inward. Strive to get the shoulders directly over the pivotal point of the ski poles. Pull the skis off the snow, keeping them parallel to the slope. While your weight is braced against the poles, pivot your skis around in the air until they point in the new traverse.

QUERSPRUNG

That's a cross-jump in English, and it's a spectacular way of making a 90-degree turn. In this one, you move down the fall line and jump between the poles.

The best way to approach the maneuver is to imagine you're going to make an extreme jet christie: Plant both poles, and while bracing firmly against them, let the skis shoot out from under you. Swing your boots up and forward, pulling up on your knees just enough to allow the heels of the skis to clear the snow—putting the skis vertical to the slope for an instant. Then fold the skis over to either side. This stunt is easiest when you've a knoll to leap from, at 3 to 5 miles per hour.

KICKTURN VARIATIONS

The reverse kickturn demonstrated in Figure 13-5 and the cross-over kickturn in Figure 13-6 are not so much stunts as good warm-up exercises for stunts (and regular skiing after a cold chairlift ride). They also have practical value because many skiers find them easier than the usual ski school kick turn (see Chapter 3).

You will find these two variations of the kickturn and other stunts easier to do, particularly at first, if you use a shorter pair of skis. Better skiers quite frequently use skis that are longer than normal for their height, and such skis are a handicap when you try to clear them off the snow and through planted poles.

At the beginning, ski school kick turn basics apply to both stunts. Make sure you've got a good platform—stamp one out if necessary—and that the ski that stays in place at the beginning of the kick turn is firmly edged. For a little extra insurance on steeper hills, angle the ski slightly uphill to keep it from slipping out from under you. Also, take your time to make sure you are set—particularly after you've kicked around the downhill ski—before bringing the

Figure 13-5. *Reverse kickturn.*

uphill ski alongside. There is no harm in pausing while you are getting familiar with the maneuver.

Although the reverse and cross-over would appear to be mere opposites of each other, the movements for each are different, mainly because we have anatomical limitations. It is relatively easy to swing the ski a full 180 degrees in a reverse kickturn; it's almost impossible in the cross-over. So let's look at each separately.

Reverse Kickturn: From a standing position lean forward from the waist and slightly uphill. At the same time, lift the tail of the downhill ski off the snow. As you start to swing the ski behind you, make sure the tail of the ski stays clear of the snow, and withdraw both poles from the snow quickly. Swing the downhill pole in an arc *outside* of the swinging downhill ski, but in coordination with it. Use what was the uphill pole as a prop, if that should be necessary to keep you from falling downhill. Since it may be difficult at first to make a full 180-degree kick, place the kicked ski about ten to twelve inches away from the other ski. This is a more stable position from which to make adjustments. Further adjustments can then be made without stepping on the other ski. The rest of the turn is completed in regular ski school kickturn fashion.

Cross-Over Kickturn. From a standing position, place the uphill pole somewhere to the rear of your boots and use it for support. Since it is almost impos-

Figure 13-6.
Cross-over kickturn.

sible to swing the ski the full 180 degrees on crossovers, make sure that after it's crossed, the ski is properly edged and you are effectively braced by your poles to keep the ski from slipping. Complete the stunt by pivoting the up-to-now stationary ski onto its tip (almost as though you were going to look at the bottoms of your skis), then swing the tip away from yourself and bring the ski alongside the other. With practice, you should be able to bring the ski around in one smooth, continuous motion without resting the tip on the snow.

Variations. Once you're proficient, you can use kickturns for real stunts. For a starter, try turning in a downhill direction, rather than uphill as is customary. Then do a series—even alter-nating between reverses and cross-overs—without a pause between turns. And for real thrills, do them while you are actually moving—slowly.

FLYING KICKTURN

Like any kickturn, this stunt is designed to get you turned around in a minimum of space, but that's about as far as the comparison should go. In the usual kickturns, one ski always remains firmly planted on the snow when the other one is in motion; in the flying kick-turn, both skis become airborne—although not simultaneously—and the entire maneuver becomes similar to the *quersprung.* Start a flying kickturn while sliding slowly in a shallow tra-verse. The downhill ski is kicked up

first and swung partially around before the uphill ski follows and is brought alongside the already airborne downhill ski. The problem is to properly coordinate this sequence of motions. If you swing the downhill ski out too far or too soon, the uphill ski will hit the tail of the downhill ski when you try to bring it up. If you don't swing the downhill ski out far enough, you may land with skis pointing down the fall line, instead of across it, in the direction of a new traverse. The timing involved in bringing the uphill leg alongside the already kicked leg also poses a problem. If this motion is late, the whole turn may be aborted. All this may prove to be a bit frustrating to master, but don't worry; in practicing you'll be cultivating a set of arm and stomach muscles of iron—physical qualities which are most desirable if stunts become your passion.

HOCHWENDE

This is another Austrian originated maneuver, and it can be translated as either high turn or high vault. In practice, the stunt is a combination of the two. Like the flying kickturn, it is closely related to the *quersprung.* Actually, the *hochwende* consists of a sequence of motions, as shown in the circle (Figure 13-8). But, for clarity's sake, the figures in the illustration have been separated. The key to success is the placement of the poles: the uphill pole is planted close to the tip of the uphill ski; the downhill pole isn't quite so far forward. To get the skis pointed in the direction of the new traverse, you have to thrust and twist your skis vigorously. If you don't, you will find your skis pointing downhill on landing—a decided embarrassment on steeper slopes.

Figure 13-7. *Flying kickturn.*

186

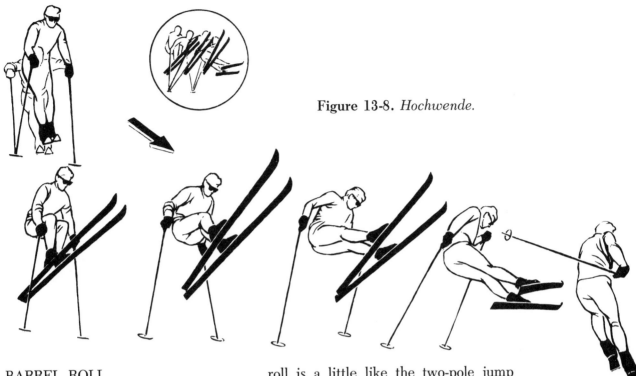

Figure 13-8. *Hochwende.*

BARREL ROLL

For a barrel of laughs, try this one on your friends when they're not expecting it. To make a barrel roll come off requires movements much like those in a forward roll in gymnastics: When springing out of the crouch to start the roll, the chin and arms must be tucked in; and the legs must be thrust back and up so that the tips of the skis don't auger into the snow. In Figure 13-9, note the position of the arms throughout. The critical moment comes when you are on your back. At that time you must twist your skis across the fall line. Planting the poles as I do will help you to get back up on your feet again.... Did we say something about using shorter skis a few pages back?

TIP ROLL

If you were good at cartwheels in gym class, this is the stunt for you. A tip roll is a little like the two-pole jump turn described on page 183, except that vigor is required to keep the ski tips pivoting on the snow. After planting your poles—crossed, with the outside pole over the inside pole—you must spring powerfully onto your poles and flip the tails of your skis around. If you don't use that extra impetus, all you'll get is that two-pole jump turn again, or a flop.

UNDECIDED QUERSPRUNG

Decisions! Decisions! Left? Or right? A straight gelande? A quersprung? Or a barrel roll? This undecided quersprung is ideal for stunters who can't make up their minds, or for those who want to mix up a lot of separate stunts to come up with one super stunt. As you can see from Figure 13-11, a lot of the stunts we've described on the previous pages are involved here. The action starts as

187

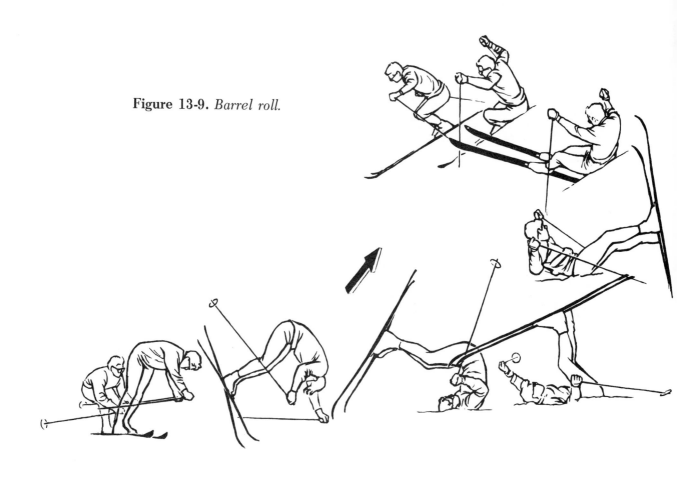

Figure 13-9. *Barrel roll.*

Figure 13-10. *Tip roll.*

Figure 13-11. *Undecided quersprung.*

189

though you are about to start a quer-sprung, except that the poles are planted as though you were about to do a Hannes jump. But once you're in the air, split your skis, the tip of your right ski to your right, the left tip to your left. When you first try an undecided, you may want to stop at the third figure illustrated. Carry on only if your muscles are limber, and your pants seams strong. You do want to continue? All right, dive forward, tuck in your chin, and roll onto your back. While you're on your back, quickly uncross your skis and try to plant your poles. If you haven't become totally confused, you'll end up back on your skis again and with the skis shooting down the fall line. When the powder is really deep, try a flying sitzmark. As you come up as shown in the second figure from the top, push hard on your poles so that your body comes parallel with the slope. Then let yourself fall flat on your back into the deep and fluffy snow. How's that for sheer exuberance?

14

FITNESS
For Safety and Strength

Design Your Own Program

Some facets of skiing are all wrong for the body. While overall it is a graceful, fluid sport, some of its activities could hardly be more effectively designed for making the body stiff and inflexible. In the first place, there's the cold. The human organism seems to huddle against the cold, to tense against it, to stiffen as though by not moving it could preserve its own pocket of warmth.

Moreover, there is the way we practice the sport. We take long automobile rides in overheated cars, then struggle out to face the cold, still stiff from being cramped into restricted space. We stand in lift lines, letting the cold attack our unmoving bodies. We take long, cold lift rides, during which active movement can constitute an actual danger. We wear heavy clothing, and fasten unwieldy equipment on ourselves, both of which restrict looseness and movement. Few of us really "warm up." Then we fling ourselves down slopes at frightening speeds, through a succession of anxious situations, tensing against the necessity of maintaining balance. To insure that balance, we attempt to apply the skiing technique we have learned, which, no matter how enlightened its

method, has trained us to think automatically in "positions" that should improve our style but actually tend to freeze us into semi-immobility.

Even the routine of modern life is out of phase with skiing. Most of us rush to the slopes at wide intervals, overexert, get sore muscles (which reinforce our stiffness), groan impatiently until the soreness passes, and then rush back again for more. It's a wonder we aren't all frozen into solid chunks of cramped muscle and jangling nerve ends by the end of the season. And so the first advice of any ski instructor, to any student, is simply, "Loosen up!" Few of us can properly respond.

We know our muscles are called upon, in skiing, for more than they're used to giving. So the more conscientious among us subject themselves to various pre-season physical conditioning sessions in an effort to ward off soreness and, with luck, prevent physical injury. What's missing in the motivation behind such conditioning is the realization that proper physical preparation can actually make a skier *ski better*. And what's missing in those conditioning programs themselves, all too often, is an awareness of what has been learned about muscle conditioning in recent years. Today's skier too often bases his conditioning labors on foggily remembered agony from junior high school gym classes of his childhood—or the latest fad perpetrated on the public by some quick-buck artist who'd have you believe that perfect muscle tone comes from ten minutes a day and no effort.

Faddish exercise routines come and go, but despite what they seem to be telling you, there is no easy way to good physical conditioning. You may be able to maintain enough elasticity and muscle tone to withstand the stress of everyday life with a fairly mild program of exercise and relaxation. But skiing isn't everyday life; it can be a tough, rigorous, demanding sport that makes some peculiar demands on the physical plant. To get the most possible fun out of skiing—with the lowest chance of injury—takes a sound physical constitution. You *can* get yourself in excellent shape for skiing, before the season starts. Here's a five-step plan on how to design your own fitness program and get more fun out of skiing without getting sore.

STEP ONE

If you are sadly overweight, with a low level of fitness, then you must use care not to create more problems for yourself than you try to solve. Little-used and seldom-stretched muscles and tendons can be easily damaged. If, however, you merely feel out of shape— such that a set of tennis, or a brisk mile walk would make you stiff the next day —then begin each of your early conditioning sessions this season with a period of muscular relaxation, like the following.

Lie on your back, a pillow under your knees and a rolled towel behind your neck to support your head. Get comfortable. Start on the neck and shoulder muscles, concentrating on letting all the major muscles go completely limp.

Relax by contrast. Tense a major muscle, as in your leg, and then let it go limp. Pause for one deep breath, thinking about relaxing that muscle. Go on to the next. Turn your head to the side, hard, for a moment. Then relax. Work systematically through your body, concentrating on, and relaxing, all the major muscles: biceps, forearms, calves, thighs, feet, jaw, forehead, chest, buttocks, everything. Breathe deeply and evenly. It helps to imagine that with every exhalation, you're sinking deeper and deeper into the floor. (Don't go to sleep.)

Once you're completely relaxed, begin stretching. Extend every limb—one limb at a time—to its extreme length, then work it through its extreme limits of motion, in every direction. Then relax it again. Work your way over your own body in major muscle groups. Some, to be properly stretched, will require that you sit or stand. Concentrate on keeping the neck, shoulders, and face relaxed as you do. Don't stretch to the point of pain, but do reach the limits of your own elasticity. You'll find that the limits of your elasticity are continually being expanded every time you go through your stretching and relaxing routine.

STEP TWO

Analyze Yourself. Sure if you think you are in fair shape, you can leap into a rigorous game of tennis or a fast game of handball. Or you can start running for a mile or two. Sure, you'll be stiff for several days after, but the soreness will vanish. Sure, but you're defeating your very purpose in so doing. Stiffness and soreness are setbacks. Rather than progressing during those days of mild pain, you are merely marking time.

Your conditioning program can put you days ahead if you go about it sensibly. And the first sensible thing to do is to analyze your present level of fitness— your strength and endurance. First, go through the relaxing and stretching routine described in Step One. Second— perform the endurance step test described below. Third—go on with the strength-building exercises on these pages. Be sure to include a few minutes of easy jogging, or running in place, to give your muscles a chance to warm up.

Analyze Your Endurance. Your heart is a muscle. It, too, must be kept in condition. The degree to which it can pump blood bears a direct relationship to the amount of strain which your muscles can endure—your endurance. And your pulse rate gives a direct clue to this endurance. Proceed with this test before getting to work on the exercises. Do not complete it if you become too fatigued in the process and check with your doctor before going ahead with any kind of program to get yourself back into condition.

First, check your normal pulse rate— that is, your pulse before any unusual exertion, but *not* after a night's sleep or a long nap. Now, get a bench or chair that is fifteen inches or so high. Stand in front of it, and put one foot up onto the seat. On a count of one, step up on the chair, bring the other foot up beside the first for a two count. Step down with the foot you started with for the three count. Bring the other foot back down for a four count. Repeat this on a four

count, thirty times a minute for two minutes. Then sit down on the chair and rest for two minutes. At the end of two minutes, take your pulse rate for fifteen seconds, multiply it by four, and jot down the product. It'll be a good index to your endurance as you go along in a conditioning program—repeat the step test with pulse count about every two weeks for future comparison. After several months, you'll have established your own norms which will be a very real clue to your own physical fitness level. (Since there is no such thing as one "normal" pulse for everyone, we won't even attempt to give you pulse rates for comparison. Compare yourself with only yourself.)

STEP THREE

Analyze Your Strength. The exercises presented here as strength builders for the muscles of skiing are the conventional ones—done correctly. Infinite variations on these exercises are possible, and you can devise your own additions and substitutions. But for the purpose of testing yourself to find which parts of your muscle structure you need to work on most diligently, we'll stick to the familiar: toe-stands, knee-bends, leg-lifts, push-ups, sit-ups, and chinning. Before getting into these exercises, we cannot emphasize enough the value of relaxing and stretching beforehand. And if it's been a long time since you've exerted yourself, then by all means turn the page and do at least a few minutes of the "stretchers" presented there. In addition, warm up for a few minutes by jogging in place.

Keep a relaxed frame of mind, keep your breathing deep and even, and do not do any exercise to the point of pain

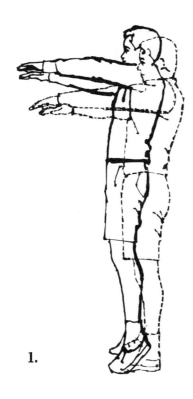

1.

or outright fatigue. Relax between each exercise for a few moments, either sitting or lying down. Do as many as you can of each exercise, until it becomes unpleasant to do any more. Count the number of repetitions you are able to do and jot down the figure.

Developing Skiing Muscles. Here are some exercises that will help to develop your skiing muscles:

1. *Toe-stands.* A great strengthener for the lower leg; helps in edge control, unweighting, and mogul-hopping, and keeping forward on your skis. Also helps develop flexibility of the ankle joint. Stand flat-footed and simply bob up onto your toes as far as you can go. Do it either one foot at a time or with both feet. Use a support now, but later you'll want to do toe-stands unsupported, to train your balance. Also, later you'll want to do them with your toes on the edge of a thick book, your heels touching the floor between each toe-stand—a great Achilles tendon stretcher, as well as a calf developer.

2. *Knee-bends.* This one builds the quadriceps, that major muscle on the top of the thigh that is so important in skiing. (If it's weak, you'll straighten your knees to rest it, and you'll be asking for trouble skiing that way.) Again, you may want to hold onto a chair or something at first. Do knee-bends with your heels flat on the floor or rocking up onto your toes, whichever is more comfortable for you. Later, you'll split your knee-bends, doing half each way. (The common current myth that knee-bends are harmful to the knee joint is true only for weight lifters doing huge numbers of repetitions with massive weights on their shoulders.)

3. *Chest-curls.* This one develops muscles in the upper part of the torso—

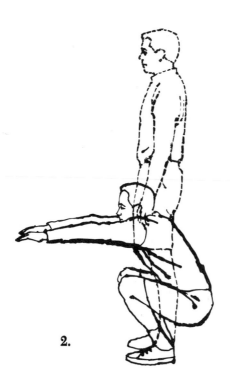

2.

the chest region and the upper abdomen —which help you to pull yourself forward whenever you forget to maintain a good balanced stance. Lie flat on your back, on a firm surface. Raise your knees, as shown, keeping your feet flat on the floor. Curl your head and chest forward and reach with your hands to touch your knees. Return your head and shoulders to the surface. Repeat.

4. *Leg-lifts.* Want to leap over moguls, with the tips of your skis hanging down, beautifully parallel to your landing slope? Then better get some strength in the muscles of the lower abdomen. Do it with leg-lifts. Numerous variations are possible with this exercise. You may raise the legs only three feet from the surface, then return them to rest for a moment. Or, you may swing them up

and overhead, to touch the surface with your toes, next to your head. Or, as shown here, keep the legs straight and press your heels toward the ceiling, stretching hamstrings and Achilles tendon. Raise and lower the legs in rhythm, pausing momentarily between cycles.

5. *Push-ups.* Great for arms, shoulders, back, and stoicism. Tones up everything you use in pole plants and climbing on skis, helps initiating turns. If you can't do a full push-up, ladies, do them from the knees up. Lie on your stomach, arms doubled and hands on floor at armpits. Keep your back stiff and your body rigid, and straighten your arms, pushing your body up so only hands and toes are touching floor. Go down, stop when chin touches the floor, then back up again.

3.

4.

5.

195

1.

STEP FOUR

Body elasticity is the single most necessary quality for safe, effective, enjoyable skiing. And we pointed out that the reaction of muscle tissue to fatigue, to cold, to pain, to mental and emotional tension, to overstress, even to overstretching, is to contract—to tighten up. The following nine stretching exercises are not sensational, startling, or in any way, new. They have been especially selected to stretch those muscles and tendons which are most apt to receive abuse, either in the normal course of skiing, or in the "normal" process of taking a nasty egg-beater tumble. If you'll only take the time to keep yourself tuned up with some of these daily "stretchers," at least you'll avoid most of the unnecessary debilitating effects of strains, sprains, and torn body tissue so often suffered by out-of-shape skiers.

1. *Ankle-bends.* An Achilles tendon stretcher. If your boots are flexible enough, yet you can't get forward when your instructor tells you to, this exercise will help. Using a desk, a chair, or the wall, position yourself as illustrated. Press your knees forward and downward, keeping your heels on the floor. Experiment a bit, until you feel an action that pulls on the Achilles tendon. Proceed gently, gradually bouncing the knees further downward. But stop before you feel pain. A variation of this exercise is simply to squat like the stereotype of a Mexican peasant, armpits on knees, and rock back and forth.

2. *Toe-touching.* A great lower-back and hamstring stretcher. It has often been said that anyone who can't touch his toes is risking a skiing accident. And don't give us any of that jazz about being proportioned wrong. Relax into it. Roll down from the shoulders and reach as

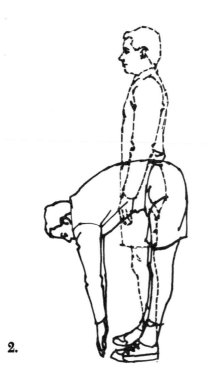

2.

far as you can, knees straight, without pain. Keep breathing deeply; hang in the head-down position and concentrate on relaxing your neck, back, and arms.

3. *Trunk-bending.* A rib or intercostal muscle stretcher which helps eliminate your spare tire. Stand with feet astride, alternately reach down directly sideways to try to touch your calf, keeping the knees unbent. Simultaneously raise the opposite hand to touch close to the armpit. This helps you avoid torso stiffness.

4. *Torso-twisting.* An intercostal and "waistline" stretcher. Stand with the feet comfortably astride. Raise your arms, with hands across your chest, as shown. Alternately twist from one side to the other, gradually forcing your elbows to circle around further and further. This is another torso stiffness preventative.

5. *Splits.* An "inseam" tendon and muscle stretcher. This is a good one for the uncertain snowplower. When the tips of the skis separate and the inside edges grab the snow, the opposing forces on each leg tend to split you up the middle. Severe stiffness along the "inseam" is bound to result if you haven't prepared in advance by making use of an exercise such as this. Stand with the feet well apart, with your left foot at right angles to the other one. While keeping most of your weight on the right foot, with the right leg straight, push your left knee forward. Gradually thrust your left knee more forward, but not so far that you feel pain along the "inseam." Reverse the position of your feet and the direction of the knee thrust to give a workout to the "inseam" of your left leg. Remember, don't force the stretching.

6. *Edging.* An ankle stretcher. Great

3.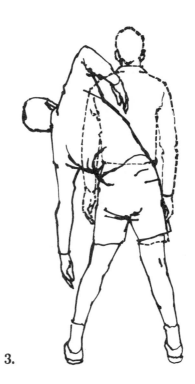

4.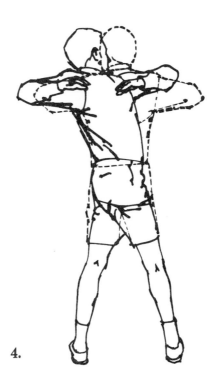

5.

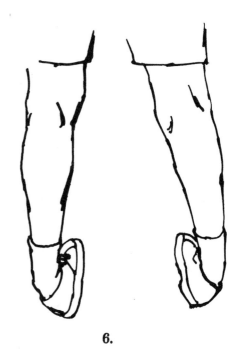

6.

for improving control over your edges, and for helping to prevent strains to the foot and ankle. Just walk about, barefoot or shod, on the outside edges of your feet, until you begin to feel a slight strain. Switch to the insides. Then stand in one place, and swing the knees from side to side, putting the weight alternately on the inside and outside edge of each foot. Combine this with a little of the Achilles tendon stretcher.

7. *Back-bends.* An abdomen stretcher that can do wonders for uptight stomach muscles. Stand three or four feet from a wall and reach up and back over your head with both hands. Make contact with the wall with your palms and lean against it. Now "walk" your hands down the wall until you reach your comfortable limit. Breathe deeply and concentrate—silly as it sounds—on relaxing. This exercise helps you avoid problems resulting from a mean clobber. Caution —if you've ever had back trouble, check with your medic before attempting this.

8. *Toe-pulls.* A thigh stretcher. You may want to stand near enough to a wall to support yourself with one hand for

this one, unless you're a Yogi. Standing sideways to a wall, lift the outside leg behind you. Reach back and grasp your toe, and pull it toward your buttocks, doubling up the leg. That may not stretch your thigh very much—when you start doing some good is when you begin to pull up on the toe. Proceed gently. And, of course, work over both thighs.

9. *Neck-rolls.* This stretches the neck, the seat of most people's tensions. And a portion of the body often subjected to stiffness resulting from the strains of falling, or simply of trying to recover from backward falls. Stand or sit in a relaxed position. Gently turn the head from side to side as far as it will go. Let it loll forward, backward, sideward. Don't force. Roll it gently around the limits of its movement. Reverse direction.

Other tune-up exercises are given in Chapters 3 to 9.

STEP FIVE

Designing Your Own Daily Program. Once you have analyzed your strength

7.

8.

and endurance you have an objective clue—a basic index—to your physical fitness. And some indication of which muscle groups need the most work. The number of repetitions you manage is unimportant except in comparison with the degree of condition you want to achieve. Your goal is to continually increase the total number until you achieve a level of fitness which permits you to go skiing without suffering unnecessary consequences.

Now, let's build a sample program. Let's assume that when you tested yourself you did fifteen toe-stands, twenty knee-bends, twelve leg-lifts, twelve chest-curls, and six push-ups, and you chinned yourself twice, and your pulse rate, at the end of the step-test, was eighty-eight. You now know that your legs are in reasonable shape, from the toe-stand and knee-bend results; your stomach, back and arms need improvement. Your endurance is only so-so.

Now, arbitrarily assign yourself a certain number of repetitions for each strength-building exercise. Select a number less than the amount you achieved

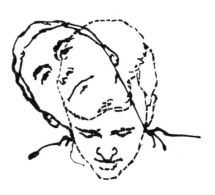

9.

199

while testing yourself. Make the number low enough to keep from discouraging yourself early in the program. Set up your routine to alternate the strength builders with the "stretchers," to develop your own, well-rounded program. We arrive at a daily cycle like this one:

1. Stretching and relaxation, as needed.

2. Warm-up—five minutes of jogging.

3. Exercise cycle: a) Toe-stands—twelve; b) Stretching—ankle-bends; c) Kneebends—six on toes, six with heels down; d) Stretching—toe-pulls, to stretch thighs; e) Chest-curls—ten; f) Stretching—back-bends; g) Stretching—rib-stretcher; h) Leg-lifts—ten; i) Stretching—torso twisting; j) Push-ups—five; k) Stretching—inseam.

4. Relaxation period.

5. Repeat exercise cycle in reverse order, steps k) back through a). Substitute other stretching exercises.

6. Endurance exercise—run or jog on the spot, for ten to fifteen minutes. Less, if you can't manage that much.

7. Cool down, walk for several minutes.

8. Stretching and relaxation.

Note that we don't specify a number of repetitions for the stretching exercises; you should simply perform the exercise until you feel you have the good from it. Note that all the stretching exercises are interchangeable, although the exercise should involve stretching the muscles that have just been contracted in the preceding exercise. You can also substitute, as we said earlier, for some of the strength-building exercises, if others appeal to you more. The important thing is to keep to the principles of stretching, of re-peating exercises in small groups, of increasing the total number of repetitions.

Your goal is more repetitions. Once a given exercise program seems easy, increase the number of repetitions in a given cycle or repeat the cycles more times. Our preference is the latter, since it gives you more opportunity to fit stretching exercises into the routine. Set yourself a goal in total number of repetitions for each exercise. When you reach it, you can then cut back to two workouts a week, just to maintain your level of conditioning.

Whatever you change—the number, type, frequency, or order of the exercises—just don't omit the first two or the last three steps. And if you have to omit everything else, keep Steps 6 and 8. If all else fails, you can arrange the pace of your endurance exercise so that you warm up slowly, go through a period of peak effort, then taper down to a cooling-off period of mild exercise, to be followed by stretching and relaxing. Endurance training can be in almost any kind of activity—swimming, rope-skipping, hiking and mountain climbing, stair-climbing (and descending), trampoline, or whatever—as long as it gives you a regularly recurring opportunity to stretch your muscles.

The endurance portion of the program has additional benefits for skiers. It builds wind, which helps you function better at high altitudes, since you can do more on less oxygen. It helps circulation, which aids in withstanding extreme cold. If you perform your program regularly, it even allows you to eat more and drink more without gaining weight—and everybody knows how important those two activities are to skiing.